American
Shaman

American Shaman

AN ODYSSEY OF
GLOBAL HEALING TRADITIONS

JEFFREY A. KOTTLER AND JON CARLSON,
WITH BRADFORD KEENEY

BRUNNER-ROUTLEDGE
NEW YORK AND HOVE

Published in 2004 by
Brunner-Routledge
29 West 35th Street
New York, NY 10001
www.brunner-routledge.com

Published in Great Britain by
Brunner-Routledge
27 Church Road
Hove, East Sussex
BN3 2FA
www.brunner-routledge.co.uk

Brunner-Routledge is an imprint of the Taylor & Francis
Group.
Printed in the United States of America on acid-free
paper.

10 9 8 7 6 5 4 3 2 1

Library of Congress Cataloging-in-Publication Data

Kottler, Jeffrey A.
  American shaman : an odyssey of global healing
traditions / Jeffrey Kottler and Jon Carlson with
Bradford Keeney.
      p. cm.
Includes bibliographical references (p.   ) and index.
    ISBN 0-415-94821-5 — ISBN 0-415-94822-3 (pbk.)
  1. Shamanism. 2. Spiritual healing. I. Keeney,
Bradford P. II. Carlson, Jon. III. Keeney, Bradford P.
IV. Title.
    BF1598.K43K68   2004
    200'.92—dc22

                                2003020599

Contents

About the Authors

Jeffrey A. Kottler is one of the most prolific authors in the fields of psychology and education, having written 55 books about a wide range of subjects. He has authored a dozen texts for counselors and therapists that are used in universities around the world and a dozen books each for practicing therapists and educators. Some of his most highly regarded works include: *On Being a Therapist; The Imperfect Therapist; Compassionate Therapy; Beyond Blame; The Last Victim; Finding Your Way as a Counselor; Doing Good, Doing Better;* and *Making Changes Last.*

Jeffrey has been an educator for 25 years. He has worked as a teacher, a counselor, and a therapist in preschool, middle school, mental health center, crisis center, university, community college, and private practice settings. He has served as a Fulbright Scholar and a senior lecturer in Peru (1980) and Iceland (2000), as well as worked as a visiting professor in New Zealand, Australia, Hong Kong, Singapore, Thailand, and Nepal. Jeffrey is currently professor and chair of the Counseling Department at California State University, Fullerton.

Jon Carlson, PsyD, EdD, is a distinguished professor of psychology and counseling at Governors State University, University Park, Illinois, and a psychologist with the Wellness Clinic in Lake Geneva, Wisconsin. In addition to serving as the long-time editor of *The Family Journal,* Jon is the author of 30 books in the areas of psychotherapy, family therapy, marital enrichment, consultation, and Adlerian psychology. Some of his best-known works include: *The Intimate Couple, The Disordered Couple, Brief Therapy With Individuals and Couples, Health Counseling, Theories and Strategies of Family Therapy,* and *Time for a Better Marriage.* He and Jeffrey have coauthored *Bad Therapy, The Mummy at the Dining Room Table,* and *The Finest Hour.*

Jon has also developed and produced over 150 commercial videotapes that feature the most prominent leaders in the field (including the professionals featured in this book), demonstrating their theories in actions. These videos are used to train the next generation of practitioners. He has also worked as the school counselor and psychologist for 25 years at the Woods School in Lake Geneva, Wisconsin.

Bradford Keeney, American shaman, is an ex-academic, an ex-therapist, and now a cultural anthropologist and a social critic. He has written classic books in therapy, including *Improvisational Therapy, Resource Focused Therapy, Aesthetics of Change,* and *Mind in Therapy,* as well as books for the general public about cultural phenomena: *Crazy Wisdom Tales for Dead Heads: A Shamanic Companion to the Grateful Dead* and *The Lunatic Guide to the David Letterman Show*. He has also written several popular books, such as *Everyday Soul: Awakening the Spirit in Everyday Life, Shaking Out the Spirits,* and *The Energy Break*. Keeney was recently appointed as a feature writer for *Utne* magazine, assigned to write on "soulful, shamanic, and outrageous sources of wisdom."

For the last 10 years, Keeney has concentrated his efforts on producing the *Profiles of Healing* series, in which he has written about the practices of prominent healers around the world. Brad is vice president of Ringing Rocks Foundation, an organization formed to advance knowledge about alternative healing practices in diverse cultures. He is also a cultural anthropologist for the Mental Research Institute in Palo Alto, California, and an adjunct professor at California State University, Fullerton.

Preface

This book tells the story of Bradford Keeney, American shaman, from his early years as the son of a country preacher, to his later childhood spent as a pianist and a budding scientist. After studying with some of the originators of cybernetics, Keeney went on to a distinguished career as a theorist and a practitioner of systemic family therapy. We follow his transformation from traditional academic to his position as one of the leading spokespersons for indigenous healers. He has been described by the editor of *Utne* magazine as the "all-American shaman, the Marco Polo of psychology, and an anthropologist of the spirit" (Walljasper, 2003, p. 46).

In this book we trace the adventures of the American shaman from one continent to the next, from the rice fields of Bali, the monasteries of the Far East, and the jungles of Paraguay and Brazil, to the deserts of Africa, America, and Australia. At each stop along the way, we witness the wisdom of the world's greatest healers as they work with their most challenging cases. Keeney is sometimes their "patient," sometimes their consultant, and sometimes even *their* healer. Wherever he goes, visions and miracle cures follow him along the way.

Through the eyes and the voice of the American shaman, you will see, hear, and *experience* how the global healing traditions can teach us revitalized ways of thinking about the challenges of everyday life. Our conversations and dialogues, captured in this story, enabled us to reflect upon the oldest traditions in the world and what they have to teach contemporary helpers and healers.

About Our Collaboration

Few books about helping others could have a more diverse team of authors. One of us (Jeffrey) is an avowed existentialist and an integrative therapist who has written a number of books about relationships and change processes, as well as texts and professional resources for therapists, counselors, and teachers. Another (Jon) is a renowned and passionate Adlerian theorist and couples therapist who edits one of the most important journals in the field and has written many influential texts and books in family therapy. And then there's Bradford Keeney—a cybernetic epistemologist and one of the heirs to the work of Gregory Bateson. Keeney was also a former family systems theorist and therapist who developed both improvisational therapy and resource-focused therapy. In addition, he was an academic who directed one of the premier doctoral training programs—that is, until he "disappeared" for over a decade.

Keeney didn't exactly vanish off the face of the Earth; he simply abandoned academia and clinical practice and has spent the last years living and working as a shaman throughout the world. This, in itself, would be a fascinating story—how a well-known and influential theorist and scholar abandoned his profession in order to devote his life to the journey of a shaman and to spend his time in the company of indigenous healers in Mexico, Brazil, Japan, Paraguay, Namibia, Botswana, South Africa, Bali, the Ojibwa culture, Louisiana Black churches, and elsewhere all over the globe. Even more intriguing would be the story of how this psychologist and academic-in-exile ended up as the "shaman's shaman," the healer whom other famous healers consulted when they were experiencing their own troubles and difficulties.

But that is not what led us on this journey together. And that is not even the most interesting part of the story that we have to tell. It so happens that Keeney has evolved a way of working with people that combines many of the features of his early training as a systems theorist and a cybernetician with the some of the oldest global healing traditions that have been practiced for thousands of years. Brad is a uniquely American shaman who has not only blended East with West, but North with South, and the 21st century with practices that have been in continuous use since prehistoric times. He turns everything we ever learned about helping and healing, everything we thought we knew and understood about therapy and counseling, upside down. He challenges our most cherished assumptions, as well as contradicts the ideas we studied, taught, practiced, and have written about in dozens of books. We don't exactly subscribe to many of his ideas (frankly, we can't even claim we understand them, because we never really understood his theories of "recursive frame analysis" and "improvisational therapy" when he was an academic), but we are more than a little intrigued and disoriented by his propositions that we might be better off doing things very differently than we are currently operating.

Some Rather Unusual Ideas

Brad Keeney presents several ideas that contradict much of what we are currently doing in the fields of psychotherapy, counseling, education, and related disciplines. Although these principles might seem strange to us, they happen to be among the most common practices currently in use by indigenous healers around the world: (1) we should be devoting our efforts to honoring greater mystery in life, rather than to promoting understanding; (2) instead of helping people who are upset to calm down, we should encourage them to become more aroused; (3) talk doesn't always help, but dancing, singing, touching, and transcendent prayer are where the action often takes place; (4) the role of helper and healer should include many facets—as guide, coach, minister, counselor, physician, musician, and trickster; (5) homework, when employed, should involve ordeals, trials, tribulations, and "shamanic tasks," none of which have to make sense to the person; (6) people in trouble take themselves far too seriously, and any intervention should take place on a level of play; (7) all helping should be a sacred enterprise, in which the spiritual world is integrated into the body, the mind, the soul, and Nature; and (8) ultimately, helping and healing are about love; they are about being a part of a community.

How This Book Came to Be

Among his many jobs (as a professor, a psychologist, an author, a journal editor, and an elementary school counselor), Jon is also a film producer who has created over 100 videos about the most prominent theoreticians in the world demonstrating their styles of practice. As part of the series on "Psychotherapy With the Experts," in which theorists first do a live therapy session and then explain the basis of their ideas, Jon had invited both Brad and Jeffrey to film their integrative theories in action. This led to a collaboration between us, in which we decided to do a series of books about famous therapists' worst sessions and what these learned from them (Kottler & Carlson, 2002), their most unusual cases and how they impacted their subsequent theories (Kottler &

Carlson, 2003), and their "finest hours" or best examples of their work (Kottler & Carlson, 2004).

We interviewed Keeney for a book about the most unusual cases of the most famous therapists in the world. As a function of his classic books on therapy *(Aesthetics of Change, Mind in Therapy, Improvisational Therapy, Resource Focused Therapy),* he is considered a notable figure by the same profession that he has chosen to challenge. You see, Brad doesn't have much use any longer for the kind of stuff that we do in our clinical practices. He finds it overly simplistic and utterly ridiculous that therapists believe that anyone can actually change as a result of greater understanding alone. He sees all the ways that traditional therapists stifle their creativity and imagination. By contrast, he feels in no way limited by a "talking cure" that Freud invented over a hundred years ago and that is surely obsolete. According to Keeney, therapy and, for that matter, all forms of healing must reinvent themselves.

Although we struggle trying to understand many of Keeney's ideas about cybernetics, epistemology, aesthetics, improvisation, and shamanism, and we are somewhat suspicious about anything that smacks of "New Age," we have little doubt about the power of his interventions. We have watched, filmed, and recorded his "traditional" therapy sessions. We have documented some of his miraculous cures. We have followed him into the Kalahari Desert to watch him work with some of the most powerful healers in the world—indigenous doctors who can cure people through touch, dance, and song.

It is among the Kalahari Bushmen that Keeney is regarded as a powerful medicine man, the White "Big Doctor" who can shake and dance with the spirit for 12 consecutive hours, long past the point where others collapse. To the Bushmen, he is an agent of the "Big God" sent to help them revitalize their ancient practices. He is a true shaman.

Although, to others, shamanism may conjure up images of New Age flakiness and eating hallucinogenic mushrooms, Keeney sees most of this as narcissistic self-indulgence. He has no interest whatsoever in altered states induced by potions or drugs; he has found that true healers are born with a gift, but it is not the sort of calling that anyone would ever choose for himself: The cost is too high. The kind of shaman that Keeney has become is the furthest thing from New Age; rather, it is Old Age, based on the most ancient traditions, which go back thousands of years. In the context of this book, a shaman is a mystic and a spiritual guide who helps and heals people through the ancient wisdom traditions. Most often, this takes place within a community context, in which dance, song, movement, prayer, rituals, and therapeutic ordeals are employed.

All throughout our journeys and dialogues together, we have remained skeptical but curious about what we have witnessed and experienced. We mention this by way of an introduction, lest the reader think that we are all a bunch of New Age screwballs. We are scientists and writers, professors and psychologists, journal editors and academic department chairs. And we have been transformed as a result of the collaboration that took place in writing this book.

Touch the Soul

Although shamanism has not been part of our formal training as psychologists and professors, we do realize that science has not provided answers to many of life's most troubling questions. After all the research that has been done during the last century, and all the many books we have written ourselves about human change, we still don't understand exactly how and why people transform themselves. And when change does manage to take place, against all odds, we are not even close to figuring out what makes it last. There are dozens, perhaps hundreds, of prominent theories out there to guide therapists, yet when all is said and done, they are only frameworks that provide illusions of truth. Clearly, our journeys must encompass far more than what is familiar and comfortable, what resides in our neighborhoods. The wise person travels lightly, without attachment to things or stable ideas; this is what allows us to keep an open mind.

Between the three of us, we've written close to a hundred books. We could fill the average household library with an impressive collection of scholarly tomes, treatment manuals, textbooks, and books about cultural phenomena. We've got almost every subject covered between us—philosophy, anthropology, sociology, psychology, theology, biochemistry, education, health, media, travel, true crime, and fiction. As authors, we've written about such wide-ranging subjects as aesthetics, cybernetics, solitude, crying, travel, serial killers, conflict, love, marriage, groups, and dozens of others. Yet with all these books, we still wonder how many of them have really mattered.

Ask yourself this question: Of all the books you've ever read in your life, all the books still sitting on your shelves, how many of them have actually transformed you in a profound and significant way? When was the last time you read a book that, after you put it down, caused you to nod your head and say to yourself (and others): "Yup. That's it. I'm different now. No turning back."

We ourselves are trying to recall the last time we read a book about what we do, as experts on change, that was in any way impactful or interesting or that truly taught us anything new. Most of what is published is a rehash of what has been said before, or it's boring, or, even if it does include the seeds of a useful idea, the effects don't last very long. If the truth be told, we are even bored with most of our own books—and we wrote them!

For the three of us to take the time and devote the energy to collaborate on another book, it has *got* to be something special. At this point in our lives and careers, we are not interested in repeating something we've done before, nor are we particularly enamored with the prospect of writing a book that is only interesting and entertaining, perhaps even informative. The challenge that we face is writing a book that matters. We want to touch you in a way that you have not been touched before. And when we say "touch," we mean that in every sense of that word—to move you, caress you, hold you, and stir you emotionally, intellectually, and spiritually.

So, if you are reading this book because you are looking for a little more than a few hours of pleasure or entertainment, if you want something more than a vicarious journey into the realm of the magical, then we are pleased to inform you that it is here. We present you with the opportunity not only to read about a subject that might interest you but to *experience* the power of healing and growth in your own life.

In the journey that follows, and the incredible stories you will hear, we urge you to keep an open mind and heart. Keep your skepticism close at hand as well—you can be certain that we will do the same. But remember: We are not asking you to reach up toward any fantasized pie in the sky. We invite you to join us in getting our hands dirty while we dig for the oldest spiritual roots, going all the way down to the earliest forms of human wisdom.

Part I

Some Conceptual Foundations

Chapter One

The Zulu Conflict

"Hello?"

"Jon?"

"Yeah. This is Jon Carlson."

"Jon. This is Mev."

"Mev?"

"Brad's wife."

"Oh, Mev. Hi. I'm looking forward to seeing Brad in a few weeks. But I've been concerned because I haven't heard anything from him confirming our appointment."

Jon Carlson was sitting in his office, catching up on case notes before his next appointment. It was a Wednesday, a busy day for seeing clients, nine of them lined up, one after the other. When the phone rang, he was just getting ready to greet the next person waiting.

"Yeah, about that," Mev said in a strange voice that immediately got Jon's attention. "That's why I'm calling."

"Is everything alright?" Jon asked, suddenly alarmed. "Is Brad okay?"

"Well, I'm not really sure, actually. I got a call from him earlier today. Or rather, it was tomorrow over there."

"Huh?" Jon said, even more confused.

"Sorry," Mev answered him in an apologetic voice. "He's over in Africa now, and I guess it's tomorrow there already."

"I see," Jon said, without at all seeing where this was going. He realized that Brad Keeney was in Africa doing some sort of research on ancient rock art, or shamanic rituals, or some such thing. So why was Brad's wife calling to tell him this?

"There's been some sort of problem with the Zulus," Mev explained.

"A problem with the Zulus?" Jon could not imagine what this might involve. Was there some war going on between the tribes? And what was Brad doing in the middle of it?

"Well, anyway, he's in the middle of something that he can't get out of. He was supposed to be home next week, in time to make your video. But now he doesn't know when he'll be back."

"Let me get this straight," Jon said, trying to restrain a laugh because this story sounded so strange. "You're saying there is some kind of Zulu conflict, and Brad is in the middle of it."

"I think there's a misunderstanding between some people over there. In addition, an elder Zulu he knows, a witchdoctor, is on his deathbed or in some kind of trouble, and wants to see Brad before he dies. I'm really worried. But he called—it was a terrible connection—and all he said is that he wouldn't be home for awhile."

A Dream, a Message, and a Gift

Keeney had gone to Africa to meet with his old friend Vusamazulu Credo Mutwa, one of the most revered medicine men in the world. He was the author of several renowned and widely circulated books about African tribal history and legends (Mutwa, 1964, 1971, 1986) and also the grandson of a high Zulu witchdoctor who had been the custodian of Zulu traditions. Credo Mutwa was considered to be one of the spiritual leaders of all healers and a beacon to much of Africa. He had also been the subject of numerous assassination plots by members of other tribes who considered him a threat.

Credo Mutwa was an old man in very poor health, diagnosed with a multitude of circulatory and respiratory diseases that were common in Africa. He was a huge, imposing figure outfitted in layers of multicolored fabrics, a bright red cape, and a large staff topped with an ornamental bird. His large, round belly protruded from underneath dangling necklaces. He wore thick glasses, from which he briefly stared intently at anyone he faced. He believed these were the last days of his life, and he was at a point where he was waiting for death to take him. He had known Keeney for many years and was waiting to see him.

Nearly a decade earlier, Keeney had traveled to Mutwa's village in Mafikeng and announced, "I have come to you because of a dream. I bring you a sacred gift. And a message."

Mutwa slowly held out his hand for Keeney to shake and studied him carefully. "I know of you," Mutwa said simply.

"The spirits have brought me to Africa," Keeney continued. "I have found a spiritual home with the Bushmen and I am honored that they have adopted me as one of their spokespersons."

The old man nodded gravely, still studying the stranger intently. "My mother's father was a Bushman. I am a descendent of the people."

Keeney replied, "I just came from the Kalahari and I was with the people. I came to Africa with two pipes that had been given to me by strong medicine men in my own country, friends with whom I work. They are of the tribe called Ojibwa." He pronounced the word slowly and watched Mutwa form it on his own lips. It struck Keeney as incredible at the time that here he was, the conduit between two powerful healers in the world, each from a different continent.

"I was confused until this moment," Keeney said, "because I brought this pipe for you as a gift of the Indian people of my own country. But in my dream I was told to give it only to a Bushman. Now I see that you are not only a great Zulu but also a Bushman." He slowly extended both hands with the peace pipe held between them.

As Mutwa reached for the sacred gift, he winced in pain. He took the pipe and examined it, nodding to himself. "I have a gift for you as well," he said gesturing to a necklace made of wooden beads. "This is a very special thing. It is made from sacred wood that has been burned while a prayer has been said to the Big God. It is only to be worn by a *sangoma*, a healer such as yourself."

Mutwa's wife, who had watched the proceedings with some trepidation, approached the tall White bearded stranger with long hair holding the sacred wooden beads. Keeney had to bend over like a knight in order to receive the necklace around his neck.

Vusamazulu Credo Mutwa, Zulu healer, wearing
the ceremonial blood necklace.

"With this sacred thing, made from the wood of the Protector,
you are recognized as a *sangoma* of our people. I will share the
Zulu sacred knowledge with you and you will also carry our
truths." With this last statement, Mutwa smiled for the first time.

"I am truly honored, Credo Mutwa, but I see you are in great
pain. I *feel* the pain in my lungs."

"You must touch me then," Mutwa directed Keeney, requesting,
in effect, that Brad use his healing powers to relieve him of his
suffering. After many years of a hard life, both physically de-
manding and politically treacherous, the great spiritual leader of
Africa was both depressed and discouraged. In spite of all his efforts, he had failed to unite his people. He was still considered an
enemy by old members of the South African police and several
foreign powers. And now he was waiting to die a very painful
death.

Keeney watched Mutwa slowly stand, with the help of his wife
and another villager. It seemed to take several minutes for him to
rise and then rearrange himself in proper form. Keeney reached
out and took the old man's hand between his own. He pressed
both hands against Mutwa's chest, the place where he sensed the
most pain deep in Mutwa's lungs. While they stood close in this

position, Keeney could feel his own body begin to shake and vibrate, an undulating series of movements that seemed to move from one limb to another and then centered deep in his belly. As they held one another and shook, Keeney began to chant and improvise songs that were inspired by his relationships with other healing traditions. The songs were directed toward Mutwa's pains, inviting them to come out.

By this time, others from the area had come to watch this strange proceeding—they didn't know what to make of this big long-haired man who was singing and shaking with their spiritual leader.

It might have been only minutes, but it felt to Keeney like hours before the shaking stopped. Mutwa looked up at Keeney, who was taller than he, and nodded his head.

"I have had a dream about this meeting," Mutwa said, "but it is also a dream of four winds that come together from different directions."

"Yes," Keeney replied, "this is my mission and my life, to help bring together the healing practices of many people."

Mutwa smiled warmly again, then turned very serious. "I must tell you something. I do not have long to live . . . even with your help." He smiled gratefully as he said this, for he was indeed now briefly free of pain. "It will soon be time for others like you to carry on the walk. There is much to do and many forces that block our way." Mutwa was a tired, dispirited man who was exhausted from doing battle with the South African police, the jealous African leaders, the governments of neighboring countries, and even the United States government, which consistently sided with authorities against his people. He spoke of his frustrations with the supposed advances of modern medicine that had no respect for the old ways. He talked about his sadness over racial tensions, the corruption of African officials, and the spread of diseases like HIV.

All throughout the day and well into the evening, Mutwa and Keeney talked of their missions and their work. They shared beliefs about their healing methods and how they worked. They exchanged ideas about the world around them and what must be done to help the people. And before the day ended, they had become fast friends.

So, this was how Brad Keeney found himself as the *consigliore,* the spiritual adviser, and the shaman to the most powerful shaman in Africa. And because of events that were about to unfold, Keeney would end up smack in the middle of some of the latest South African conflicts that were waged, not with spears, but with automatic weapons.

Dangerous Journey

It was clear to Keeney that Credo Mutwa needed spiritual help for this last stage of his life, more than could be provided by his own powers. During their next talk, he revisited an earlier discussion.

"I remember a story you told me," Keeney said, getting right to the point, rather than continuing their discussions of political unrest in the country.

"Yes," Mutwa said, nodding his head gravely.

"It was a story of your own teacher, the woman who initiated you into this world."

"That was Mynah. My aunt. She was the last surviving daughter of Dingane, the Zulu king. She became a *mulozi,* one who is guided by the whistling spirits."

"Yes," Keeney pressed, "I remember you saying that she was your mentor, the one who first taught you to be a great healer."

"That is so. She was a great healer of our people. When she was a child, her father, my grandfather, had a secret bag that contained his most sacred objects. He had become very ill and was concerned about what would happen to the bag after he died; it must be destroyed. The bag was then taken far into the land and hidden. Mynah was instructed to go out and let the spirit lead her to this bag. She fasted for many days and was gone for a long time. When she returned, she told a story of being led to a large termite hill, where she felt the spirits draw her. She reached inside the hill and retrieved the bag, which had been unmolested by the insects. Ever since then, she had become the keeper of my grandfather's sacred medicine."

"I notice that you said she *was* a great healer. Is she no longer alive?"

"Sadly, this must be so. She would be over 100 years. I have not seen her in 30, or maybe 40, years."

"Are you certain she is no longer with us?" Keeney pressed him. "Maybe we should go look for her?"

For the very first time, Mutwa's eyes lit up like a child. "You really think so? You think we should go find her, do you?"

Keeney looked intently in Mutwa's eyes, magnified by the thick lenses. "Yes, Baba," he said, "that is what we must do." In fact, Keeney held out little hope that this old woman could possibly be alive at age 100, given all the disease and conflict that would have come her way over the years. Yet Keeney reasoned that it was not crucial that Aunt Mynah still be alive, but rather that Mutwa had a mission, a reason to go on living. In such spiritual journeys, it is the search that is important, not the goal.

"Do you have any idea what you are asking, my son?" Mutwa shook his head at the impossibility of such a pilgrimage. "Do you know the place of my ancestral home?"

"I do not," Keeney admitted. "But that does not matter. We will go there." He said this with such finality, and such intensity, that Credo Mutwa felt he had no choice but to agree.

What Mutwa had not explained at the time was that his ancestral village was exactly in the middle of the most violent and dangerous place in South Africa. They would have to travel down a road that was occupied by dozens of snipers who would ambush people on sight. To add to the mix, apartheid may have just been declared illegal, but that did not stop various groups from killing one another.

This was also an especially dangerous time for traditional healers in Africa. They were being hunted by police for fomenting revolution. Some radical fundamentalist missionary groups had gone so far as to encourage the use of fire-burning "necklaces" to kill these primitive witchdoctors, who were an affront to good Christians everywhere. There was gossip of a large bounty on Mutwa's head for any assassin who could bring him in, dead or alive, but preferably dead.

For this reason, Keeney and Mutwa would have to travel with bodyguards. These were largely mercenaries who had worked for various regimes and now hired themselves out to protect important figures. Three bodyguards would be accompanying them on this trip through KwaZulu-Natal Province, all of them equipped with Uzis and automatic pistols strapped to their ankles.

"You guys got any rocket launchers, too?" Keeney kidded Wil, the guard in charge of their security. Whether it was because he didn't understand the question, or he preferred to keep his armaments secret from a possible enemy, Wil just stared at Brad with an expression that chilled him. Brad had already heard from Mutwa that this man was a professional assassin, someone who had killed many people for his previous government employer. Keeney actually felt very grateful that Wil was now working for them.

They loaded up the convoy with their equipment and weapons. Credo was outfitted in his most impressive ceremonial Zulu gowns. Beads and necklaces weighing more than 70 pounds were draped around his thick neck and hanging off his shoulders. Keeney thought about asking Credo if he could present a rather less conspicuous appearance for the journey—after all, this was like proclaiming to all the world, and especially to all the marksmen waiting along their route, that this was a witchdoctor worth a sizable bounty.

Credo Mutwa and his entourage of bodyguards, assistants, and family members, with Keeney in tow, began the long trek across the desolate land. They traveled the back roads as much as possible, barely cleared spaces that were pocked with ruts, strewn with boulders, and overgrown with brush. They were hoping to avoid the gauntlet of snipers and bandits along the main road and so took a lesser-known route that went through the mountains.

It had grown dark. There was a cloak of fog so thick, they couldn't even make out the edges of the road, a circumstance for which Keeney actually felt grateful. He knew there were long drop-offs just inches from the spinning wheels that were trying to gain some purchase in the soft dirt. Wil and the other bodyguards held their weapons ready, fingers on the triggers, but with safeties on, lest an inadvertent jolt set off the guns. Previously, they had been scanning the cliffs, watching for possible ambush sites, but that now proved impossible: There could be a whole army of mercenaries and Zulu warriors standing just ahead and there was no way to see them. By now, they could barely make out the front of the vehicle just ahead.

"Do you think we should stop?" Keeney asked the driver. He had tried to follow their route on a map, but the roads they were traveling were not even shown.

The driver just shook his head vigorously, as he hunched over the steering wheel, attempting to peer into the fog. Keeney looked toward Wil, who shrugged. "If we stop," he said, "those who are following us would be very pleased."

"There's someone following us?" Keeney asked, trying to keep his voice as calm as possible. After all, he was now not only an initiated Bushman shaman but also respected by the Zulu. He must show courage.

Wil shrugged and looked out into the fog as well. It was obvious that the game plan was to move as fast as possible to stay ahead of anyone who wished them harm. Keeney's concern about their navigation was interrupted by a conversation taking place between Credo Mutwa and a woman in the entourage. Nobela had been brought along for just this occasion: She was known for her ability to go into trances in order to allow herself to be guided by the spirit. She was doing this now, Keeney noted.

"Credo," Keeney asked Mutwa, "what's going on?"

While staring out into the fog with everyone else, Mutwa shrugged. Keeney was not sure exactly what that meant. Did he not know what this woman was doing? Or was he saying he didn't care? Between waiting for the snipers to start shooting or the van to go rolling off the side of the cliff, Keeney felt panic starting to well up inside him. Yet Mutwa seemed calm. So did the others. Taking deep breaths, Keeney quieted himself, in order to remain as still as possible. It would not do to disrupt the energy flowing in this precarious situation.

Nobela was an ageless woman, maybe 30 or 40 or 60—Keeney couldn't tell. She was wrapped in a shawl that covered her head, and the whole bundle seemed to be rocking, much as one would see among Orthodox Jewish rabbis during prayer. Keeney noticed that although she was also staring out into the direction of the fog, her eyes were closed. And she was pointing to the driver which way to go.

"Go to the right," she said, "this way, over there." As she moved her arm in that direction, various string of beads encircling her arms and torso began to rattle.

The driver turned to the right without giving it a thought, although none of them could see a thing beyond the front of the van.

"Good," Nobela said. "That is far enough. Now you must go carefully here because there will be a boulder blocking the way. There will be no room to pass it on the left so you must stay to the right." As she was giving these directions, Keeney looked again and noticed that her eyes were still closed. This was such an amazing show that for a minute, he forgot the danger they were in. Even the bodyguards were transfixed, not quite believing their own eyes: They were being led through this treacherous territory by a woman in a trance with her eyes closed. Wil had been a guard to Nelson Mandela; he had never seen anything stranger than this.

Shopping for Goats

Mutwa was sitting quietly in his seat, arms crossed, as if this type of foggy journey happened all the time. After a period of time, he announced that it was time to stop.

"Are you certain?" Wil asked him. He was becoming increasingly nervous because being in control is what guided his ability to do his job. Now he had no idea where they were or what enemies they might face just within striking distance.

"We must find some goats," Mutwa then announced. "Up ahead we will find them."

"Goats?" Wil asked, the same question that was on Keeney's mind. What on earth could they need goats for at a time like this?

"For the sacrifice," Mutwa explained, "We cannot visit my aunt without a gift of greeting and celebration." Keeney noted that by this time, Mutwa was referring to Mynah as if she was alive. Did he know something? Keeney wondered.

Several hours later, they arrived at a thatched hut in the Babanango region of KwaZulu-Natal province, what used to be called Zululand. The settlement was situated on a ridge of mountains that overlooked a wide expanse of plains. Because the fog had lifted by this time and the sun was rising, they could see forever.

The hut was circular, not unlike an igloo, only it was constructed of dried mud, with a roof made of twigs and sticks. Mutwa and Keeney got out of the van, followed by the others, and approached the entrance. Inside, four women were sitting around, one of whom was indeed Mynah, around 100 years of age, who was in the process of making final preparations for the end of her life.

Mutwa embraced his long-lost aunt and spiritual mentor, and her small body looked as if it had been swallowed up by his hulking flesh. They hugged one another and would not let go, eventually breaking out into a dance to call up the spirits. This reunion proved not only to be the salvation of Credo Mutwa's spirit, because he had long since given up his own will to live, but it renewed Aunt Mynah's commitment to postpone her own death a little further. They pledged to one another that they would continue their struggle to bring together all the people of Zululand and greater Africa, to unite their spirits.

Keeney watched this reunion with awe and not without a certain satisfaction that he had insisted that his friend make this important journey. Later, when they had a chance to talk together about what had happened during this journey and what it meant, the great healer turned the discussion to Brad's own life.

"You must be brave," Mutwa told Keeney. "You are carrying an important message to the people, but it is not one that everyone will accept. The empires of the world try to stop the spirits of the mother, but we must not let them. It is the same with medicine. People do not respect the old ways."

Mutwa paused for a moment, warming himself to the story that was to follow. "Some years ago I saw a doctor who told me he would have to cut off my leg. I asked him why and he said it was because I had a cancer named melanoma. I told them that was a beautiful name, like that of a pretty girl. I told this doctor that there is no way that a beautiful girl named Melanoma would kill me. The doctor just thought I was crazy.

"So I went to the land and I started to make a sculpture of this beautiful girl named Melanoma. It was to be as high as three people and as big as a house. I worked on it day and night until I became so exhausted that my family tried to keep me restrained. But I would not let them.

"When I finished the statue of Melanoma, the large things on my leg went away. In Africa, we call this skin disease Md-lazubada, the one who devours you. But we never say this name lest we awaken his hunger. We believe that cancer like this is not a disease at all, but a living creature that must be contained. And the way to contain this thing is to build an image of it, to lose yourself in its creation and thereby forget what has happened to your body."

By now, Keeney was used to such stories so he waited patiently.

"I see," Mutwa said, "that you are waiting for an old man to finish."

"No," Keeney protested. "Not at all. I was just . . ."

"That is fine. That is just fine. But this is what I want to say to you: My time is over and now it is your time. You must be the one to tell the people about the old ways. You must be the one to continue the work of Mynah, and myself. You must become a bucket that holds the sacred water of the Zulu and the scarce raindrops of the Bushmen, as well as the healing waters found in other places that you go. You must learn their ways. And you must teach their ways to others, as you have done with me. Among other things, I want you to tell my life story. It will hold some of

Vusamazulu Credo Mutwa and the Statue of Melanoma
he built to cure his disease.

the old forgotten knowledge from my ancestors." (Note: Keeney did write a biography of Mutwa, which was published several years later [Keeney, 2001a].)

Mutwa touched his chest as he said this, referring to his healing session with Brad, which occurred upon their first meeting. Since that time, and because he and Keeney had shared many other healing sessions together, the pain had been kept at bay. This was even better than having to go out onto the land and build another statue.

"Finally, I wish to say you are like a son to me, a holder of my teachings." With those last words, Vusamazulu Credo Mutwa, great healer of the African continent and spiritual leader, touched Brad's shoulder one last time and looked deeply into his eyes. It was then that Keeney saw Mutwa's eyes roll back into his head, with only the whites showing. He then began to sing his most sacred song, leaning toward Keeney, coming closer until he draped himself over the White man's body. He then placed his lips to the top of Keeney's head, blowing hard into the hair.

Keeney felt Mutwa's warm breath, and his huge bulk seemed to swallow him, just as the shaman had done with his Aunt Mynah.

Brad felt lost in his embrace, a little boy being held by his father. He felt himself shaking uncontrollably, as the vibrations ran between and through them. The power and the sensation became so strong that he could not catch his breath. The last thought he had before losing consciousness was that it was time to go home.

Chapter Two

Dancing under the Stars

"We're just about out of fuel."

"What do you mean, we're out of fuel?" Keeney shouted over the sound of the engine. They'd been lurching along for hours, driving through the heart of the central Kalahari Desert, the second largest expanse of endless sand in the world. They were probably still in Botswana, unless they had somehow crossed over into Namibia. It would certainly be easy to do, because what had earlier passed for a road now dwindled to a track in the sand.

"Keep going," Keeney ordered, trying to line up the map with some recognizable feature of the landscape. But it all looked the same—as far as they could see, endless brush and sand were speckled with a few spooky-looking camelthorn trees. If they didn't figure out their location soon, they'd end up sleeping in the truck until someone else came along.

Peter was a colleague and a fellow professor at the University of South Africa in Pretoria, where Keeney had been working as a visiting professor. One condition of his appointment had been that they arrange for someone to take Keeney into the Kalahari so that he could spend time with the Bushmen, the oldest practitioners of shamanic healing in the world. Peter had graciously volunteered for the job, and although he might have been an able academic, he had done a questionable job of planning for this journey. They had neither the proper equipment nor the necessary spare parts if something broke down. Now they were about to run out of gas in the most remote place in the world. There'd be no rescuers any time soon.

"Look! There!" Peter pointed in the direction of what appeared to be a road heading west toward some trees and possible shade.

"No, Peter, just keep following straight," Keeney insisted again. He looked over at Nelson, their third companion, sitting in the back seat. He was a university student who had come along as their interpreter. Hearing no advice from the only native African present, Keeney insisted again, "We're getting close. I can feel it."

Dreams of Africa

Peter looked sideways at his companion, still intrigued with hearing about Keeney's hunches and dreams. He'd already heard the story of how this whole trip had come about. Keeney had been working as a professor at various universities in the United States, teaching family therapy. He had by this time abandoned much of his academic training as a scholar and a psychologist and was recasting himself more along the lines of a cultural anthropologist, if not a practicing shaman. As part of this journey, he began spending more time with Native American medicine men, fasting and praying, and was an active member of an inner-city Black church. He was also learning to pay more attention to his dreams, as a guide for his waking life.

Sometimes, Keeney would dream a phone number; when he awoke, he would call the number to see who was waiting for him on the other end of the line. These encounters never failed to interest him. He also hid a secret life from his academic colleagues when he sneaked off to reservations in South Dakota and Canada to meet with respected healers and spiritual leaders of various tribes. These led to some unusual dreams, which he began to trust more than ever.

One night Keeney had a dream of Africa. He dreamed about a place in Southern Africa, in the desert, where the old people lived, the oldest known healers. The next morning he awoke determined to learn more about these people. He took books out of the library and looked for similarities between their practices and what he was familiar with. He read about the shaking and dancing that cause such ecstatic body movements. And he learned as much as he could about their spiritual beliefs. Something about the Bushmen drew him. And by this point, he had stopped questioning his visions.

Not more than 3 weeks later, a letter from the university in South Africa came in the mail, asking if he'd like to come over as a visiting professor to teach his theories of change to undergraduate and graduate students. They had been using his books as texts in their courses. Keeney was mildly amused by this fortuitous invitation but not really all that surprised. Things like this had happened to him before.

"Sure," Keeney wrote them back immediately. "I'd be delighted to come over. It is truly an honor. But I have one condition: You must arrange for me to visit the Bushmen."

So now, here they were, enroute to Keeney's dream: finally meeting the holders of the most ancient wisdom of shamanic healing. It seemed, however, that this trip was about to have an abrupt and inauspicious end. The needle on the fuel gauge was so far below empty, it had fallen off the dial, no longer visible at all. Their last fuel can had already been emptied into the tank. This was it. It was time to start looking for a place to sleep for the night. If they conserved their water, maybe they'd be lucky enough for someone else to come along.

A few minutes later, they saw a settlement in the distance.

"There it is!" Keeney said excitedly. "That's it!" He compared the location to the map, where he had marked the exact location of the place he had seen in his dream.

An Unusual Greeting

The truck was making such a racket on its approach that villagers came out of their huts to see what was going on. Keeney noticed a few scrawny men, wearing dirty brown pants, squatting on their haunches, watching impassively as the vehicle sputtered closer. Several women, one with a baby attached to her back, were kneeling on the ground, pulling up grasses and examining their roots for something edible. And in the center of this village, Brad noticed a group of older men standing together, watching them impassively.

Keeney actually bounded from the truck before Peter fully came to a stop. He strode toward the men who were conversing. While Peter waited in the truck to see if it was safe, Nelson, their interpreter, ran to catch up with Keeney. "These crazy Americans!" he thought to himself, not for the first time.

"Come on, Nelson," Keeney whispered urgently. "I want you with me when we greet them."

Keeney walked right up to the three men standing there and found himself drawn to the one in the middle, an older man with a wrinkled face and white, short-cropped hair. Without giving the matter any thought, Brad put his arms around the old man, who embraced him in return. As soon as they made contact, Keeney felt himself begin to shake—his arms, his upper legs, but mostly his stomach and chest. It was as if the two of them were connected by a current of electricity—which, in a sense, they were.

Once the two companions saw what was happening, they, too, grabbed hold and started to shake. The three Bushmen began to sing. It was music from their hearts, starting soft and gradually building up volume. Every once in a while, there was a deep, resonant "Mmmmmmmmmm," like the sound someone might make after tasting a delicious morsel of food.

Other men in the village started to approach, seeing their friends—who all just happened to be the three main shamans of the community—shaking with this wild-looking White man who had appeared out of the desert. They began fluttering their hands over the four shaking men, making sympathetic music and sounds. This seemed to draw out the women of the village, who began singing and clapping a syncopated rhythm that got the men's feet moving. Now everyone started dancing.

Both Peter and Nelson stood watching this spectacle with their mouths open. One moment they were lost in the desert, and now they stood watching a spontaneous tribal healing dance in the middle of the community. As of yet, Nelson had not had the opportunity to translate anything: Keeney seemed to be doing all right on his own, with his dancing and shaking.

Sweat was pouring off their bodies, as the men danced and the women clapped and sang. Nelson explained what was going on, for Peter's benefit, but Brad was out of earshot, hooked into another world altogether. Then Keeney thought that perhaps it would be a good idea to introduce himself. After all, here they were, all moaning and hugging and vibrating together, and they didn't know one another's names. Surely, this was some breach of protocol.

If the three shamans did not seem surprised by Keeney's visit, it was later explained to him that they had also dreamed of this encounter; they had been waiting for him for some time.

Keeney approached the oldest of the men again and gestured for Nelson to translate. "My name is Bradford Keeney and I come from a land far away, not on this continent."

"We know who you are," the old man said. "I am Mantag. It is from my grandfather that I receive my vision. It would be the same for you."

As soon as Nelson translated these words, Keeney felt a chill. It *was* from his grandfather that he had inherited his spiritual sensitivity. Grandfather Keeney had been a country preacher and a spiritual leader for his community. He was the most significant figure in Brad's life, the family legacy from which Brad drew his inspiration.

"This is so," Keeney answered and then examined the old man further. Mantag was dressed in worn, filthy, brownish-grayish rags that hung on his thin, emaciated frame. Nothing about his appearance would enable anyone to guess that he was the most powerful shaman among the local Bushmen.

"Welcome home," Mantag said next.

"Excuse me?" Keeney turned to Nelson, not sure he understood what the man had said.

"He said to you, 'Welcome home,'" the translator repeated, uneasy about this whole interaction. He wondered what a White man was doing way out here and why he wanted to bother these people. The Bushmen were often treated as worse than vermin, even by other Africans, who disrespectfully considered them remnants of the Stone Age. Nelson had earned admittance to one of the most prestigious universities on the continent, so he could not understand why this foreign doctor wished to come to this godforsaken place.

Keeney again felt a chill. Welcome home? What did *that* mean?

Seeing his confusion, Mantag cocked his head and pointed toward a tree at the edge of the community. It was a majestic camelthorn tree, draped with thick branches. "This is where you can live," he said. "And when you die, that is where your soul will return."

Keeney visibly paled. He looked at Nelson for a reaction, but like most young Black Africans, when in the presence of a White man, Nelson was careful to hide his true reactions. Peter, on the other hand, seemed to be even more freaked out than Brad was.

Mantag placed a hand on Keeney's shoulder and leaned in close, almost as if to get his scent. "Soon we will dance," he said.

Visitors

The Bushmen lived in simply constructed round huts, perhaps a little more than a body's length in diameter. There were thick branches stacked together like logs, then held together by mud and grasses. Grass was piled on top as a roof. Around the perimeter of the camp, the Bushmen had placed a rough fence of camelthorn branches, the sharp points facing outward. This was designed to keep lions and other predators from getting inside.

Nelson explained all this to Peter and Brad, then muttered to himself that it was too bad it didn't do much to keep the black mamba out.

"What's that you said?" Peter asked.

"Black mamba. It's a snake," Nelson answered.

"I *know* it's a snake, but what's that got to do with the fence?"

"Nothing really. I was just thinking about when I was a child and I lived in a place like this. We had a fence made of camelthorn to keep away the lions. But it did nothing to keep away the black mamba."

"What's this about the black mamba?" Keeney now asked, overhearing the conversation while he was helping to set up camp under the tree that would become his ancestral home.

Nelson became even more serious than usual. "When I was a boy, one of those things came into our village. They grow to be 9 feet long and they are most vicious. It is said they have enough venom to kill a whole group of people. They rise up high off the ground, then they strike not just once, but they will attack many times one after the other, killing anything within range. They are so fast, you cannot even see them strike."

This only reminded Keeney where he was—in Africa—in the wildest place that still existed in the world, living with the oldest people. And yet, when he thought about it, he realized that Mantag was right: He *did* feel as if he were home.

While they continued to set up their camp, people from the village walked by to see what the strange White doctor was doing. Kids visited, of course, because they were curious. But Keeney was also surprised to see that most of the adults, especially the older men, came by to pay their respects. It was all very exhausting and overwhelming, so the visitors turned in early for the night.

From a Dream

The next morning, they were sitting inside their tent with cups of tea, delighted that neither a lion nor a black mamba had breached their perimeter.

"Had any more of your dreams last night?" Peter asked Keeney in a teasing voice.

"As a matter of fact, I did," he answered, then took a sip of tea. Brad took the jests in the spirit in which they offered. He realized that Peter was a very different scholar from himself, an empiricist and an observer. He was a teacher of psychotherapy and a skeptic, not prone to believe in any of the types of things that attracted Keeney's attention. And this dream business Peter considered the most puzzling of all.

"What was it, then?" Peter asked him, eager for the latest installment of a world he didn't quite know how to evaluate.

"It wasn't a strange dream this time," Keeney said. "It was rather simple. I dreamed that we would have a guide among the Bushmen to lead the way. His name is Tweelie or something like that. He pronounced his name to me. . . ."

"In the dream, you mean?" Peter teased.

"Yes, I know it sounds strange, but I heard his name in my dream."

Peter nodded, watching the sun rise over the edge of the horizon. It was a huge red shimmering ball.

"I was saying that he spoke to me in the dream, but with the clicking, sing-song language, it was hard for me to say it back right. I think it's Tweelie or Twilie or something like that."

"Good then," Peter laughed. "I'll keep an eye out for such a chap. Maybe we should just call the name out to the village and see who comes running."

Brad laughed good-naturedly. He liked Peter a lot and knew that his friend respected but did not understand his visions and dreams and shaking.

Usually, an indefinite period of time would elapse between his dreams and their realization, but this time it was soon after they prepared to begin their day that another man from the village came calling.

"Damn," Brad whispered to Peter, "I know this guy. I swear I've seen him before."

He was a tall, angular man, the tallest Bushman they had yet seen. He was not like the others, who were mostly shamans wanting to make contact with the new doctor in town. He approached with a huge smile that spanned the length of his narrow face. He had a sparse goatee and a mustache—little curly threads that, on first impression, made him seem younger. He turned toward Nelson, who was watching him suspiciously, and spoke with Nelson for a few minutes, their voices clicking in that beautiful rhythm and cadence of the Bushman language.

"This man has come to help you," Nelson told Keeney. "He says he wants you to meet his people. He will do everything he can to make this possible. He wants to help the Big Doctor in his work." Before continuing, Nelson explained that the title "Big Doctor" did not refer to Keeney's size but to his stature among the other doctors of the village. "This man tells me that they have never met anyone with so much power to shake. They want you to know there will be strong dancing tonight."

Keeney was absolutely drawn to this new visitor's amazing smile. Whereas other Africans he had met in the bush had somewhat restrained and muted expressions, this man smiled like the sun they had seen earlier—bright and blinding. He held out both his hands to the visitor, and said, "I am Keeney, and it is good to know you."

"I am Twele," the man answered and then stopped when he heard the other White man, Peter, gasp.

"It is an honor to know you, Twele," Keeney answered, not skipping a beat. He turned to look at Peter and winked, as if to say, "Do you believe this?"

As it turned out, this was actually a turning point for Peter, the empiricist and scientist, who, for the rest of the journey, let go of some of his assumptions and just watched the show unfold. He

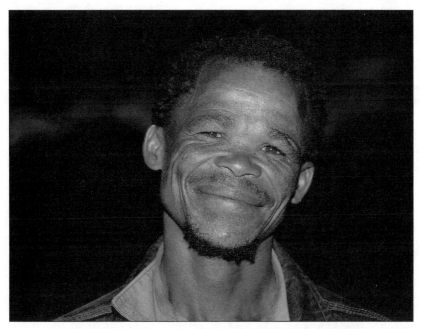

Twele, Keeney's Bushman friend from Khutswe, Botswana.

still remained on the outside, an observer like Nelson, but he was totally enraptured by this adventure, which was so different from anything he had known in his own country.

Twele moved into their camp, just as the dream foretold, and became their invaluable guide from that day forward. His first task was to prepare the White doctor for the ritual during the evening. Whereas, previously, other Bushmen had danced for anthropologists, this healing ceremony would be unique. They were going to a dance expecting a stranger, not to mention a White man and a non-African, to deeply participate in their secret ways, which had been passed on from one generation to the next, since the first humans were born.

Heating and Cooling the Nails

The first thing that Keeney noticed later, when they settled around the fire, is that there were not a lot of rules or piety, such as one would expect in a sacred and religious ceremony. People seemed jubilant and playful, almost as if they were hanging out at the pub. Everyone was just gathering and laughing.

Keeney leaned over to ask Nelson about the conversations going on around them. "What are they saying?"

Nelson seemed embarrassed at first, reluctant to answer. "The women—they are teasing the men about whether they are going to be good lovers tonight after the dancing is over."

The kids were playing and running in circles. Dogs walked through the circle that was forming, until chased away by kids throwing stones at them. Just outside the big circle with its huge bonfire, little fires were started, where some of the older men were sitting and heating drinks. There was an atmosphere of gaiety, with no hint that the most holy and powerful of all sacred rituals on the African continent was about to take place.

Once it became dark, the women sat down to join the group. Keeney heard one of them swat at a mosquito, which seemed strange because he had seen no mosquitoes during this season. Then he saw that it had been a scorpion. He tucked his legs farther under him, hoping to present less of a target. After one last look around to check for marauding lions or black mambas, he focused his full concentration on what was unfolding around him. He had never been more excited about anything in his life, except perhaps the birth of his son. In a way, this was the birth of a new son, a new part of himself.

A few people began to sing and clap, as the women had done when they first greeted him the day before. More and more women joined the song, until they were all together, clapping in rhythm and singing the song that had been sung here since the beginning of their people.

While the women continued to sing, the men began to rise and dance slowly around the edges of the circle. It was a simple movement, a little two-step shuffle like you might see at an Indian ceremony, but with an African rhythm. The older men danced the basic step, while the younger ones showed more flair, moving their arms, strutting their stuff, entertaining the women. It was then that Keeney rose to join them, situating himself in the line between Twele and Mantag, his two guides.

So far, what he had seen was what might be shown to visitors, tourists, or anthropologists, the kind of thing they demonstrate in documentaries. The Bushmen rarely, if ever, show outsiders their most powerful expressions of the healing dance.

It is when a shaman feels the energy in his body that the healing dance begins. This is first reflected in the music, which becomes more intense in volume. The clapping takes on a crisp and piercing staccato rhythm. The mood around the campfire changes completely, from one of playfulness and celebration to deadly seriousness: It is dangerous business calling out the spirits.

"What's happening?" Peter asked Nelson anxiously, noticing the abrupt changes taking place. Nelson, in turn, asked Twele to explain the transition, which was then translated back to Peter.

"It is now that the healers . . . ," Nelson hesitated a moment, considering a choice of words. There really is no exact translation for what the Bushmen call their healers. The titles "doctor," "witchdoctor," or "shaman" are all not quite right, so he chose "healer" for now, which also did not really fit.

"The healers are feeling the power now. It rises in their belly," Twele said, putting his own hands on his stomach to test the current action. "I feel my hands become hot in the dance. The power also comes to my feet and they move of their own accord."

"Is that what is happening now?" Peter asked again, noticing that Keeney's own movements in the dance were becoming more erratic and jerky.

"Yes, see the Big Doctor?" he pointed toward Keeney. "He feels the power from the Big God. I only feel the power during the dance, but some—like Keeney and Mantag—they have the visions and are visited at other times."

Twele then went on to say that the Big God plants arrows and nails in the bellies of the chosen ones. Nelson stopped to explain that although Twele used the word *nail,* they used to refer to *thorns,* as in the sharp branches of the camelthorn tree. There are only two ways to get such arrows and nails—from the Big God, or from another, more powerful shaman who has many such things in his own belly.

"When you see the others touching Keeney," Twele said, pointing out how others during the previous days and this evening had been fondling and hugging him, "they are not so much being affectionate as they are feeling and receiving the arrows and nails in his belly. They say he has many."

"But the witchdoctors, the healers—they look like they are in pain." Peter was referring to the bent-over movements in the dance, in which a few of the men were gasping and holding their abdomens, almost as if they had stomach aches.

"Yes," Twele nodded. "When the healing dance begins, the nails begin to heat up and become very, very hot. I feel this, too, when I dance, although not as strong as others."

Peter surreptitiously felt his own belly, but nothing was there except a little indigestion from dinner. However, there was no doubt that the witchdoctors who were dancing seemed to be in great agony—and great ecstasy.

"When the nails become hot," Twele added, "they start to rise in the body and they climb in the chest. The heat becomes like steam that comes out of a hole in the head. The steam falls to the ground, where it cools again, forms another arrow or nail, and enters the body again through the feet of the dancer."

At this point, Peter noticed that a younger man who had been dancing right behind Keeney started to jerk in convulsions, screaming in pain, and then ran out of the circle into the bush. Peter looked nervously over his shoulder to see the man writhing on the ground. "Is he okay?"

Twele nodded gravely. "Yes, he will live. But no, he is not good right now. The younger ones cannot tolerate the nails and arrows when they dance. It frightens them. They lose control and start to shiver."

As a psychologist, Peter recognized the classic symptoms of an anxiety attack, in which the central nervous symptom goes into emergency mode, igniting a whole range of protective mechanisms that people experience as anxiety. That was what seemed to be happening to those who were relatively new at this shaman business.

Peter could now see several of the older men kneeling over the writhing man. They were waving their hands over him, then massaging his stomach. One of the men was taking his own sweat and rubbing it into the man's arms and neck.

"That is how they cool down the nails," Twele explained.

Peter turned again and saw that Keeney was obviously feeling the arrows in his belly, for he was dancing around like a marionette that was being jerked at the end of a string. It no longer looked like he was dancing but like he was being danced. Peter could see from Brad's expression that he was surprised by what was happening, as if this was totally outside of his control.

The second this automatic dancing began, it was as if the others had radar. The other healers knew that Keeney had been grabbed, even if he didn't know what was going on inside his own body. Before this point, it had been as if the energy were playing with him a little, jerking him around, so to speak. But now he was clearly in the zone. First one leg started jerking, then the other. Then his chest began rippling and vibrating. By this time, Twele had run over and was now holding him, drawing strength from his energy. He placed his right hand on Brad's belly, and Brad later swore that it felt like hot coals that singed him all the way to his core. He was then surrounded by the other healers, all of whom were rubbing their sweat into his body, touching him, pressing their foreheads against his. Others were like human leeches, attaching to his neck or back, sometimes making sucking sounds as if they were extracting the energy from within. It was as if Keeney were a nuclear source of spirit energy, and the whole tribe wanted a piece.

The dances have cycles, because there is no way that a human body could sustain this sort of jerking and shaking and dancing continuously throughout the night. After several hours, everyone else had crumbled to the ground. People were lying in heaps, some sleeping, others panting in exhaustion. Only Keeney and the old man, Mantag, were still dancing, as if there was no limit to their energy; the Big God would not let them go. Keeney's movements, at this point, were becoming more subdued. His last conscious thought was that it felt as if he'd known these people all of his life.

Shaking the Fears Away

When Keeney awoke the next morning, he had no recollection of how he had gotten back to his camp, much less inside the tent. Peter was already gone, so Keeney reckoned he must have been unconscious for some time. He recalled that after he passed out the first time, he was awakened again by the sound of music. Just when he thought he might rest his weary arms and legs, and his fiery stomach, he was lifted off the ground again by the puppet strings. The dancing and shaking had begun again in another cycle. And so it continued throughout the night. At least, that's what he thought had happened, unless it had all been another one of his crazy dreams.

"You up?" Peter called from outside the tent, hearing Keeney groan.

"I think so," he mumbled, feeling numbness in his arms and legs.

"That was some party, huh?" Peter said, sticking his head through the tent flap. "I had no idea you were such a wild man."

"Neither did I," Keeney answered. He was expecting to be hung over, but he felt surprisingly well rested, except for a slight numbness in his limbs. But that was not unusual, considering that he never exercised or worked out. Somehow he had kept up with the strongest healers in the community, many of whom had been doing this their whole lives, even though he could barely walk a few miles without stopping to rest.

Peter handed Brad a mug of hot tea and sat on a stool by his cot. "That was probably the most remarkable thing I've ever seen," he said to Keeney. "And I've seen a lot." He shook his head as if he still couldn't believe it.

"It was something, wasn't it?" Keeney looked at his friend and was surprised to see that Peter had tears in his eyes. Peter was a social scientist, an ethnographer. He was always on the sidelines, as an observer, just as he had been last night. But he was rarely affected emotionally—much less spiritually—by anything he witnessed and recorded.

"It's just as good as it gets," Peter said, wiping a sleeve across his face. "Thank you for this."

Now Keeney remembered that this was how the night had ended. Each of the other witchdoctors had approached him solemnly and thanked him for the dance. Their bellies felt full of arrows and nails, and they ascribed this to the White Big Doctor's power. Brad felt self-conscious about the whole thing. He felt as if he hadn't done anything; something had been done *to* him—he was just a passenger along for the ride.

"Hey, my pleasure," Brad answered and then took a sip of steaming hot tea, which warmed his stomach but nothing like the preceding night. "I'm glad you're with me. Who else would believe this?"

Peter scooted his chair closer. "So, what was it like out there? You must have been terrified. I mean, you were being surrounded by a dozen African witchdoctors who were all grabbing you and rubbing their sweat all over you. And you were jerking around for hours. . . ."

"You know, it was really the first time I *didn't* feel scared."

"Huh?"

"You know what Mantag first said to me when we arrived? Welcome home. That's what it feels like for me here."

Peter nodded but really had no idea what his friend was saying.

"I've had these sort of shakes my whole life—but never with others who were shaking, like what happened last night—but still . . ." He stopped for a moment, unsure of how much to reveal.

"Ever since I was 20, I've occasionally experienced something like this when my body starts shaking. It used to freak my wife, Mev, out because the bed starts vibrating. She just tells me to stop and it goes away."

Peter laughed in appreciation, trying to picture this. Here was this internationally known theorist and intellectual, one of the most highly regarded family therapists in the world, the guy whom the university had brought all the way over from America, and he's actually a secret witchdoctor. And not *any* shaman, but now recognized as a Big Doctor by this gathering of Bushmen. It was beyond merely weird.

"Last night was the first time I felt no fear. It was all so familiar to me. It was natural."

"But what about that guy who was freaking out with the convulsions? He looked terrified. Heck, I was so scared at one point I wanted to leave, but Nelson made me stay."

"That younger man," Keeney explained, "was a new initiate. He didn't understand what was happening to him. But I've been feeling this way my whole life."

Peter nodded but still didn't seem to understand.

"Look," Keeney said. "Last night I remember Mantag came up to me during a quiet time in the dance. He was speaking to me in his language. At first, I was just mesmerized by the sounds—it is such a beautiful, otherworldly language, with the clicking and all. I'm not saying I understood everything he was saying, but I knew he was asking for help. So I told him in English that I understood and I followed him. I don't know where Nelson was; maybe he was with you."

"Yeah, Nelson was with me the whole night. I wouldn't let him leave my side for a second. I wanted to know what was going on. Man, it was really out there! You gotta admit that."

Ignoring the question, Keeney explained that he could understand much of what Mantag was saying. Mantag told him that there was someone in difficulty—not the guy whom Peter had seen earlier, but another one. So Keeney followed him to where this man was lying on the ground, moaning and shaking as if he had a fever.

"We must help this man," Mantag said. "He is in deep trouble. We must bring him back."

Keeney nodded his understanding of what must be done. All the doctors piled up on top of the man, with the "patient" at the bottom of the heap. Keeney joined the pile-up, starting to shake the mass of intertwined limbs, imitating the chants of the others.

"So," Peter interrupted, "now you're saying that you understand their language?" He said this with a tone of voice that was no longer skeptical but, rather, teasing. By now, Peter would believe that anything was possible with his friend the Big Doctor.

"No," Keeney smiled. "I'm not saying that. It's just that sometimes, through gestures and sounds and . . . well, just a feeling, sometimes I understand what they are saying to me."

"Well, whatever is going on here, I just want you to know I'm grateful."

"Sure. It's a delight."

"So," Peter continued, turning serious. "What was it like last night? You know, when it was all going on. I mean, do you realize that we witnessed the oldest healing practice in civilization? It was the most elemental form of spiritual worship."

Keeney nodded, trying to put into words what he was only beginning to make sense of himself. And then there was a part of him that didn't want to explain this, didn't want to even think about it.

"It was like I was shaking from the bottom of my feet," he began tentatively. "At first, I could feel this little flutter in my hands. Then they started to vibrate. It was like the percussive clapping and the singing were entering my body.

"I can see now why they say there are arrows in their bodies because I could feel this shivering sensation moving up and down, like the swell of waves."

"But since these people have never seen the ocean," Peter pointed out, "naturally they would use a metaphor that is familiar."

Keeney looked at his academic friend, amused that he had once again adopted his pedantic tone. "Yeah, it's like waves. Then you get chills. You get whipped. You get the jerks. It is like lightning hits you. Then Twele was explaining to me that over the years, the doctors get a lot of tension in their bellies as the movements get things pumping."

"And that's what happened to you?"

Keeney nodded. "But the really strange part is you can't speak while all this is going on. You lose the ability to talk. There were a few times I opened my mouth to talk, but only sounds came out, no speech. It is like my whole being regressed to its most basic level."

"Sort of like a precognitive state," Peter said.

"Once that started, I remember the doctors came over and took their sweat and starting vibrating my legs. I was trembling and then I felt this wild vibration in my thigh. It was like I was a complete gigantic massage machine. Then my feet were jerking up and down. It was like a string was attached to my ass and was pulling on it."

"Like a puppet."

"Yeah. Just like that. But it was weird because the whole thing was kind of effortless. It didn't feel like I was expending any energy. It was like I could have danced all night."

"You *did* dance all night."

"Right. But I mean I didn't feel tired. In fact, I feel remarkably refreshed right now! But I'm hungry! Let's get something to eat."

The Gift of Touch

The two of them were sitting at a makeshift table, finishing breakfast, when Mantag approached the camp.

"The people are very happy," he said, embracing Keeney and then smiling at Peter. "It was a strong dance."

As Nelson translated this phrase, he explained that this was the supreme compliment that a Bushman would offer another.

"God gave you the gift of your hands," Mantag continued. "I would like you to touch me with your hands."

Keeney looked at the old medicine man in amazement. He was coming to him for a consultation, from one shaman to another. This was truly an honor, and Keeney told him so.

Mantag nodded, then explained that he had been having trouble breathing and wanted to know if Keeney could help him. Brad thought for a moment. He almost laughed to himself, wondering if this would be practicing medicine without a license. That struck him as particularly funny because these people had never seen a doctor in their lives.

Keeney felt embarrassed by the request. He had no sense of himself being a doctor. In fact, if anything, he had been systematically stripping away his previous professional roles as a psychologist and a family therapist because of his discomfort with being in the position of expert, rather than helping people to draw on their own healing resources. Moreover, he had no understanding of what his power was all about. All he knew was that he shook all the time, and he was very happy to discover that he had found a group of people who also did this and liked it.

Brad looked over at Peter after the translation, almost as if asking his permission. Peter just shrugged. He seemed to be saying, After everything else that has happened here, what was the big deal?

Keeney walked over to the old man and wrapped his arms around him. They both waited for a moment and then the rumbling began, gentle at first, then undulating. It was the dance again. The two of them held on to one another as if they were being jerked around by a tornado, which in a sense they were. At this point, Keeney had no idea what was going on, but, eventually, the chaotic energy settled into a rhythm. Now it felt like they were under this waterfall of energy, a pulsating curtain of water. It was totally exhilarating and euphoric, and when the two of them broke away, Mantag grinned and walked away.

Keeney had not heard whether Mantag's respiratory ailment improved, but what he did notice over the next week was a lineup of people from the village who wanted Keeney to shake with them, install more arrows in their bellies, or pass on some of his spirit. Peter and Nelson watched with increasing amazement as the pilgrimage to their camp continued.

Keeney agreed to offer whatever help he could to those who approached him. With some, he would hug them and shake a little. One time, he was shaking so strongly with a smaller man that he literally picked the man up and lifted the man over his head. None of it made sense to Keeney, but by this point, he had stopped trying to understand it. In fact, he learned that he could not make himself shake; he had to wait for it to happen. And as for the origins of the supposed cure for an assortment of ailments, he couldn't begin to sort that out. Was the shaking somehow unsettling the disease, as the Bushmen believed? They felt that sickness resulted from dirty arrows in the body that needed to be cleaned or removed. Or was this a simple case of the placebo effect, in which the patient's own belief system acted as the impetus for self-cure? Keeney didn't know and didn't much care. Whatever he was doing seemed to happen effortlessly and naturally. And most important, it was familiar and valued by the Bushmen.

Years later, when he spoke to another shaman, Mabolelo Shikwe, he learned more about the larger meanings of the healing dance.

Shikwe walked around wearing an old, beaten-up hat that may at one time have belonged to an officer in the army or maybe even a bus driver. He carried with him an instrument called a *sigankure,* which is sort of a one-string violin made from the tail of a wildebeest.

"My own healing song is the same as from my grandfather, and his father before him. The song always starts out the same, but then changes as the dance progresses. It becomes spiritual after we become more serious about the dancing. That is when we sing about the Big God above, the one who made you to be born. The Big God speaks to me and tells me what to say and how to heal each person."

Shikwe talked at length about the source of his power and how the strength of it varies in each person. "You must have a strong heart to be a healer. You must be mentally and physically well. The Bushmen of the Kalahari know each other's hearts. We also know the hearts of others in the world. You must open your heart to have a good heart. There can be no jealousy or bad intentions inside you. You must look after everyone. That is the key to healing."

Keeney couldn't think of a single thing that the old man had said that didn't strike him as true about the practice of psychotherapy or any other healing. To the Bushmen, the dance was not just about healing but also about building a sense of community. That is where touch becomes so important, because people literally stay in close contact with one another by pressing their bodies against each other and sharing their sweat.

The Paper

As they were packing up their camp, making preparations for the return to Pretoria, Mantag came to say good-bye.

"The people, they are very happy that you have come," he said. "I have been very ill during this past year. I did not believe that I would live much longer. Now that you have come, I feel the strength in my belly again."

"I, too, am glad that I have finally come home," Brad responded warmly. "And I am so grateful that you came to me first in my dream, and then in this beautiful place."

"All the healers," Mantag continued, "they are still so surprised that the Big God made a White Bushman. Even though it was told in a dream, some of them still do not believe such a thing could be possible." Mantag smiled, as if he had never been one of the skeptical ones—it was as if he had been waiting his whole life for such a thing.

"Please tell them that I am just as surprised as they are. This was all totally unexpected. And I feel so honored that you have welcomed me to be one of your people and brought me into your rituals."

"No, Big Doctor, it is *you* who must receive our thanks. For you have done so much for our people."

Mantag and Keeney just stared at one another for a moment, shyly, knowing that they might never see one another for a long time. They had become like brothers. Finally, Twele broke the silence by shaking his head and clucking his tongue.

"What?" Keeney asked him. "What were you thinking?"

"I was just thinking how the people, the healers, are so surprised that the Big God made not only a White Bushman but a Bushman shaman. This gives us all hope that some day all people can dance together."

Just as Mantag turned to walk away, Keeney was struck by a bizarre idea, yet one that made perfect sense at the time. "I wish to give you one last thing before I leave," he said formally.

Mantag reached out his hand as Keeney presented to him a small, rectangular piece of stiff paper. The old man looked at it curiously, seeing the black marks that were similar to the rock art that his ancestors had carved into caves. But rather than pictures, there were inscribed small, intricate lines that were bumpy in texture.

"If you ever wish to give me a message," Keeney said, pointing at his business card, which was held reverently between Mantag's thumb and forefinger, "send one of the young men to take this to the Park." He was referring to the Botswana Department of Wildlife, which administered the game reserve in the central Kalahari.

The last that Keeney saw of Mantag, he was walking slowly toward the village, carefully examining the raised marks on this strange piece of paper.

The Word Spreads

It was soon after this experience that word leaked out at the university that Bradford Keeney was a White Bushman witchdoctor.

Traditional healers from all over South Africa, Namibia, and Botswana came to meet him and to shake with him. A photograph of him in a ceremony appeared in *Time* (Gwynne, 1997) and his work with the Bushmen was given a mention in the *New Yorker* (1995) magazine, generating a lot of attention. Meanwhile, Keeney tried to figure out what he should do with all this: Should be become the first missionary for the Bushmen and shake everyone he could find? He had been told, upon leaving the Kalahari, that he should spread the word of the healing dance. Was that now to be his mission?

Now Keeney had time to reflect on what had happened in the Kalahari. What had he learned from all this and what did he want to do with his gifts? He was trying to sort out these new insights in light of all his previous training as a psychologist. According to current thinking in the field, when people are experiencing emotional or spiritual problems, they are told that they need to relax. They are instructed to meditate, to practice yoga, to relax; sometimes they are given drugs to help them to calm down. It is believed that people's lives are overstimulated and what they need to do is to rest and find some tranquility.

Yet everything he had learned from the Bushmen was just the opposite: It was through arousal, not relaxation, that changes and healing took place. It is at the highest state of excitation, when every neuron is firing, that people transcend their daily lives into spiritual ecstasy. Just as they had been doing for thousands of years, the Bushmen were achieving the highest states of pure consciousness in an almost effortless way of uniting their community. This was nothing like what others do at the Harvard Divinity School, at a Tibetan monastery, or in other places of spiritual worship, except perhaps in churches of African descendents right here in North America.

Bradford Keeney was forever transformed after this first visit to Africa. He decided thereafter to spend the next years of his life finding other people who keep their traditions alive, who shake with the spirits. He would go to the most remote parts of the Amazon, to the outback of Australia, to rural Louisiana and South Dakota, and to any place where he could find teachers among those who had been forgotten. He'd had quite enough sitting at the feet of the intellectuals and academics; it was time to learn from those who lived a deeper truth.

The Message Returns

Later, after these events took place, a letter arrived for Keeney, postmarked in Botswana. The letter had somehow found its way from his previous university and been forwarded to his current address.

> *18-11-92*
> *Bradford,*
>   *I have been requested by Mr. Mantag Kefeletswe to tell you that he is still kicking and alive, even though at a very low standard. He still remembers you as his saver [sic] and he is still expecting help from you. If you still remember him, could you please write me and I will convey the whole information to him.*
>   *I am working for the Wildlife Department stationed at Khutse Game Reserve as Assistant Game Warden. I have been here for two years.*
>   *You are welcome to visit Khutse any time to see the old man, Mantag, who insists his days are numbered.*
>
> *Yours Faithfully,*
> *Odumeleng Radar Kaketso*
> *Department of Wildlife*
> *Molepole*

Keeney sat staring at the letter, tears pooling in his eyes, as he thought about Mantag and the Bushmen of the Kalahari. He could see the old man as clearly as if he was standing in the room. He could feel Mantag's strong, sinewy arms wrapped around his neck when they hugged and shook. He could smell Mantag—smell his musky, sour scent as their sweat was exchanged by rubbing it on one another's bodies. He could picture him perfectly, looking quizzically at the square card Brad had given him, the card that would summon his old friend, who, if he could not come home, would send words instead.

Without a moment's thought, Keeney immediately sat down and wrote a letter to Mantag, in care of the assistant game warden.

> *Dear Mantag,*
>   *Thank you for sending word to me. My friend Peter, who came with me to see you, has made arrangements to send you and your people some food and clothes.*

The fire still burns in my belly. I will forever be thankful for your accepting me and giving me a home under your tree. It remains my true home and I carry it with me in my heart.

After I left you, I met a great African healer named Credo Mutwa. He said the spirits told him I once lived with the Bushmen in the Kalahari and had returned to find my home with you. He also told me about death. He said it was just a door to another life. I believe that you and I will always be connected, no matter which worlds we live in. This is our destiny. I believe I will be in touch with you whenever either one of us crosses over. The spirits make that possible.

I love your people and I believe you have the most to teach the rest of the world about how to live. If we don't listen to you, we will all die. I am giving much of my life to encouraging people to support and learn from your people. You were the first people of the world, the first to learn how to heal, how to love, and how to live together. We must be led by your old ways of knowing and being. The wings of our hearts make us one.

All my deepest respect and love,
Brad

Keeney visited the desert of the Bushmen many years later. When he arrived, the whole village turned out to dance and celebrate the return of the Big Doctor. The first of those to greet him were Twele and Mantag's wife, Gabanthate. They embraced and rejoiced in seeing one another again after so many years.

"Yes," Gabanthate said, before Keeney could even ask his question. "Mantag did receive your letter. The game warden read it to him. It made him very happy. He never let go of that letter. He held it next to his heart. He was holding it when he died. We buried him with that letter."

Brad began crying at this news, so Gabanthate held him tighter. They hugged and rocked in this way for several minutes, her own grief returning to join that of her husband's friend.

"I want to tell you about Mantag's power. No one taught him how to be a healer. He went into the bush one day when he was a young man. It was there that the Big God talked to him and gave him the power. He would dream thereafter about special medicines that would heal others. He knew where to find these things. He became our strongest doctor. He was not only a strong man, but a good man. And now his spirit is very happy to see you again. He waits for you by the camelthorn tree that is your home."

Keeney looked over toward the tree that had first been pointed out to him by Mantag so many years before. Things grow slowly in the desert, but he was sure that it was stronger than it had once been. It was a good place to call home.

Brad felt a gentle tapping on his shoulder. He turned to see his old friend Twele, grinning broadly. Keeney showed him the photographs and the manuscripts he had written about the lives of the Kalahari Bushmen shamans (Keeney, 1999c). Twele and his friends gathered and jumped with jubilation at seeing their photographs and hearing how their stories were recorded.

"Come walk with me," the guide from his dreams said. "Let us talk about Mantag and the times we spent together. Then let us dance."

Keeney nodded, still looking out over the African plains. The sun had gone down and there was now a slight chill in the air. The last of the light had now faded to pastel layers of orange, pink, yellow, powder blue, and into black. "I once heard," he said, now looking at Twele in the soft light, "that when a Bushman shaman dies, his heart comes out in the sky and becomes a star."

Twele clapped his hands and shouted in delight. "Yes, it is so," he said. "Tonight we will dance for the stars."

Chapter Three

What It Means to Be a Shaman

"What the heck is that?"

We might be excused for a little overexuberance after spending 36 hours cramped on airplanes before finding ourselves literally dropped into one of the most remote places on Earth. We rendezvoused from all corners of the Earth. Jeffrey arrived from Southern California, via stops in New York, Johannesburg, and Windhoek, and then took the bush plane out into the desert. Jon came from the opposite direction, from Thailand, Cambodia, and then Malaysia, to Southern Africa. And Brad from still a third direction—South Africa, where he had been meeting with tribal leaders.

"An ostrich," our guide said. "A black ostrich."

Our first sign of wildlife in Africa. We had spent 2 hours flying across the Kalahari in a small plane before boarding a truck for the hour-long ride to the camp where we would be living; so far, we had yet to see a single indication of life anywhere.

We pulled into camp just outside the Bushman village. There were tents set up by our outfitters underneath a towering baobab tree. This was one of the places where Keeney had first discovered his powers with the Bushmen 11 years earlier. We had returned to the scene to have a look, to see for ourselves the American shaman in action.

Shamanism in a Bottle

Keeney has definite reservations about using the word *shaman* to describe the work that he does. The very word *shaman* conjures up images of a voodoo witchdoctor casting spells or a wild-eyed anthropologist tripping on peyote. Also disturbing to Keeney are the ways the term is thrown around in the context of weekend workshops held in suburban retreat centers, where lost men learn to bang drums or hang out in sweat lodges or hot tubs to find their long-dormant shamanic powers. For many of them, it is all about accessing power.

Jon stepped in to offer Keeney a challenge, "If you hang around shamans most of the time, aren't you also seen as a shaman? If you walk and talk like a shaman, it seems to me that you are one."

Keeney warmed to the topic, gazing out over the African savannah. Storm clouds and lightning were lined up along the horizon.

"Most people think that shamanism is about some journey south of the border to smoke a cactus, or go further south and eat a vine that takes you on a hallucinogenic trip." He shook his head in disgust. "They think that there's a magical plant that automatically gets you to heaven. The sacramental use of plants requires a deep immersion in a cultural context, with its sacred songs, prayers, stories, and myths. There's no such thing as an 'over-the-counter' or 'instant coffee' spirituality. This has not been my journey."

Keeney's point is that many people prefer to find shortcuts. When they feel down or dispirited, a choice may be made to use alcohol, recreational drugs, or psychiatric medication—to boost morale, so that it isn't necessary to invest in the hard work of figuring out what's missing in your life and what needs to be done to get yourself on the enlightened path. It's the same with shamanism in a bottle.

Keeney has already seen enough heartbreak in his life as a result of substance abuse and addictions—with family members and friends and more clients than he can possibly count. Just as some people try to medicate their pain and boredom with chemicals, so, too, do some wannabe shamans use these ancient healing practices as an excuse to get high.

"That's not to say," Keeney laughed, "that I don't *look* like I'm on drugs when I'm out there dancing and shaking." This is meant half as a joke, half as a warning. We'd already heard plenty of stories and seen films of Keeney dancing with the Bushmen, and he *did* look like he was flying out of his mind. At times he would crouch over, balancing on his tiptoes, bellowing and chugging. Keeping himself grounded in the sand, his whole body would shake from deep inside his chest—legs, arms, torso, and neck gyrating as if in a seizure. Then the other shamans would dance over to him and literally tap the kinetic energy from his chest, attaching themselves like leeches, drawing a part of him into them, as well as depositing their own ancient spirits into his belly.

Defining Shamanism

"I have no difficulty being identified with the people I hang out with," Keeney acknowledged, when we pressed him on his reluctance to use this term. "My issue is that in our culture the term *shaman* is typically understood in ways I don't connect with."

On the one hand, there is the Carlos Castaneda (1973) crowd, including those who munch on psychedelic plants and write popular books on "tales of power." On the other hand, there is "Harnerism," created by Michael Harner (1973, 1982), who once consumed psychedelic plants in the Amazon and then came back to say that the core of shamanism is a technique for accessing inner power that may be taught in a weekend workshop. He also claimed, as an aside, that shamanism didn't necessarily have anything to do with a belief in a Higher Power. He went on to create a copyrighted Harner technique of shamanism that is commercially marketed.

None of the indigenous practitioners of spiritual medicine whom Keeney has ever met fit the image of what Castaneda or Harner described. Instead, he has found that shamanic practitioners almost universally speak of their profession as being based on direct contact with God (or the gods) and see prayer as the bridge to that connection. When divine contact is made, the body shakes and the sacred gifts come forth.

"I don't want to say that other people using the term are wrong," Keeney clarified. "I'm only saying that the shamans I have met are different from what is being taught in today's popular books and workshops. The shamans I know are, first and foremost, more like saints of love than wizards with magic wands."

"Is a shaman the same as a mystic?" Jon pressed.

Keeney nodded. "Sometimes the two do overlap." He looked thoughtful for a moment, looking so intently out toward the horizon we thought he'd spotted another wild creature. This was our first visit to Africa, so we were anxious to see a giraffe or a lion or at least an elephant.

"But I don't want to get into academic hair-splitting," Keeney said finally, "when we try to differentiate spiritual categories of experience. Finding your way to ecstatic communion with the divine characterizes both shamanism and mysticism. Sometimes you fall into a trance, or dance, or both, or simply get an inspiration or a vision that alters the core of your being."

It is Keeney's belief that Harner and Castaneda got off to an unfortunate start by playing the role of academic anthropologist, rather than being pilgrims seeking love and inspiration. Perhaps they were also overly reliant upon the historian of religion Mircea Eliade (1968), who arguably overemphasized, with great literary liberty, one aspect of shamanistic experience—the imagined journey to a spirit world, either in the underground or in the sky. According to Keeney, many scholars took that type of experience as the key definition of shamanism, that it is mostly about a magic journey, but neglected the dimensions of love and spirituality that are at its core.

Of course, there may be a significant difference between the theory of shamanism and its actual practice. Such as with all healers and helpers, some shamans fall far short of the ideals. They may be manipulative and may pervert their status in the community, in order to act as a broker to the gods, the pathway to power or favors.

"Authentic shamanism is always a voyage into the unknown," Keeney elaborated, "where no one, including the designated shaman, knows what he or she will experience. Any talk of a core experience or a core method is discourse about a routinized form of spiritual practice that, more often than not, has lost its spirit and soul. That's what we often find in cultures that have lost their way in modern times. Their spirit has dried up and their practices have given way to barren ceremony. This is arguably what many anthropologists find in their fieldwork, and more sadly, it may be what they try to teach others when they try to start a new pseudo-spiritual commodity."

"Okay," Jeffrey interrupted the rant. "Enough of this! This is starting to sound like a sermon. I don't have any problem seeing you as a shaman and wish you would stop apologizing for the term. I understand that people can mean different things by the label, that there are even negative connotations associated with it, in terms of being some sort of drug-addled flake. We'll call you a shaman, and as we do so, understand that to the indigenous peoples you work with, this also means 'healer,' 'doctor,' and 'guide.'"

But Keeney wasn't quite ready to give up on this point. He is so tired of feeling defensive about the nature of helping, as it is practiced among indigenous peoples around the world. Therapists in the Western world are so uncomfortable with anything that smacks of religion and see "love" as a four-letter word that is un-scientific and unmeasurable. "Keep in mind," Keeney added, quoting the scholar Casanowicz (1926), "that the Siberian Tungus word for shaman, *saman,* means one who is excited, moved, or raised."

Keeney believes that this definition is descriptive of the shaman's shaking when excited by a realization of spirit. Under the influence of the divine, shamans become "the artist, the priest, the dramatist, the physician, all rolled into one, who develop the abilities beyond others to dream, to imagine, to enter states of trance" (Larsen, 1976, p. 9). Through an altered consciousness, the shaman gains access to the world of spirits and ancestors in order to cure, divine, discover, invent, solve problems, and provide hope and salvation.

Another translation for the Tungus word *saman* is "inner heat," and an alternative etymology comes from the Sanskrit word *saman,* which means "song" (Hoppal, 1987). These two definitions, along with the primary one of "body excitation," are the key characteristics of a shaman. Taken together (inner heat, shaking, and song), these three phenomena comprise the core experience of the shaman. "Shamans," Keeney said with a laugh, "are hot shakers who try to catch a song." Or more formally, he adds, "shamanism is the evocation and utilization of aroused (and enhanced) spiritual experience for the purpose of inspiration, guidance, and healing, typically brought about by feelings of body excitation and inner heat while performing spirited rhythms and music."

"Wait a minute," Jon inserted, while Brad was catching his breath. "Isn't the whole idea of traveling the spirit world a key theme for shamans? Correct me if I'm wrong, but that's what I always thought."

"Sure," Keeney agreed. "Traveling the spirit world happens for shamans, but only as a consequence of being driven into ecstasy by internal heat, shaking, and song. Yet as dramatic as those trips are, they are not the core experience of shamanism. Whether or not a shaman has a flight into the spirit world may be irrelevant. What is probably more accurate to say is that 'magical flight' is a metaphor for the movement into altered consciousness."

A person becomes a shaman either by hereditary position, referred to as the "lesser shaman," or by being spontaneously called, referred to as the "greater shaman" (Eliade, 1968). "Greater" refers to the observance that the spirits or the gods have chosen someone to be a shaman by setting in motion a spontaneous experience in a person's life that transforms his or her way of being in the world. The initiation of the latter begins with an experiential lightning bolt that shatters the common reality of the recipient. Someone may face a divine light or have a divine encounter while fully awake. This shakes the core beliefs of the person and puts him or her into a crisis that typically results in a long "shamanic illness." In this dark night of the soul, the initiate experiences death and resurrection, usually several times, until he or she feels reborn into a new way of being.

Keeney explained further that as one becomes comfortable with the spirit settling into the body, the shaking becomes more stabilized, waiting to be released upon ceremonial invocation, rather than seizing the recipient in an unexpected, chaotic, and out-of-control manner. All authentic shamans go through this grueling process of being awakened by spirit and then enduring the crisis of holding onto the spirit until it settles down and can be harnessed for shamanic activity. This gives some idea of how different true shamanic initiation and training are from weekend social activity at a workshop. "No one in their right mind would pursue the real thing," Keeney said. "This is what most shamans have told me. It is both a curse and a blessing to be brought into the shamanic world of experience."

As we will later discuss, Keeney was hit by a shamanic crisis when he was 19 years old. Like the Mongolian shamans of old, it took him many years to learn how to live with the shaking force that lived within his body. His dreams took him to many indigenous elders around the world, who gave him further instruction and sometimes oversaw ritualistic ordeals that served to deepen his shamanic capabilities.

Keeney has undergone numerous periods of fasting in the wilderness and in an isolated ceremonial room, sometimes up to a 5-day period, while supervised by elders from an indigenous shamanic tradition. During his training, he was told, from time to time, to go hunt for a variety of shamanic items that had to be obtained within a short period of time, from a complete set of crocodile teeth, to an otter skin, a bear claw, and an old leopard skin, among other things. He has been ritualistically buried and rebirthed, been asked to make great financial and personal sacrifices, and been placed in states of consciousness that took him to the edge of madness.

Part of his training required strict tests that showed a community of shamans that he could diagnose the sickness of another person by feeling it in his own body, divine through dreams, tap into the secret symbols and sounds of a healing tradition, and spiritually travel into a dreamtime world that held certain teachings and answers that had to be expressed to the elders. He also had to demonstrate the ability to awaken the life force, or *n/om,* in others, through bringing forth body shaking and heightened consciousness in those who gave the test.

He did all of this while studying, working with, and writing about some of the great psychotherapists of our time. As his academic career flourished, the calling of his shamanic roots never ceased. Eventually, he left academic psychotherapy to be with traditional shamans. In a tribute to his teachers, Keeney has published an encyclopedic collection of biographical studies of many of the shamans he was involved with, arguably comprising the most ambitious fieldwork of diverse shamanic traditions ever undertaken. (See the *Profiles of Healing* multiple-volume series published by Ringing Rocks Press, in which Keeney interviewed and focused on the work of a Lakota medicine man, a Japanese master of *seiki jutsu,* numerous Kalahari Bushman healers, several Guarani shamans of the rain forest, a Zulu high *sanusi,* a Dine medicine woman, various shakers of St. Vincent Island, two elder healers of Brazil, traditional healers of Bali, and other projects in the works with an Argentinean folk healer, a Mexican curandero, a Kundalini yogi, an Aboriginal healer of Australia, members of an African American sanctified church, and a North American hypnotist familiar to most therapists—Milton Erickson.)

New Age and Old Age

Keeney had made it all too clear that there was a huge difference between what is called "New Age" versus "Old Age" shamanism. All three of us are cynical about so-called New Age movements of the month, in which people flock from one fad to another in search of spiritual enlightenment. They look everywhere for the latest gimmick that promises them Nirvana, heaven on Earth, or the chance to be a godling themselves. To Keeney, this is all narcissistic indulgence, the glorified idealization of the self.

The shaman's journey actually parallels the classic ways of the world's great religions—it is about getting past yourself, rather than trying to go more deeply, neurotically, obsessively inside yourself. "The history of shamanism," Keeney explained, "is about the dismemberment of self. You must go through your own death." He smiled. "That is one hell of an ordeal, I gotta tell you. I can't imagine anyone deliberately choosing this kind of journey."

Keeney has found that pop shamans and pop psychologists are similar to religious fundamentalists, who argue that if you memorize the right answer and scripted propaganda, you, and only those like you, will be admitted to heavenly success. All of these "lazy" approaches end up as businesses that aim to bring in the money/offerings/donations, while seeking converts with "I-have-the-truth" evangelical zeal. "I have been very lucky to have stayed away from the success hucksters," Keeney said, chuckling, "and to have hung out with authentic shamans. My grandfather warned me to be suspicious of anyone who had achieved monster success. Small is not only beautiful; it is usually true. The genuine ones, those on a journey of and for spiritual light and love, never, ever give importance to beginning with a core technique, answer, truth, or understanding that claims to maximize success of any desired outcome. They more humbly start with a dedicated search to awaken and open their hearts."

"When the lightning hits, the journey starts," Jon summarized.

"Exactly. If you become lit with spiritual fire, you find your vision and understanding transformed. Now you can read the Bible, the Torah, the Koran, the Upanishads, or even the collected works of Freud or Jung or Erickson, and see, for the first time, the spiritual mysteries they were meant to reveal. Fundamentalists, on the other hand, want us to start with the textual encounter and then believe that reading will prepare them to receive spiritual blessings. They have the process inverted and this can become dangerous. Scriptural knowledge read by cold hearts easily leads to vicious condemnation of others and if unchecked may erupt in a holy war. For this reason, I suggest that religious books contain a warning on their cover: 'Do not read unless your heart has been converted to forgiving and loving others.'"

"What about reading a book such as this?" Jeffrey asked. "Aren't there dangers of something similar for our readers? Might they believe, mistakenly as you suggest, that it is possible to learn shamanism by reading a book, trying an exercise, or attending a workshop?"

"You have to jump off the cliff that holds your everyday mind and expose yourself to the spiritual storms. Like Benjamin Franklin, you have to send a kite into the sky during a lightning storm and hope that lightning travels down the line into the key that is tightly held in your trembling hand. That's the key that opens the door to spirituality and shamanism. When it arrives, you'll be knocked over and knocked out. You won't understand what the hell is going on, nor should you try. You will be both thrilled and scared. No words will help you communicate what happened. That's how shamanism begins, at least in the traditions of our oldest known cultural healing practices."

The Big Doctor

Speaking of ordeals like jumping off a cliff, we were about to arrive at the spot near the village where we were to live for the next week. Just as we began to set up our camp, a runner from the Bushman village was sent to tell us that they were gathering for the big dance.

"These people we are going to see," Jeffrey asked Brad, with a certain anxiety, "what do they make of you? I mean . . ."

". . . You're this big White guy," Jon finished the thought. "You come roaring out of the sky in this big bird that swoops down. This is the same exact place where they made the movie *The Gods Must Be Crazy*, about the Coke bottle that fell out of the sky and how it affected these people. And now you come to them, claiming that a dream led you here."

"I know that sounds really weird to you guys," Keeney admitted, "but trust me, this makes perfect sense to the Bushmen. This sort of thing is known and respected in their culture."

Indeed, it may sound strange to us that dreams take on such importance to the Bushmen and indigenous peoples, when to us they are a mere source of amusement or perhaps, to the Freudians, a few clues to the unconscious. To many shamans in general, and Keeney in particular, dreams are as real as anything in human experience.

"Okay," Jeffrey acknowledged, more than a little skeptically, "let's just say that all this is true. But still: How is it that the Bushmen accepted you so readily into their tribe and have given you such honors? When you visit them, the people line up to be touched and shaken by you."

We can see this is difficult for Brad. After a few false starts, we can tell he is struggling to put his thoughts into words in a way that we can understand and in a way that he doesn't come across as arrogant.

"Well," Jon stepped in, "after all, the Bushmen don't just see you as a doctor, but as a strong doctor, one of the Big Doctors. And, you *are* a giant in the midst of little guys."

Ignoring the comment, Keeney explained that he is seen as a strong shaman not because of his physical size or because he has white-colored skin—there have been other visitors to their village in the previous decades—mostly, Ivy League anthropologists studying this group of people, which is supposedly one of the last remnants of hunter-gatherers in their natural habitat left on the planet.

"They don't treat me this way because I am big or clever," Keeney said. "Heck, I don't even speak their language. It is because the strength of a shaman is judged on the basis of who is left standing at the end of the night and, more important, whose heart is most open. Who can shake and dance for 12 straight hours without dropping to the ground in exhaustion?"

"So they are awed by your endurance?"

"That's part of it. When I hook up to whatever spirit is operating around that fire, my energy is inexhaustible. This connection is made possible by opening your heart and feeling love for everyone. Most of the doctors, the shamans, can shake for a few hours at a time before they drop like trees hit by lightning. They rest or sleep wherever they fall, then rise up and begin again. But I can go all night. And this just amazes me." Brad looked down at his body and said with a laugh, "I just can't explain it myself."

What he meant by this was that he is one of the few people left in our culture who may be exercise-aversive. He has never worked out and never done anything to stay in shape, except walk to where he needs to go; even then, he may fatigue easily. But when he is in the shamanic ceremonies, the spirit simply grabs him and won't let go. He dances and shakes as if his body belongs to someone or something else. And, truthfully, the Bushmen who have been dancing like this all their lives have rarely seen anything quite like it.

It is not just with the Bushmen that he feels this endless supply of spiritual and physical energy; it is the same when he is dancing and singing in a Black church in Louisiana or in a Native American ceremony.

"It is such a sweet thing," Keeney said, thinking about his last visit to Bushmanland, "to go to bed the next morning after a night of dancing. I have no idea what happened or why. But I love being in this kind of experience. But when I am back home, or with you now, it can feel somewhat embarrassing to talk about this."

Later, when we have the opportunity to interview the elders, the shamans, and the chief of the village, we ask them the same questions. How do they explain someone like Keeney in their midst?

Cgunta, an old wrinkled man of indeterminate age, explained how someone such as Keeney is chosen. "God can give such concentrated power directly to a human being and make him or her a shaman, and, in turn, a strong one who has the power to serve as an intermediary can give it to someone else. When a person gets this power directly from the Big God, it is extremely powerful. These are the greatest shamans. When you receive it this way, it may throw you to the ground as if you were struck by lightning. In addition, you may see a big light and be shown how you will help others."

Keeney nodded agreement with Cgunta. We were all blown away by this lovely old man, stooped, wrinkled, bent over, rail skinny, but a shaman who can literally outlast anyone in the village during the ceremonial dances. He looked each of us in the eye and smiled, holding his thumb up in the universal gesture of affirmation.

"Shamans like Cgunta feel something vibrant inside themselves," Keeney added to the discussion. "There may be a tingling sensation that comes on your skin, a sudden jerk of your leg, or a twitching of your finger or eyelid. In many indigenous cultures, these experiences are taken as evidence of the presence of spirits. Whether it's a butterfly, a bird, a bear, a moose, or the Virgin Mary, I regard these images as sacramental expressions of relationship and intimate connection. For example, when I had a vision of an eagle facing me on a cliff during the midst of a fasting ceremony, it was such an emotional impact that it became expressed or localized in my arms and shoulders. Now, years later, if I pray and become mindful of that eagle, I may feel that part of my body begin to move, imitating the movement of a bird's wings. I do not purposefully choreograph this movement. It happens without conscious intention. Here the experience is a sacrament of relational connection. It is an invocation of ecstatic knowing, a somatic expression of a shaman's tactile vocabulary."

Cgunta then lost interest in this discussion and hunkered down into a bit of shade. He was resting to save his energy for the evening's dance.

The Ostrich Egg

Some of the children from the village followed Cgunta to see what the strangers with the Big Doctor were doing. They saw Jon fiddling with his tape recorder and Jeffrey snapping pictures. Some children, who could not have been more than 8 years old, were carrying babies on their backs. They watched us intently but smiled and averted their eyes every time we looked their way.

Keeney talked more about the burdens that come with the gifts of dreams and visions. "This is a story I've heard around the world from other shamans and medicine people. Nobody wanted to be this way. Nobody wants this calling. I know there are herds of people rushing to one workshop or retreat center trying to find their shamanic calling, but if they had any idea what comes with it, they'd run screaming in the other direction.

As much out of boredom as from continued interest in the subject, Jeffrey returned to their earlier subject of his first encounter with the Bushmen. Jeffrey was also feeling increasingly nervous about what was waiting for them at the ceremony. In a moment of playfulness, or perhaps serious intent, Keeney announced to all the shamans that Jeffrey was ready to learn more about being a shaman, ready to dance with the spirits and take the "arrows in his belly," the intensely painful ritual that is part of the proceedings.

In truth, Jeffrey was not much of a dancer, and he was reluctant to admit it. In fact, ever since the confirmation and bar mitzvah parties of his youth, when he was expected to do the twist, the frug, the pony, and other such moves that still look silly in old movies, he avoided dancing whenever possible. He wondered what would be expected of him during the shaman ceremony. Would he have to writhe on the ground with arrows in his belly? Would he have to keep a reasonable beat to the chanting of the women folk? How embarrassing to show these people how little rhythm he had? Maybe, he hoped in a silent prayer, the Spirit would grab him as it did Brad on a regular basis.

"So Brad," Jeffrey asked, to keep his mind off the coming trials by fire, "what's your relationship like with these people? How did you explain to them why you showed up in their camp?"

"I told them I had a dream," Brad said.

Jon groaned. "Not another Keeney dream?"

"It was a pretty boring dream, as far as these things go. Nothing dramatic. I just dreamed that I was staring at an ostrich egg."

"An ostrich egg? Like from a bird?"

"Yeah. The egg was just suspended in the air in front of me. I stared at it. And then it cracked open into two halves."

"That's it?" Jon said, clearly disappointed. "There was just an egg that split open and *that's* what led you to the Bushmen?"

"Lemme finish. I stared at the two halves of the ostrich egg and I noticed that each one had jagged edges. The right half was completely white, normal looking."

"As far as ostrich eggs go," Jon inserted.

"Right. But the left side had these two stripes on it. One was red and the other was green. Then I woke up."

"That's it?" Jon pressed. "You saw an egg. It opened. You woke up? Incredible!"

"Well," Keeney laughed, "you might not be impressed, but the Bushmen sure were."

"This meant something to the Bushmen?" Jeffrey jumped back in to hear the end of the story. He knew this was going to be a good one, even with the slow beginning.

"Yeah. As a matter of fact, they went crazy. I was still standing there in front of the elders, the biggest doctors in the village, and the translator was telling them the story of my dream. And then they started whispering to one another. Their voices got so loud and animated, and their gestures became so wild, I started to get worried. It was like I had just announced that their team had won the World Series. They started dancing around, and then other people from the village heard the word and they came running toward us."

"So, what the hell happened?"

"Well, I had no idea at the time, but it turns out that a dream about a broken ostrich egg is their most sacred dream. It's a secret that they've never told anyone about; only the strongest doctors talk about it to themselves."

"Come on, Brad," Jeffrey said, "you mean you never read about this anywhere and through the power of suggestions, it entered your dream. . . ."

"I swear," Keeney answered. "I had no clue what this was all about. They finally confided, as much to one another as to me, that this dream about an ostrich egg with stripes was an image shared by their fathers and grandfathers since the beginning of time."

"And there's no way you could know this?" Jon asked, joining Jeffrey's skepticism.

"It has never been recorded," Keeney answered patiently, in that tone of voice that indicated that he didn't care if we believed him or not or that he wasn't even sure he believed it. "No one ever knew this. It has never been recorded. And these are among the most researched anthropological groups in the world."

"Okay," Jeffrey asked, "so what's it mean? What's the big deal about a broken ostrich egg, anyway?"

"The Bushmen told me that it symbolizes that the ropes are open."

"The ropes?" This was getting more and more obtuse and complicated. Where the heck did ropes come in?

"Yeah, ropes," Keeney said patiently. "On all the rock art discovered in southern Africa—some of it the oldest known human drawings—the ancestors of the Bushmen depicted their spirit world by showing ropes to God, lines that shoot up from the shamans dancing to the spirit world in the sky." (See Keeney, 2003a.)

"Those are the vertical lines," Jeffrey pointed out. "What's with the red and green bands?"

Pleased that he had been paying attention, Brad showed an appreciative grin. "The colored bands represent horizontal ropes. They told me that red typically means evil and green means good. The most powerful shamans can climb those ropes to meet God. It is through the dancing and shaking that this is possible."

Only some of this made sense to us, but we got the main thrust of the idea. Apparently, Keeney, this southern-bred preacher's son from America, was visited in his dream by a symbolic ostrich egg, which only made sense to other African Bushmen who were the continent's most powerful witchdoctors. And by telling his hosts about this dream, he was immediately accepted as one of them. Incredible!

The Bushmen believed instantly that Keeney was indeed one of them, a shaman chosen by the Big God. When many in the village lined up to be healed by him, to have him infuse their spirits with his own energy, they opened more than their hearts. Although the Bushmen have been studied by anthropologists more intensely and thoroughly than any other culture, one of the Bushman shamans confessed that no outsider ever has been experientially inside their most spirited healing dances.

"The dances we show visitors," the old Bushman said with a cackle, "are entirely for show. These people travel to our communities and they expect certain things. What they see in the dance is smooth and entertaining; it is usually not the dance of the Big Doctors."

Such a dance is jerky, chaotic, and often excruciatingly painful. The shamans are attempting to do no less than heat metal arrows and feel these burrow up through their feet, into their bellies, and up through the top of their heads, where sometimes smoke can be seen as the arrows exit toward the heavens. The dancers are in excruciating agony and ecstasy, writhing on the ground, needing to be held down lest they spin out of control or burn up from the internal fire.

So Keeney was accepted among the Bushmen as a Big Doctor, a most powerful shaman, because of a dream he had, because of his stamina as a dancer, and, most important, because of his big heart. He loves them and they know it. We knew this was only a small part of what was going on. What we witnessed showed us quite a number of things. When Keeney walks among the people, he smiles, engages, touches every one. He brings them gifts of food or blankets, and, certainly, this would make them rather glad to see him. But others came to visit with such offerings as well, and none of them were invited to dance, nor were they treated like a Bushman.

Healing Through Arousal

Not unlike the ways we conceive of group therapy, support groups, or "12-step" programs, the tribal dance is not just about healing but also about building cohesion among members. One shaman talked about how, when he feels the power rising in his belly, making his feet dance, it makes him feel like crying and reaching out to all around him. "Our hearts overflow with love and caring for one another. This is a time when no one can have a bad feeling for anyone else. It is one of the ways the dance heals our community. If, during the course of everyday life, people start feeling upset with others, they can call a dance to make things better. The good feelings from the dance take away all the irritations and disagreements that come into our lives."

The dance is by no means similar to what one has seen in the movies or in documentaries on public television, in which the tribesmen move with gorgeous rhythm and amazing grace. This is a dance that is so shocking to the uninitiated that villagers keep their distance and avert their eyes. They huddle together and watch with both fascination and caution, to witness what the spirits will offer.

Keeney again reminded us how interesting it was that the Bushmen, and so many other indigenous healers he had studied, actually do the exact opposite of what we do to help people in our culture. Psychologists, social workers, doctors, and other health professionals routinely do things to calm and tranquilize people when they are agitated or upset about something. We prescribe Xanax and thorazine and Prozac. People attempt to medicate and calm themselves down with alcohol and other drugs when they feel upset. We teach people to do meditation and relaxation training. Psychotherapy is all about helping people to de-escalate their conflicts, see things in a more serene light, calm down, relax, *tranquilo.*

Yet in ancient cultures, the shamans often advocate something quite different: They instruct people who are troubled and disturbed to rev up their energy even further. People are invited to dance away their troubles, to share them with the community, not through talk, but through movement. People become so aroused, they literally begin shaking and convulsing, sometimes needing to be visibly restrained by others, cooled down, before they jerk up again as if pulled by the strings of a puppetmaster.

In order to communicate in a meaningful way with others, the Bushmen believe you must be maximally aroused—your emotions at their height, your spiritual energy ratcheted up to the highest possible level, and your body fully alive.

"You cannot send thoughts to others," a Bushman shaman explained, "without first being filled with feeling. The arrows in your belly must be hot and your heart fully awakened." Then, and only then, can the deepest messages be expressed between people and become completely realized.

The Burden

In this discussion of what it means to be a shaman, it is quite apparent that this role carries similar burdens and responsibilities that are shared by helpers and healers everywhere. "Whether among Ojibwa medicine people or Amazonian shamans," Keeney said, "those with healing power all say that every imaginable plague will come after you."

Keeney is talking about far more than a little burnout or compassion fatigue. He means that physical illnesses and incredible sickness can befall a shaman who battles demons. In fact, in most cultures the shaman must go through a rite of passage far different from the graduate school experiences that we put our own helpers and healers through. The shaman must go through a sickness from which he or she will either recover or die (spiritually, if not actually physically).

Keeney returned to his amusement over all the New Age nonsense related to people wanting to have visions. "When something like that really happens, it can mess up your life."

"How do you explain this?" we asked. "In a former life, you were an academic, a scientist, an empirical scholar."

Keeney shook his head. "I used to make a living trying to explain things like this in a rational way. But there is no explanation that enables us to fully understand what it means. There are things that have happened to me that I can't believe even though I know that they happened to me. If I believed these things, I would just have to completely . . ."

Keeney stopped and considered for a moment just how to put this into words. "Look, I don't believe in all the crap that people claim to see. I can't imagine believing in UFOs. Never will. Even if one picked me up and flew me away, I still would not believe that it happened. I refuse to believe in that kind of thing. There are some things that I have theories for and other things that bankrupt my ability to make sense of what is happening."

Keeney suggested that one reason why this sort of work with indigenous shamans has been largely overlooked by psychotherapy scholars is because it is associated with the same sort of skepticism they attribute to otherworldly phenomena. And this is strange to him, considering that almost all of us have visions and dreams and the shakes, even if we choose to deny and ignore them—perhaps for good reason, considering the burdens that come with them.

With practice and experience, Keeney has not only learned to bring forth shamanic experiences virtually at will in the appropriate circumstances but learned to embrace, rather than to fear, them. In a sense, he has developed a shamanic immune system that protects him from the worst of the emotional-spiritual fallout. This, of course, is what all professional helpers and healers learn to do if they are going to survive for any time in their work.

Any beginning helper or healer in our culture will feel frightened, dispirited, exhausted, and overwhelmed by the burdens of professional practice. The same is true for apprentice shamans. The first time a Bushman initiate tries to accept the arrows in his or her belly, this individual may run screaming out of the circle and may need to be literally tackled to the ground and rejuvenated. But with experience, the shaman eventually learns how to negotiate the trials and the challenges of the journey.

In our culture as well, it is hoped that helpers and healers learn to lose their fears of failure and of self-destruction. They begin to see the unknown and their most challenging clients as opportunities for continued growth, rather than as burdens.

The Shaman's Dance

There is less difference than we might imagine between the ways we use the word *shaman* and the words *helper* or *healer*. Ultimately, Keeney has settled on the word *shaman* to describe his type of healing work because he feels less restrained by a role that embraces theology, spirituality, and kinesiology, rather than the social sciences, as its base.

Keeney does not wish to glorify or overromanticize the work of shamans over the traditional work of conventional therapists, teachers, physicians, and clergy. "I have met just as many frauds and quacks in indigenous cultures," Keeney said, "as I have in our own world. There are some truly magical helpers and healers in our culture, just as there are in the Amazon, the Kalahari, or the Tibetan peaks."

In whatever locale or healing context, helpers and healers must still deal with the toxicity they encounter on a daily basis. We must protect ourselves against what shamans call evil spirits, negative energy, or vengeful ancestors; we must find a way that we can live with the pain we feel in others.

It is ego and self-centeredness that get in the way. Shamans have no sense of self in this way; they are merely agents of their community, selected by the spirits. They don't choose this path; it was chosen for them—often with their kicking and screaming along the way. As you will see in the chapters that follow, the shaman's dance is magical, powerful, mysterious, and haunting. But it is not always what you'd expect.

Chapter Four

The Psychiatrist Wanted to Be a Priest, the Psychologist Wanted to Be a Shaman

After returning from Africa, Keeney resumed his academic responsibilities, all the while continuing his furtive but passionate study of indigenous healing. He was convinced that if his colleagues discovered the nature of his research interests, he would lose a significant amount of credibility. He had worked hard to establish himself as a force within the family therapy community, authoring books, presenting at conferences, and collaborating with some of the biggest names in the field on ways to apply cybernetic theory to clinical practice.

As a result of the popularity of some of his books, especially *Aesthetics of Change, Improvisational Therapy,* and *Mind in Therapy,* Keeney was invited to lecture in venues throughout the world. Among his most devoted followers was a group of mental health professionals in Brazil, whose members repeatedly asked him to visit in order to do workshops and seminars on resource-focused therapy, the current name for his style of work.

Although Keeney was tired of talking about therapy in its traditional forms, he saw these professional trips as opportunities to deepen his research interests into shamanic healing among indigenous peoples. Thus, just as he made it a condition of his appointment in South Africa to have the chance to visit with the Bushmen and the Zulu, so, too, did he use trips to Brazil to meet with shamans in the Amazon region. Nevertheless, up until this point, he still viewed himself primarily as a family therapist who was venturing a bit far afield.

The Audience Was Restless

The auditorium was buzzing with excitement in an assortment of languages—English, Spanish, and mostly Portuguese. Character-istic of the Brazilian people, and particularly of those who make a living as therapists, the various hand-and-arm gestures looked from the stage as if a riot was about to break out. In truth, the people in this collection of psychiatrists, psychologists, and social workers were nervously excited because they had traveled from all over the country to see Keeney in action. This was one of a se-ries of lectures and workshops that he had held throughout Brazil and other countries in the Amazon region.

It had been Keeney's custom to conduct his sessions before large audiences by demonstrating therapy with a family and then using the interaction to speak about the concepts that were in evidence. On this particular day, the audience was becoming rest-less because, even by the fluid standards of Brazilian time-keep-ing, it was well past the appointed starting time.

The Call for a Volunteer

"Excuse me," Keeney yelled out over the chaos before him, "could I have your attention?" As soon as he spoke, the assigned transla-tor repeated the message in Portuguese, this time using a micro-phone at full volume.

When the noise quieted down a bit, Keeney turned on his own microphone and tried again. "May I have your attention?" he cried out. He waited patiently, arms at his sides, literally vibrating with energy. It was Brad's method before a "performance" to put himself in a trance state of sorts, a place where he could clear his mind and spirit and concentrate fully on whatever unfolded. As a master of improvisation and an avid student of shamanism, he had learned that rather than making himself "still" or relaxed, as some might advocate, he would literally shake himself with rip-pling energy. He could feel his arms, upper legs, back, and neck start to gently undulate. When he felt the sensation in his belly, he knew he was ready.

"It appears . . . ," Keeney began again, this time speaking in a soft voice that practically required everyone else to stop talking if they wanted to hear, "that our volunteer family has not shown up this morning." He waited for the translation, settling into a cadence and rhythm so that the words that came forth out of the translator's voice appeared to be from his own mouth. Although many in the audience understood some English, Keeney's approach is so nuanced with subtle meanings that it was important for the full range of his speech to be clear.

"I was wondering if we might have another volunteer," Keeney continued. "Is there someone in the audience who would like to come up here for a session?"

The buzz in the audience ratcheted up again to a deafening level. Who would have the courage to walk up on stage and talk about their innermost thoughts and feelings, their unresolved issues, in front of their peers? To do so would risk humiliation and loss of face at the highest level. And because Keeney was known to be somewhat unpredictable and spontaneous, there was no way to know what might happen.

The chorus rumbled on for a minute or so, while participants talked to one another about this extraordinary invitation. In Brazil, where there is considerably more stigma attached to seeing a therapist or even to revealing personal problems, it was highly unusual to expect that a professional of high standing would risk being so vulnerable on stage. To add even more tension to the enterprise, it was clear to all those present that the whole proceeding was being recorded on video and audiotape. Because Keeney's previous tapes had made the rounds all over Brazil, there was little doubt that this session would eventually be seen by thousands more than the few hundred audience members in the room.

A man stood up with his right arm raised above his head. He had a regal presence and was dressed in a shirt and a gray jacket, the collar embroidered in purple. He was an older man in his 60s, balding, with a bulbous nose and sun spots speckled on his head and face. Everything about him proclaimed his pride and dignity.

Keeney recognized him instantly, as did the rest of those present: He was the grandfather of all psychotherapy in Brazil. He was a psychiatrist and a psychoanalyst of international repute, perhaps the single most prestigious figure in the field. Keeney had run into him at other professional conferences, but their previous interactions had been rather formal. Brad wondered why the older man was walking toward the stage; perhaps to cajole someone in the audience to come forward?

There was an audible gasp in the room when the participants realized that the esteemed doctor was, in fact, volunteering to be the client.

The Confession of Failure

Keeney walked across the stage to greet him, not with a formal handshake but a warm hug. "Hello, Vincente," Keeney smiled. "Thank you for coming up here. I am touched that you decided to have a conversation with me. I am sure that being with a man of your stature, I will learn a lot."

Brad waited for Sabrina, the translator, to convey this ritualized greeting to the distinguished doctor. He knew it was extremely important that he do everything possible to help the man retain his dignity in what was obviously a difficult situation. It was equally clear to Keeney that Vincente had agreed to come on stage because he genuinely needed to—he was obviously in great distress.

They arranged their chairs facing one another, with Sabrina's chair next to Keeney. They had worked together several times before, so they both had tremendous confidence and respect for one another. Sabrina had become quite expert over time at conveying not only Brad's words but his unspoken messages.

"It is indeed my privilege," Vincente responded with a slight bow of his head, "to have an opportunity to experience your work. I have great admiration for the things you do."

Keeney smiled gently. "Just begin anywhere you would like."

"I have come up here because I have struggled over the years and have had much pain." Vincente visibly grimaced as he said this, leaving no doubt that he was in tremendous anguish. "I have been a father to many people in this field. I have been a teacher and a training analyst. I have enjoyed some success with my patients and my students. And . . ."

Vincente hesitated for a minute, looking out at the audience, as if he just realized once again where he was, "I feel the goodness of my family of students who are here."

"You have certainly been a great father to the generation of therapists in this country," Keeney agreed in a soft, respectful voice. He wanted to take this very slowly, not sure where things were going.

Vincente nodded, acknowledging the respect. "This may be so. But I have been a complete failure as a father to my own son. I have found confusion and anguish. I am at a loss as to why I have not been able to raise a healthy son."

Keeney could feel the whole room shift after this disclosure. Vincente was about to confess a bombshell, an aspect of his private life about which nobody had an inkling. He was always a private man, a man of dignity, yet someone who was not inclined to reveal much about himself. Keeney just waited, breathing, staying still. A minute passed. Then another.

"My son," Vincente said, almost as a sob, "my son . . . he lives in a mental hospital. He has been diagnosed as a schizophrenic." He looked up at Keeney and stared deeply into his eyes. It was now as if the two of them were completely alone. There was no audience. No translator.

Deeper in the Zone

When Keeney gets in his most therapeutic zone, he does not so much tune out distractions as tune into the persons he is with. He enters a trance, in which, though his body is buzzing with energy, his mind becomes completely still. He becomes completely absorbed in the moment. It was from this position that he could feel all the love in the room for this great man. He could feel the energy from all those present, wanting so badly for Vincente to share and release his burden. And yet . . . there was absolutely nothing that Keeney could think of to say to him in this moment. This was someone who was a master at understanding relational difficulties. What could be said to him that would really matter, that he hadn't thought of himself?

It is rare that Keeney feels moments of impotence when he is doing therapy. He is usually quite successful in achieving a sort of Zen-like noncaring that leads him to care deeply without being hooked by a person's "stuff." Yet in this moment he felt totally powerless, almost frozen. But he didn't think, "I need to do something" or "I've got to do something for this man." Instead, he embraced the feeling of not-doing that had come forth.

Keeney waited patiently, going deeper and deeper into a state of doing nothing, not unlike the Buddhist practice of "deep listening." Here he was, trusted by this wonderful man who was in such pain, and in front of an audience, being videotaped, the whole world waiting for him to work his magic, and he felt there was absolutely nothing that he could do. Like any other therapist who does not know quite what to do or say, Brad prompted his client to continue the narrative.

Vincente spoke for the next 15 minutes, telling story after story of the patients he had seen who presented symptoms similar to those of his son. "There was one young man," he said, "who was a paranoid schizophrenic. He showed up at my office one day with a revolver in his belt and a wild look in his eyes."

The audience laughed in appreciation at the cavalier way that Vincente faced what appeared to be a very sticky situation.

"I came here to kill you," the patient said to the doctor.

Vincente nodded to his patient, thinking that he had no idea what to do in such a situation. "I had no weapon," he explained to Keeney. "I had no way to defend myself. So I decided to face my death calmly. I put my faith in God and waited for the bullet."

"Before I kill you," the schizophrenic said to him, "I want to know one thing. Are you married?"

Vincente considered a number of possible responses to this volatile young man, most of them psychoanalytic interpretations to switch the focus back to his patient as he had been trained to do. Instead, he answered honestly. "Yes, I am."

"And do you have children?"

"I do," Vincente nodded to the agitated man. "Seven children." He looked the man straight in the eyes and waited to see what would happen next.

The patient looked down at the seated doctor, his hand on the pistol, seeming to listen to some voice directing him in his head. Suddenly, he relaxed. He sat down in a chair, put the gun on the table next to him, and began to talk about his troubles.

As Vincente finished this story, he crossed his arms and waited for the audience's appreciative reaction. Keeney still remained stone-still, listening and staring intently with his piercing blue eyes. He was sitting, Budda-like, hands resting on his knees, back perfectly straight, appearing not even to blink. During the preceding 15 minutes, he had not said a single word. Keeney just listened to the doctor's stories of disturbed patients he had tried to help and wondered where this was all going and what he should do or say next.

Quicksand of Despair

"I need to get deeper into the zone," Keeney thought to himself. He began heating the arrows in his belly, waiting for the spirit of his imagination to grab him. For the next minute that he stared intently at his volunteer patient, Brad concentrated all of his energy toward trying to sink deeper into the moment. It was then that he realized that he would not come up with anything clever or brilliant. "If I don't know what to do," he thought, "then maybe that is telling me I should not do anything at all."

Keeney found himself thinking about what an interesting experience this was for him. Usually, he could come up with a thousand ideas about what to do. He is a jazz pianist, for God's sake, a master at improvisation!

"The hell with it!" he said to himself. "Let's just sort of jump off the plane of trying to figure out what is going on, and just sink deeper into being absorbed by the experience of what this man is feeling and living. This is sort of like someone who says: 'My problem is my son died.' What can I say to such a person? There is nothing to cure. That is just like what Vincente just admitted: 'My son is permanently stuck in a mental hospital.' What is there to say after that? He is saying that his son is way beyond curing."

Keeney took a deep breath, then another, trying to sort out what was going on inside himself. He then asked Vincente to talk more about his son. It was the most horrible story he had ever heard. The boy had tried killing himself many times. He had tormented his family. He had so many different problems, it was a wonder he was alive at all. And as the doctor related the details of the situation, Keeney could feel himself, and everyone else in the room, sink deeper into the concrete floor. No one was moving. For the next 10 minutes everyone sat completely still as Vincente talked about one tragedy after another.

Keeney does not usually let people go on at any great length about their problems. His resource-focused therapy is all about helping people to move away from their problems, and all the gory details, and instead focus on what strengths they have available. If you allow people to dwell on the theme of "my life is a problem," then they tend to feel greater helplessness. Keeney's preference is to wait for some glimmering or clue of something that has been resourceful in their lives and then to jump all over that as leverage to dig for more.

In talking about his strategy, Keeney recalled the story of R. D. Laing, the great anti-psychiatrist, who had been asked to work with a chronic catatonic schizophrenic in front of an audience of medical students. She was wheeled onto the stage where he had been waiting in a chair. The first thing he said to her was, "I understand you have quite an amazing skill of remaining still."

Laing went on to maintain this resourceful view of what the woman had been doing all these years—her remarkable ability to remain immobile. He eventually helped her to get a job as an artist's model so that she could put her skill of stillness to work. This story reminded Keeney of his own evolution away from a traditional psychology that seeks to understand problems.

"Talk about problems," Keeney explained, "or talk about solutions: They are really the same thing. If you are a solution-focused therapist, then you are always in the middle of problems because they are inseparable. As long as we keep looking at pathology, then that is what we will see. That is what irked me about the *DSM (Diagnostic and Statistical Manual of Mental Disorders)*. It makes it seem as if these diagnoses are real, which only saturates a person with problems. I'd much prefer to move on to what resources a person has available."

In spite of this preference for moving away from a focus on problems, Keeney sat before his patient utterly paralyzed. He allowed Vincente to go on and on about the problems that he and his son had faced together. Although he wanted to stop the barrage of complaints, he felt powerless to do so. As things proceeded, he felt himself sinking into a quicksand of despair.

Trusting Intuition

If, from Milton Erickson, Keeney had learned the value of utilizing a person's resources, and from Gregory Bateson he had learned about the larger systemic forces at work in any presenting problem, then from Carl Whitaker he had learned to trust his unconscious process. Each of these three great figures in the history of family therapy and healing seemed to come to Keeney's aid at a time of great need. It was as if he could feel their presence in the room, whispering to him, even if he could not quite make out

João Fernandes de Carvalho, one of the most renowned
faith healers of Brazil. He is uncle to José Carlos,
a psychotherapist who hosted Keeney's clinical
workshops in Brazil.

what they were trying to say. Yet the one thing that all three theo-
rists shared in common was an indomitable trust in their own in-
tuition. He also had learned to use his faith, from the renowned
Brazilian faith healer João Fernandes de Carvalho (see Keeney,
Hands of Faith, Healers of Brazil. Philadelphia: Ringing Rocks
Press, 2004).

"Excuse me," Brad finally interrupted Vincente. "I don't know
where this is coming from, but there is something on my mind. It
is sort of an idea that popped into my head that won't go away.
With your permission, I would like to ask this question."

Vincente nodded solemnly. In some ways, he was probably grateful that his long, sad story had been stopped.

"I don't know what led you to become a psychiatrist, but before you began medical training, I was wondering if it was ever the hope of your family that you become a priest? Even before you pursued medical studies, I wonder if, as a child and as a young adult, you had your heart set on becoming a priest?"

"Yes, that is so," Vincente answered, more than a little surprised by the direction the conversation had taken. "Everyone expected me to be a priest. That is what I always thought I would do." He stopped for a second, then looked quizzically at Keeney: "Why did you ask me that?"

"I don't know," Brad shrugged. "It just came to me. It was just an idea that popped into my mind. Furthermore, because I can only be honest with you, and because you are being so honest with me, I lost track of what you have been saying for the last several minutes—I wasn't listening to you. It all just sounded so horrible that I felt myself sinking into a place where I no longer felt that I could be a therapist for you. So I took off my therapy hat and just checked out. Then this question popped into my mind. I don't know where it came from, but I have learned to trust these things."

Vincente just nodded, puzzled but still intrigued by Keeney's probe about his former career aspirations.

"So," Keeney pressed, "is there something about what I said that is important to you?"

"As I said, it was always my family's desire that I become a priest. I had it in me, but I didn't have enough faith. Everyone said I was a natural, that I should be a priest. But I had a crisis of faith. I didn't believe enough to be able to do that so I became . . ."

". . . a secret priest," Keeney finished for him.

There had not even been time for Sabrina to translate this before Vincente challenged him in heavily accented English: "What do you mean?"

"Maybe you are a priest, but you don't tell anyone. Not even yourself."

"Yes," Vincente nodded. "Maybe this is so."

"A priest knows a lot about suffering."

Vincente listened, riveted on Keeney's eyes. He was no longer looking at Sabrina, impatient with the translations, and was willing himself to understand the words directly from Keeney's mouth.

"What is the biggest story for a priest?" Keeney pressed.

Vincente took a deep breath and continued to stare.

"The Heavenly Father has a son He is unable to save," Keeney said softly.

As soon as he said these words, Vincente started weeping. Keeney was concentrating as hard as he could on the doctor, but he could not help but notice the sounds of others in the audience crying in sympathy.

Then the most amazing thing took place, something that Keeney had never done before. He remembered a dream he had had the night before, a very disturbing dream that he could not shake off. He saw the beginnings of a connection between what he had dreamed and what was happening that moment. Here was a man who thought he was a failed father but also someone who believed he had failed his own family by not becoming a priest. Yet in some ways, he *was* a priest, living out a unique drama.

Suddenly, Keeney felt slapped in the face by his own dream of the night before. He began to weep as deeply as the doctor was.

"This is most peculiar," Keeney said softly, brushing away his tears. "You are taking me into completely new territory."

The Reversal of Roles

Vincente signaled Brad to continue what he was saying, although they now seemed to be in the strange position of exchanging roles.

"From the first time I observed you in places we have been," Keeney said, "I have seen how people respect you. Before I even knew who you were, I noticed how much others admire you. I saw how they hugged you and shook your hand. You were like a father, or grandfather, to many people. In fact, I am feeling that right now."

Vincente, forgetting his own problems for a moment, smiled warmly at Brad, reaching out to him.

Keeney continued, "I had a dream last night that really disturbed me. And I feel absolutely compelled to tell you about it and to ask your help."

Vincente nodded, encouraging him to continue.

It is only in retrospect that Keeney might see that he was taking a one-down position with his client, allowing the esteemed psychiatrist to maintain his dignity and sense of control in an extremely emotional, vulnerable situation. By asking for Vincente's help, it was as if Brad was showing respect and giving the man time to regain his composure. But none of this was actually going on inside his mind at the time; instead, he simply felt compelled to abandon his traditional role as the expert therapist and instead to share from his own heart. He had no idea where this might lead, but it reminded him of the ways that some of the shamans he had worked with might proceed.

"Usually, when I dream of my grandfather," Keeney said, "he touches me with such love that I wake up weeping, drenched in tears. He died of a cerebral stroke and was bleeding from his mouth. But in this dream this morning, I was lying in bed with him. When I was a little boy, sometimes I would stay at the home of my grandparents and they would let me sleep with them. This was such a special treat." Keeney smiled wistfully, remembering the sweet times with such clarity, it was almost as if he was in their bed that very moment.

"In my dream, I was an adult, but I was lying in bed next to him, looking at him. I was feeling so proud of him. He was so wise. He had so much love. Then, all of a sudden, blood started pouring out of his mouth and covered me. I was stunned. And ever since I awoke this morning, I've been feeling uneasy and disoriented. I wonder if you could tell me what this means?"

"What do I know?" Vincente shrugged. "What can I tell you? Some foolishness of my own? I have heard a Chinese saying that people cannot flee pain because pain grabs people by the feet. To face pain, rather than to run from it, is to triumph over it."

Keeney nodded at this bit of wisdom, wondering if Vincente realized that he was talking to himself as much as to his therapist-now-turned-patient.

Interestingly, there was a parallel process linking the two men on stage. Both came from families with strong religious ties, in which the men had been expected to go into the clergy. Like Vincente, both Keeney's father and grandfather had devoted their lives to the Church.

Vincente reached out to touch Brad. "Your dream seems to be saying that your grandfather wants so much to give you his life's blood."

Keeney was so choked with tears, he was unable to speak. "I loved my grandfather more than any human being I've ever known," he said finally. It was at this point that he also realized that he had never before felt more like a therapy patient than he had at that moment, on stage, where he was supposed to be demonstrating his skills as a therapist. He completely lost sight of his original goal and yet trusted where things were going—not for his own sake but for the benefit of his patient—who was now his doctor.

The Patient Cures the Doctor and Thereby Cures Himself

Vincente began to talk about the meaning of the blood in the dream and the symbols of faith, the sacrament of blood in the Christ story. He began to reframe these images, showing how someone may crucify himself so that another might live, as well as receive other sorts of gifts altogether. He made the dream a resource. In other words, Vincente unconsciously began practicing Keeney's own therapy—not only on Brad but on himself!

Keeney began weeping deeply, sobbing in grief over his own losses, but also for his patient-doctor. Vincente walked over to him and embraced him. As they held one another, you could also hear quite a few others in the room crying.

After they returned to their chairs, Vincente was the first to speak again. "I could have never heard this unless I had said it myself."

Rather than to steal the stage back and point out what had happened, the parallel process that had just occurred, Keeney decided to remain in the role of patient so that Vincente might retain his dignity. Whereas previously Brad had been involuntarily thrust into the position of examining his own unresolved issues with this grandfather, with the corresponding loss of faith, this time he chose to stay in the patient role. Vincente now felt empowered once he took on his familiar doctor role, explaining to Keeney the nature of his problems while he was also talking to himself. This way, he could remain the supreme grandfather to everyone, including to Keeney.

"You are like my grandfather in so many ways," Brad told him. "He was such a magical person to me. When he died, I never really recovered from the loss. Every year I have a dream where he visits me, or I see him, and each time I sob for hours and hours. It's a sense of how much I loved him. I am crying out of my love and I don't want to be over that."

It was at this point that Vincente stopped being a therapist and began to become a priest. "Tell me about another dream when your grandfather came?"

"The other dream that I remember is confusing. I found myself at his home, the parsonage where he had been a pastor. I asked myself, What am I doing here? I thought it had been sold. I noticed that there was a letter in the mailbox so I opened it and it said: 'The keys are on the basement window.' I went to the basement window and there were the keys to the front door. So I opened the front door and the house was empty. This is the place where I woke up."

Holding his hands like the steeple of a priest, Vincente responded, "He is waiting for you to continue the good work." This was said exactly in the tone of a clergyman, not as a therapist or a doctor.

Vincente went on to talk about the ways that grandfathers can be so special. He was touched that Keeney saw him in ways that reminded Keeney of that special man.

"You realize," Keeney said, changing directions, "that you are not talking to me like a psychoanalyst and you are not talking to me like any psychotherapist I have ever heard. I am unable to be a psychotherapist with you. I don't feel like a client with you. You are being a priest."

Just as he said those last words, Vincente broke down completely. The two of them stood and embraced one another again, both of them crying, weeping, sobbing from the depths of their souls. By this time, Sabrina came up and joined them, putting her arms around both of them and crying herself. The whole audience could be heard weeping in chorus.

As they broke away, holding one another at arm's length, Keeney said, "I expect you to continue being a wonderful priest to all those people whom you have already ministered to, and to all those who have yet to meet you. You should tell no one that you are a priest because it makes your ministry even more humble and even more authentic."

The two of them embraced one more time, and then Vincente shuffled slowly off the stage, down the steps, and out the back door. Keeney remained still, his back to the audience, wondering who he would be when he finally turned around to face them. He had taken one step into the shamanic world of dreams, while keeping another foot in the world of psychotherapy. Would he ever dare show the world what it looked like to shamanize without concern for whether what he did was perceived as psychotherapy or something else?

Chapter Five

Healing
through Touch

"We wonder," the man said timidly, "after the performance the other day . . ."

"You mean the demonstration on stage," Keeney corrected. He noticed that the man seemed nervous and hesitant. He recognized the man as one of the organizers of the workshop for therapists that had taken place, in which Keeney had worked with the psychiatrist who had wanted to be a priest. The feedback had been universally positive, even ecstatic, and Brad knew that they wanted more.

"Yes, of course. Demonstration. I am sorry. Please excuse my English. Sometimes I select the wrong word. Of course, it was not a performance but rather a demonstration. And a beautiful one at that." He stopped for a moment, cocked his head. "Did I say the right word—beautiful? Is that correct?"

Keeney smiled. "Sure. That's perfect. Thank you for your support."

"We were wondering," the man continued, "whether you would consent to return and do another perfor—ur, *demonstration?* We could schedule this any time you want. It could be . . ."

"I'd be happy to do this for you," Keeney reassured him.

"We would be most grateful. But this time . . ." He hesitated, either looking for the right words or trying to be very careful about how he phrased the next part. "This time we would like to advertise that you are not doing therapy."

"Not therapy?"

"That is correct. This time we wonder if you would show the way you do healing. As you know, many of us are physicians and we work with patients who have many physical problems, many of them quite severe. We have heard you speak of your work as a healer and that is what we would like to see."

"Sure," Brad responded. "I can do that."

The Shaman Comes out of the Closet

Actually, Keeney was not feeling nearly as comfortable with this invitation as he sounded. This would be his first public "performance" (as the organizer would say), the first demonstration of his work as a healer or a shaman, and not as a psychologist. In a way, it would be his "coming out." He had not been practicing therapy, in the traditional sense, for some time, but he was not exactly announcing this to the world, afraid that he might be written off as another New Age quack.

The audience may not have realized it, but Keeney had not actually been doing therapy with the psychiatrist who wanted to be a priest. In his heart he was being a shaman, operating from his intuition, doing what he had been trained to do in his work with healers all over the world. He merely pretended he was doing therapy because that was what people expected from him. But now there would be no disguising his intentions. If he would truly practice as a shaman, that meant using fewer and fewer words to work his healing and instead relying on the ancient traditions of touch and dance and shaking.

Keeney quite liked the idea of actually showing other professionals what he had been doing for some time, but he was still worried about how he would be received. By this time, he had stopped thinking like a psychologist altogether. And he certainly did not behave like any conventional therapist when he was working with clients.

Before appearing on stage or doing any sort of work with a client, Keeney would first prepare himself in private by doing a Bushman dance and shaking his spirit. Or he would sit, Japanese style, and let vibrations run through his body. Sometimes, he would chant in the style of a Native American medicine man, presenting a fairly eclectic mix of traditions in a single warming-up process.

"Make me a vessel," Keeney would pray to himself, "allow me to be useful to this person." When he was doing this, he was never sure to whom he was praying—to the Christian God of his father and grandfather? To the Big Doctor in the Bushman sky? To the Spirit of the Guarani? Or to the Higher Power of any of a dozen other traditions he had studied? No matter. He would go into a trance state, so that by the time he sat down with a client, he felt like his energy was operating at 10,000 megawatts. He could feel it rippling in waves from the bottom of his feet to the top of his head. It was all he could do to restrain himself from jumping up to shake and dance. He just allowed the energy to radiate through him as he had been taught in Japan, a more subtle form of handling vibrations, rather than the gross motor movements of the Kalahari Bushmen. He would put himself in "the zone" where he felt hypersensitive—not only to what was going on around him but also to what was inside him.

During the evenings before any "performance," Keeney would invite himself to dream in vivid ways and then pay close attention to how these images might guide him. In the case with the psychiatrist who wanted to be a priest, this story was as much about Brad's transformation into a spiritual healer as it was about the doctor's own neglected religious roots. The audience recognized this, and that is why he had been invited to strip away the trappings of his previous profession and show the world what he had become. Keeney had finally come of age.

The Driver's Seat

"There is a family we want you to see," the organizer told Keeney, as he was preparing to go back on stage. The room was packed once again, this time with many of the doctors and psychologists who had attended his previous demonstration, plus an assortment of newcomers who had heard about what had taken place before.

"That's fine," Keeney said, shaking the tension out of his arms and shoulders, moving his neck the way an athlete might before a race.

"No, you don't understand," the nervous man explained. "There is a family we want you to see, but they aren't sure they want to work with you."

"I see," Keeney said, immediately intrigued with the situation. He had heard that there was a boy who was dying of bone cancer and had just weeks left to live. The doctors had already amputated one of his legs. He'd lost one eye and was blind. And the cancer had metastasized to the rest of his body. The family members had come with their son to meet this famous healer, this American shaman. But, apparently, they were now having second thoughts.

"They are outside," the man said, pointing to the back door. "But they do not want to come in. They are feeling—how you say—*protective* of their boy."

"Okay," Keeney answered, understanding perfectly why they might be reluctant to bring their dying son, with all their accompanying grief, on stage in front of a roomful of strangers. "Why don't you ask the people here to wait a bit, and I'll go outside and see what's going on?"

There was a van in the alley behind the building. Keeney could see the boy sitting in the passenger seat up front and his parents both sitting in the back. The boy looked at Keeney through the window and gestured for him to take the seat next to him. Interesting metaphor, Brad thought to himself, in that the vacant seat that was open to him was as the driver, the pilot of the vehicle. He didn't think that was a coincidence.

Keeney went around the front of the van, opened the door, and settled in behind the steering wheel.

"*Oi. Bom Dia,*" Keeney said, greeting the family in the traditional Brazilian way. "*Como vai?*" As he said these words, he turned first to face the parents and then looked into the boy's eyes.

"*Voce fala português?*" the boy asked in an unexpectedly self-assured voice, asking him if he spoke Portuguese.

"*Falu um poco,*" Keeney said with an apologetic shrug and pointed toward the translator.

Keeney had expected a walking corpse, someone on the edge of death. Indeed, the boy was frail and painfully thin, but he was gorgeous, even radiant, with huge sparkling brown eyes.

As Keeney looked into Miguel's eyes, the boy reached over and touched the back of Brad's hand, which was resting on the console between them. At first, the gesture was tentative, almost flirtatious—running a finger down the back from the wrist to the knuckle—light as a feather. But then, as he saw Keeney smile warmly, he began touching his hand less timidly. They had yet to say another word to one another.

The translator was standing just outside the window, waiting for a signal, but Keeney waved her off. Likewise, Miguel's parents in the back seat were craning their necks over the seats to see what was going on in the front.

Keeney knew ahead of time that there was little that he could do for Miguel and his parents, in the sense that there was no cure possible; there was probably even little to say to them that had not yet been said before. But he sensed immediately that talk was not what was needed in this situation—by either the boy or his family. He sensed that what they needed most was touch and to be intimate with one another, in a way that they had not been before. After all, there was so little time left. Miguel had already signaled his own desires in the strongest possible terms, by beginning his relationship with Keeney through the contact of their hands.

Brad and Miguel kept gazing in one another's eyes, holding hands, sometimes smiling, sometimes just looking at one another intently. All the while, his father and mother kept watching nervously from the back. The translator, still standing outside the window, remained mute, shifting her weight from one foot to the other.

Suddenly, Miguel broke contact with Keeney and shifted painfully to turn around to face his parents. It was obvious he was in terrible pain, hobbled further by limited leverage of only one leg. "Momma," he said in a soft voice, "can he help me? Can this man help me?"

Momma hesitated for a moment. She could see the hope in the boy's eyes, the way he was looking so animated, more so than he had in many weeks. "I don't know, my son. The doctors have said this is a good man. They say he knows things. They say he can do things."

"But Momma, can he help me? Can he make me well?"

"Honey, I don't know if he can do that. We've talked about the situation before, that the cancer is . . ." Momma seemed to gulp for a moment, as if there was something caught in her throat, but it was obvious she was fighting back tears. ". . . is advanced," she continued. "We have tried so many different things. They have not helped. Maybe this man can do something. Maybe he can help us." As she said these last words, she shrugged and looked at her husband, as if she was saying they had absolutely nothing to lose.

It didn't strike Keeney that Miguel was actually asking his mother for her opinion. Rather, he was telling her that he trusted this American doctor. Even though they'd only been together for a few minutes, Brad felt he was in that special zone that many healers and therapists feel during pure empathy—when you can almost read someone's mind and heart, when you know what the person is thinking and feeling almost before he knows it himself. In this instance, Brad could hear the boy talking to him inside his head, saying, "This man will help my parents hear what I don't know how to say to them."

It was the father who spoke next, but again not through words. Keeney looked toward the back seat and saw a large man sitting calmly and peacefully. All throughout the conversation between Miguel and his wife, he had been nodding supportively. He seemed to decide right away that this was going to be alright, and he was waiting for his wife to feel similarly reassured.

"I feel better now," Momma said, looking out the window toward the translator. The host of the conference had by this time come outside as well, wondering what was going on and whether the program would proceed as scheduled. Although Momma continued to talk to the host and the translator, and Keeney couldn't actually understand the words she was saying, he could tell their meaning, that she was giving consent. "I do have one condition," she added, then waited for the translation. She was now looking at Keeney directly. "Before you speak to our son, I would like you to talk to us first. Miguel can listen, but first you talk to us."

Keeney nodded his agreement. He realized that she was being appropriately protective. Although things had gone well so far, she wanted to audition him further before he tried anything with her son. They had already had plenty of heartbreak and were terrified that this might somehow make things worse.

Back on Stage

"Okay, let's get started," the host called out to the audience, settling them down. We have the special opportunity now to work with a family." He took a few minutes to reorganize the stage now that the family filed in. The mother walked in front, head held high. The father followed, carrying Miguel in his arms. Keeney noticed that as they made their way toward him, the father had a noticeable limp in his left leg, the same one that Miguel had amputated.

Interesting, Keeney thought.

Once they settled themselves into chairs, and the translator took up her position next to Keeney, the session began by thanking the family for coming. "I know very little about your situation," Brad said, "except that you have a sick boy. Please tell me in your own words what you want me to know."

The father and the mother looked at one another to see who would begin. The father took the lead. "I wish to begin with the matter of our son." This all began 2 years ago. I brought him to an orthopedist who did exams. Then, just a few months ago, we learned that our boy has cancer, cancer of the bones. We knew this was a terrible disease, a very quick disease."

The father then recited the story of their search for answers and help for their son. They consulted the best specialists they could find. They took him to doctors, who treated him with chemotherapy and radiation. Still, Miguel became sicker and sicker. He began losing energy and could no longer move around very easily. "Finally, they took his leg," the father said.

The father looked at his wife to see if she wanted to continue the narrative, but she seemed to be having a hard time holding herself together. She signaled for him to continue.

"We went to São Paulo to find more doctors. But they told us that no matter what they did with medicine, the cancer would keep eating our boy. And that it would kill him." As he said this, he seemed to apologize.

Keeney gestured for him to continue. While this story was unfolding, Keeney was concentrating all his energy on listening to the father but was also watching the mother and the boy. He was trying to feel their spirits and listen to their hearts.

"We feel a deep sadness," the father said in a formal construction. "We feel so much grief." He looked at his wife, but she could not meet his eyes. She looked down at her hands.

Keeney glanced over toward Miguel and noticed that he did not seem to be listening to his father speak; he was staring intently at Brad during the narrative, watching him, studying him.

The father went on at some length about the awful journey they had lived through together during the previous years—the disappointments, the terror, and, finally, the end of hope. "I asked God not to take my son," the father said in a hoarse voice. "But He . . . but it is not to be." He dropped his head.

Keeney waited for the father to regain composure. Once the father and his wife and their son all looked at Brad, he smiled with all the love and compassion he could possibly communicate that was in his heart. He knew he was not the only one in the room who was so moved by their tragic story; he could see people in the first rows wiping their eyes and shifting uncomfortably in their seats.

"Clearly," Keeney addressed them all, "this is a family where everyone has so much love for one another. You have been through some terrible things and have tried to keep everyone together." Then he turned to the mother: "Would you like to share some words with me? What is in your heart?"

"At the moment," she said, "I prefer just to hear."

Keeney nodded. "You seem to carry the strength of your family with your silence and calmness."

Momma laughed. "Well, that's what I think. But my husband thinks I am explosive."

Miguel and his father both laughed at this.

Again addressing the mother, Keeney clarified, "So you both have different ways that you each contribute to the family."

"Yes," she agreed. "We each complement one another."

Except for the brief pre-interview in the car that had taken place on a nonverbal level, so far the session on stage was proceeding in a standard, traditional (for Keeney) format. He was inviting each family member to share his or her experience and tell the story. He was listening intently for themes of strength and resources in the family members, rather than focusing on problems. And he was naming and reflecting these resources so that they might draw on them more effectively.

"I noticed when I met your family outside in the van," Keeney said, talking now to the father, "that your wife was the protector. She wanted to make sure that what happened to your family was good. She did not want all of you to come in here unless it felt safe to her. She needed to check me out first."

The mother agreed that this was so, that she does serve in this important role for the family. And all the while she was talking, her husband and son were nodding in agreement.

Like Father, Like Son

"Let me tell you a bit about the way I work," Keeney said. "I will openly speak to you what I feel. I want to begin by telling you how I was moved when I first met you as a family. I was deeply touched by looking into the face of your son. There is a radiance he carries. There is a light in his face. You know this light. You must. He is very special that he carries this light. He touched me."

As Keeney said these things, he spoke slowly and deliberately, waiting for the translation to occur so that he could read how the various family members were responding to these statements from his heart. He could tell that they were making contact with one another and that he had earned their trust.

"I felt your love for one another," Keeney continued, "but it was the light in Miguel's face that touched me the most." He looked at Miguel as he said this but was careful not to dwell there too long, because he did not have their permission to go there yet. "Immediately, when I first looked into Miguel's eyes, I felt my whole body tingle with an awareness that this special person is a teacher. When I see him again, right now, I feel this again. He is extraordinarily sensitive and pure in his heart."

Keeney could see both parents nodding their heads. Finally, the mother felt ready to speak for the first time since they had moved to the stage.

"You truly see my son," she said. "I believe he does have a very special mission. If only God would give him more time. If only . . ." She paused for a moment and then began to ask questions in a beseeching tone. "Why is this happening to us? Why to my son, my beautiful son? He is such a good boy. People have always told us how sensitive he is, even from the beginning of his life. He has so much to give to the world. I asked the doctors why he must be so sick. I asked a spiritualist this question as well."

Keeney noticed that the mother had moved the discussion away from a focus on the family strengths and resources and began dwelling, even wallowing, in the family pain. Ordinarily, this would be something he would attempt to redirect away from the negative, depressing aspects of this situation; after all, at this point, with only a few weeks or months left to live, there was hardly any purpose served by casting blame or asking why things happen. Sometimes there just are no reasons to explain things.

Yet Brad also recognized that the mother needed to be heard. She needed a place, especially a public forum like this, filled to capacity with doctors and healers, to tell her story. He honored this need by listening to her questions. Finally, he asked her, "Have you thought about writing a letter to God and asking Him for the answers to your questions?"

"I did that," she said. "I sat down and wrote a letter to God."

"And how did He answer you?"

"The answer was to have faith."

Keeney nodded. "Your words confirm even more what I feel about your son." He then asked her: "May I say something to your husband? You see, mothers know something very, very deep about their children. Unlike your husband, or any man, you carried this child inside you. You have a special connection to your son that has led to a deep understanding. You knew before anyone else that Miguel had this gift. I don't mean that he can teach knowledge but that he can teach about life—and about death. Because you know this about him, you want all your questions answered. You can't stop asking questions."

All the while Brad was "holding" the mother, letting her know that he understood her experience, the father was waiting to get into the conversation. "I also had many questions," he said. "I also spent many days in a hospital—19 days. This is when I lost my leg." As he said this, he pointed to his left leg, the one that he had been favoring when he first walked into the room carrying his child. Then it hit Brad that the father and the son had *exactly* the same disabilities. Each had lost the use of their legs. Now that he had studied the father further, he noticed that he was also blind in one eye. As the cancer spread in the boy's body, it first affected the same exact places that were weakest in the father!

"I have learned," the father said, "to not ask the questions that so bother my wife. I see no purpose in them. I try to show Miguel that he must be strong, that to ask 'why' will only make him depressed. I know if I let this go on, my family would be destroyed."

"May I interrupt here?" Keeney said to the father. "Maybe you have become used to it, but to me it is miraculous to see what has happened in this family. Through his illness, your son now has the same body that you have. It is unbelievable! He now has one eye and one leg just like you. When you carry him around in your arms, it is as if the two of you make up one body."

"The story repeats itself," Momma said.

"Exactly! It hardly seems possible. In fact, it is so improbable that it even draws more attention to there being something very special that is going on in this family. Cancer makes the son's body in the image of his father. I have never heard of such a thing before. Have you? Do you realize the odds of that happening?"

Both parents hung on each word. There was something here that gave them hope at a time when they had abandoned all possibility of such hope. This was not about some fantasy that their son would somehow be miraculously cured but rather that there might indeed be answers to the questions that plagued them the most.

"And that's not all," Keeney said to the father, waiting for the translation. "As if that is not amazing enough that you gave your body to your son, but he gave you something as well."

The father looked quizzically, trying to figure out what this American healer meant by this statement.

Keeney paused one beat, two beats, building the drama. "Your son gave you something as well. He gave you his capacity for empathy, his feelings. This is just as miraculous. Your son may be dying, but he is still trying to teach you."

"It is an exchange of sorts?" Momma asked.

"Indeed," Keeney answered with a nod. "It is like a transplant. Like a spiritual transplant. It is more than just teaching. It is something beyond understanding."

"I do understand this," Momma said. Her husband nodded as well, signaling that they were ready for the next stage.

From Talk to Touch

It was now time to switch gears, to move into the realm of true healing. So far, this conversation had been designed to accomplish several things. First of all, it helped Keeney to gather information and build a relationship with the parents so that they would trust him enough to move on to the healing. Second, he was able to emphasize the strengths and the powers of this family, rather than dwelling on the depressing details of their beautiful child who had just weeks to live. After all, what could he really do for them at this point? How could he be of greatest service to help them heal one another at this time of greatest crisis?

"I am certain that you are both aware how much your son loves to touch," Keeney offered. He had not only observed this during his own interaction with Miguel, but all throughout the previous conversation the boy was leaning over and touching his father, who sat next to him, grabbing the father's arm, stroking his hand. "He is very sensitive to touch and being touched."

"Yes," Momma answered. "He has always been this way. Very dear. He especially likes the touch over the eyes."

"I can see this. So let me ask you: In the way that each of you has felt Miguel's touch and has felt him touching you, you know the special feeling this brings? Yes, I know that you do. It is like his heart touching your heart directly. Do you know this touch with each other?"

Each of the family members nodded solemnly.

"I can see that Miguel has taught you to touch as well. All throughout our talk together, I have seen the two of you holding hands." Keeney went on to tell them about how special they were as a family to show love in this way. He wondered if they worried what would happen after the boy was gone, whether they would still hold one another in this way. As he offered this statement, he noticed Miguel nodding his head vigorously, saying that this was *his* greatest worry.

"I am going to tell you something now that you have probably forgotten." He made certain to make eye contact with the parents, to wait until after they heard the translation and prepared themselves for what would follow. "As soon as your son was born, you have been preparing yourself for the time when he would someday leave. Am I right?"

They both nodded.

"You just didn't think it would be this soon. And you are worried that after he is gone, you will lose the touch that you have when he is with you."

All three of them held perfectly still, almost afraid to move. Keeney was saying out loud what each of them feared the most to say out loud.

"What you have both forgotten is that your son learned how to touch from the two of you. He is your teacher just as you have been his teachers. All of his beauty, his sensitivity, his loving touch came from you."

Keeney could feel all the members of the audience hold their breath. This was the moment. This was the critical juncture where he had named and verbalized what the family members were most reluctant to talk about—what would happen after Miguel was gone and how they would go on without him.

The Circle

"I want to confess something to you," Keeney said to the family, looking at each person individually. "I would like to share two things about my life. The first thing I want to share is that although I taught psychology and counseling in a university for many years, I have had the opportunity to travel all over the world to study and be with some of the greatest healers. In Africa, the Amazon, Asia, all over the world. The people I lived with all carry this gift of touch, the same one that is so strong in Miguel."

Miguel tried not to smile, but it was obvious he was proud of this compliment.

"This gift of touch brings forth a feeling of love and the feeling of healing one's whole being. I took one look at your son and this family and I knew that this same touch that I have experienced in every corner of the earth is present in your family.

"The second secret I want to tell you is that I have never felt fear about anything except one thing. Only one thing has frightened me and that is the death of my son. He is now about the same age as your son. So when I see this boy . . . Whew! . . . I am knocked over. I say, Are you coming into my life to touch me in some special way? How can this be for me?"

An interesting role reversal took place for the next few minutes, not unlike what had transpired when Keeney had self-disclosed with the psychiatrist who had appeared with him on stage previously. It was almost as if Brad's decision to reveal himself in a transparent, authentic way invited the people he was helping to reciprocate their own caring for him. This created a more egalitarian relationship, one founded on mutual respect and love, rather than that of an expert treating a patient in a one-down position.

Keeney thanked the family members for their openness, for sharing their concerns and deepest feelings with him. He thanked them as well for being willing to hear him and allow him to join them. "I am wondering, now, if you are ready for me to work with you?"

Not a word was spoken in response, but each of them—father, mother, and son—nodded in agreement that they were ready for what would follow.

"I am going to say something about how I feel. I am going to offer you something. Your family—not just your son, but your family—has a mission. This mission is about keeping alive this pure gentle touch. This touch brings people to feel like one. This touch provides a moment that lasts an eternity. It transcends time. It lasts forever. It helps you through every challenge that comes your way, through every pain that comes to you. This touch is greater than all the calamities that can happen to you. This touch is the purest love."

As he spoke these words, Keeney's voice rose in power and pitch, not unlike the way a preacher would sound in an old country church, not unlike how his grandfather might have sounded with his congregation. Keeney's face and body became more animated. He began to vibrate, although he was the only one who would notice this—if he had been in a place where he could have observed such a thing. But in this zone, in this state, Brad was humming in pure energy. He was speaking, but it was as if something or someone else was forming the words.

"I believe that your family has been chosen," he said with passion. "I will say this again. Your family has been *chosen* to keep this touch alive. Without even being aware of what you were doing, you taught this touch to your child. I, too, know this touch. It was taught to me by my grandfather. I have felt it from great healers throughout the world."

The family members seemed spellbound by Keeney's words. They seemed to react even before what he said could be translated. It was as if they knew what he was saying without understanding his language.

"If you are ready, I want to offer you something. I want you all together to experience this touch. I want you to feel what it is like to feel together with your whole family. I'd like to show you what I have learned and help you to use this power to keep yourselves together and in touch. Would you accept this gift?"

Again, each of the three of them nodded solemnly, as if they were taking secret vows.

At first, Keeney slowly reached out and put his hand on Miguel's head, then brought it down to the back of his neck. Miguel smiled immediately. He brought his own hand up to touch Brad. Then

Keeney working in an ecstatic healing ceremony hosted
by Stephen Larsen (the biographer of Joseph Campbell).

their heads came together, touching at the points of their noses
and foreheads. They sat perfectly still like that for a minute, then
another, touching heads, breathing one another's air. Brad leaned
in farther still, so that they might hug closer. He could feel his own
body start to vibrate and shake, just as had happened when he
danced with the Bushmen of the Kalahari. Yet he tried to restrain
the movements, not wanting to alarm Miguel's parents—he
sensed that the boy himself would not be the least disturbed by
the shaking, but he wanted to be careful to do nothing that would
upset any of them.

Keeney could no longer be sure which of them was shaking. Together, they felt like one, their hearts beating together. They
began stroking one another's backs, holding on literally for life.

Brad began to make sounds, the same rhythmic chants that he
had heard all over the world in Botswana, Bali, Paraguay, or the
Ojibwa reservation. Miguel, in turn, matched the vocalizations,
humming to a tune inside his own head.

Reluctantly, Keeney broke contact with Miguel. He moved back and signaled that he wanted the parents to join them. He invited them all to put their arms around one another, to hold each other, to touch one another. Initially, Keeney joined them in the circle, then he moved away, leaving them to embrace one another more closely. He made subtle adjustments in their arms and gestures. He directed them not to speak but to communicate only through their touch, to show their love by the way they held on to one another.

Keeney could hear sobs in the audience and could see people crying. He ignored these distractions but felt affirmed that what was going on at this moment was indeed as moving and powerful as he thought it was. As he watched the parents hugging their dying boy, he thought about his own son and their relationship. Through years of conflict with his ex-wife, who had struggled with alcohol abuse, his family had struggled to maintain its own intimacy. Forgetting the circumstances, a part of Keeney felt deeply touched by the closeness that this father and mother were feeling toward their boy.

The reality of this session was that there was nothing he could do about the boy's cancer and impending death. All he could do was help the boy to feel as if his life had some meaning and help his parents come to terms with the inevitable. Keeney wanted the mother and the father to take their son's gifts and be touched by them, even after the son was gone.

Looking back on the way things unfolded, Keeney had taken a problem that was framed in a hopeless way—"Our son is dying"—and instead helped the family members to see the wonderful gifts they had been given. Keeney didn't see this as his idea at all. From their first contact, Miguel had signaled to Brad that he wanted Brad to sit in the driver's seat, to be his co-pilot. Furthermore, Miguel had shown Keeney with his first communication that he preferred to talk with touch, rather than with words. Keeney heard Miguel's voice speak through his hands and say, "I want you to help me heal my family. I sense they will be lost after I am gone. I want you to show us how we can be with one another during my passing, and how my parents can live together without me."

Keeney had seen before how people give up their own struggle when they face death. He had heard them say that in their last days, the biggest source of their discomfort and suffering was seeing loved ones suffer while dealing with their own loss. In a sense, it was Miguel's death that would save his parents.

Postscript

Miguel did not die in a week or two, as had been predicted by his doctors. He survived 7 months, during which period he had more than enough time to teach his parents how to live after he was gone. The boy's death served as a bridge that allowed his parents to be touched by his love and, in turn, by their own.

Chapter Six

The Circles of Life

Some Conceptual Foundations

Looking at Brad Keeney, one would never guess that he has had one of the most intellectually diverse and challenging academic backgrounds imaginable. Dressed in his customary sandals, chino pants, and untucked short-sleeve shirt, he looks more like a safari guide than a scholar. With his dimpled smile and long hair constantly falling into his face, he appears unpretentious and accessible. In fact, he often prefers the company of people who are illiterate.

Yet Keeney's body of work includes volumes that are among the most challenging in our field. They are dense and complex theoretical books, combining the most esoteric nuances of cybernetics and advanced epistemology. Even today, study groups still meet regularly to try to decipher the subtleties of *Aesthetics of Change,* his landmark theoretical work.

Keeney had the privilege of working with some of the last century's most notable and charismatic intellectual figures. Early in his career he was adopted by two mentors—Gregory Bateson (1972, 1979) and Heinz von Foerster (1974, 1981), who have been most responsible for developing and advancing cybernetic theory. Once he moved from theory to practice, Keeney joined forces with

Carl Whitaker (1982; Whitaker & Napier, 1978), one of the most innovative pioneers of family therapy.

Theoretical Foundations

It was with a certain amount of trepidation that we asked Keeney to explain the conceptual foundation for his ideas. Although he can be one of the most playful, down-to-earth fellows imaginable, once he lapses into his cerebral zone, a lot of the time we have no idea what he is talking about. Reading his books has only made us feel more bewildered. Maybe we are too impatient or are undisciplined thinkers, but when we dip into some of his books, it feels as if we are reading Greek. Indeed, understanding some of his more complex ideas does require learning a whole new language.

Thus far, we have shown some of the ways that Keeney operates in his work, on stage, while behaving in the role of healer, teacher, and shaman. What may appear at first to be rather whimsical, spontaneous therapeutic actions are, in fact, informed by a long tradition of complex ideas. Like any experienced healing practitioner, Keeney's actions, which seem so casual, intuitive, and effortless, have been shaped by decades of study and practice.

We were resting in the shade of the only substantial tree within view. The Kalahari Desert is among the most desolate, inhospitable places on Earth, and this was the middle of the summer, with temperatures well above 115 degrees Fahrenheit. Because it was during the night that the action took place in the Bushman village we came to visit, the days were spent resting and saving energy for the dance.

We had Keeney's full attention and indulgence. He had set aside the next few days, from sunrise to sunset, just to answer any questions we wished to ask him and to explain any idea about which we felt confused. We had done our homework, taken profuse notes, and formulated a list of areas to pursue in depth. Except for the nights that we set aside to dance with the Bushmen, all of our allocated time was scheduled to develop Keeney's ideas and explain them in a way that could be more easily accessible.

And we were just the guys to do this job. Brad trusted us. We could push him a bit, and he liked to push back. We were both skilled teachers and writers who were used to explaining complex ideas in a more easily digestible form. Besides, being stuck out in the middle of the Kalahari, there were no distractions—no phones, no television, no Internet, heck, no electricity or roads. No visitors, unless you counted the snakes, the ostriches, the jackals, and an occasional elephant. Just hundreds of square miles of desolate country, the Bushman village, and our own little camp.

We had 20 hours of tape, a recorder, and plenty of spare batteries. We had a cook who would supply us with food and drink. We even had some Windhoek beer chilling in a cooler. And we had some blessed shade in which to hide from the desert sun.

Theoretical Love at First Sight

There are several theoretical cornerstones upon which Keeney has built his career as a scholar, a theoretician, a family therapist, and a shaman. Abraham Maslow's work (1969, 1970) was the very beginning for Keeney, the transitional influence that led him away from science and engineering to the study of psychological phenomena. He had been most impressed with Maslow's idea that human experience could be studied based on people's resources and strengths, rather than on their troubles and weaknesses. That single concept would later form the core of Keeney's writings as the innovator of resource-focused therapy.

"What struck me most about Maslow's research," Keeney said, "was that in his language, self-actualizing people transcended simple dichotomies. You couldn't categorize people in simplistic terms of being either selfish or altruistic. They were somehow both. As unhealthy or healthy, they were somehow both. As intellectually aloof and street-smart, they were somehow both—but they transcended these dichotomies."

Keeney was first exposed to Maslow's body of work while an undergraduate at MIT. He had originally planned a career in biomedical research but soon became more attracted to psychology. Carl Jung was especially appealing to him, not so much his theories as his autobiography (Jung, 1961), where he showed great courage as an explorer of his own deep unconscious.

"Jung took great risks confronting those issues about which shamans and visionaries are so familiar," Keeney remarked. "In that way I was exposed early to a psychotherapist who operated as a shaman, particularly during his generative years exploring unconscious processes."

Even with the humanistic foundation of Maslow and the spiritual foundation of Jung, Keeney still felt frustrated by the limitations of psychology. It was then that he was first introduced to the work of Gregory Bateson (1972, 1979), the noted anthropologist and epistemologist. It seemed that everyone Keeney encountered pointed him in the same direction—Rollo May (1976) claimed that Bateson was the most creative thinker since Socrates.

The more Keeney delved into Bateson's writings, the more fascinated he became with Bateson's ideas. Rather than relying on psychological metaphors for describing human behavior, Bateson contended that the stuff of human relationships needed its own descriptive language—a language that could be attentive to pattern and process in a way that was analogous to the biological world.

Bateson's ideas are very complex, so Keeney stopped for a minute to consider the best way to describe the essence of the theory that first attracted him. "He was asking the big questions of biology in a philosophical way, which included human behavior and human interaction. Remember, Gregory Bateson was a 'naturalist,' an old-fashioned observer of natural history, someone who walked through the woods, carefully examining its snakes, insects, plants, and trees."

Keeney explained Bateson's wide interests, which crossed all disciplines and which would later lead him to assemble the eclectic research team of Jay Haley and John Weakland, with consultants and outside participants like Alan Watts (1961), Paul Watzlawick and Don Jackson (Watzlawick, Beavin & Jackson, 1967), John Weakland (Watzlawick, Weakland & Fisch, 1974), and Jay Haley (1973), and Milton Erickson (Erickson & Haley, 1967) in their seminal studies of schizophrenic patterns of communication (rather than of schizophrenic people!).

Keeney remembered Gregory Bateson's early days, when the anthropologist was sent into the field in New Guinea. He had been exploring a number of themes related to the organization of social interaction, and he was searching for data that could support or refute his hypotheses.

"While collecting his data," Keeney explained, "Bateson ran into another anthropologist, Margaret Mead, who had the data he was looking for but not the theory to explain what she had found."

Mead's husband was sick in his tent with malaria. Gregory and Margaret met to compare notes, and it was theoretical love at first sight. They began a passionate dialogue that resulted in several professional collaborations and, eventually, romantic love and marriage. They later were part of an elite group of scholars that gave birth to the new science of cybernetics, which became a formal way of looking at patterns of interaction. Rather than describing and analyzing behavior in terms of discrete units called behavior, and simple linear causality, cybernetic theory introduced the idea of circular causality, with its interactive effects.

Meeting His Mentor

Keeney became disillusioned with science while at MIT and found himself less and less interested in the formal, routine, and boring classes he was forced to take. He dropped out of school to launch a career as a jazz pianist, reading more and more books on philosophy and cybernetic theory. It was Bateson, more than anyone else, who captivated his imagination. Brad decided that he just had to meet this man.

"Is this Gregory Bateson?" Keeney asked on the phone. He had been thinking for weeks about the possibility of somehow meeting this new mentor.

"Yes," the resonant British-accented voice answered.

"*The* Gregory Bateson?" Brad asked again.

"Yes," the voice answered, this time impatiently.

"My name is Bradford Keeney. And I have been deeply moved by your ideas. I was wondering if I could have a meeting with you. At your convenience, of course." He stopped and, hearing only heavy breathing on the other end of the line, added, "It would mean a lot to me."

"I am sorry," Bateson responded, "but I am simply too busy for such things."

"I'd like just five minutes of your time," Keeney persisted. "I just want to ask you one question."

"Well," Bateson hesitated. "Five minutes, you say?"

"Yes, that's all I ask. Just five minutes of your time to ask you one question."

"I suppose you could come to my home. But I have to take my daughter to dance class. You can sit in the car while I take her to the lesson."

So Keeney traveled across the country, flying into San Francisco and then renting a car for the drive to Ben Lomond (near Santa Cruz), where Gregory Bateson lived. This house was owned by his publisher, Science and Behavior Books, which was allowing this eccentric but brilliant scholar to stay there. His collection of seminal essays, *Steps to an Ecology of Mind,* was already considered a classic.

Keeney knocked on Bateson's door, to be greeted by a tall, disheveled man with long, whitish hair. "Yesss?" he said in a drawn-out manner, looking like the perfect specimen of the absent-minded professor.

"Hi. I am Brad Keeney."

Bateson looked at his visitor for a moment, then said, "Of course, you are."

Keeney stood in the door awkwardly, waiting for a signal as to what to do next.

"Well, come in, come in, why don't you?" Bateson said. "I'll make you some tea."

Keeney entered the home to find it almost completely barren of furniture. The living room was stacked with books from the floor almost to the ceiling. There were manuscripts spilled over the floor, reams of paper. An old piano was pushed into the corner of the room, and it, too, was covered with so many books that the keyboard was not visible. When they walked into another room, Keeney saw with amazement that he was viewing one of the most extraordinary libraries in the world. Gregory's father, William Bateson, had developed a lot of the early vocabulary for the science of genetics. He had left his entire collection of scientific books to his son. In fact, Gregory was named after the famous geneticist Gregor Mendel (Lipset, 1980).

While Gregory was growing up in Britain, the Bateson family had been a neighbor to the Huxleys and the Darwins. In this very library were original first editions of Darwin's work. There were collections of drawings scattered about that had been made for Bateson and Margaret Mead during their field studies in Bali. Keeney just stared at all the treasures with his mouth hanging open. It was just the sort of eccentric, chaotic environment that he imagined would house such an original mind as Bateson's.

"This way," the older man announced, weaving his way through the maze of books and artifacts, until they arrived at the only place available to sit in the whole house—the dining room table.

Bateson fixed them both some tea, and they sat staring at one another across the table. "My daughter, Nora, will be home shortly," Bateson said. "Then we will go."

As soon as the 12-year-old girl arrived home from school, the three of them piled into a dilapidated old Volkswagen van that had been loaned to Bateson by a friend. The bumper was made out of a piece of wood. When Keeney looked askance at this strange mode of transportation, Bateson explained unapologetically that he had never owned a car or a house, and he never would.

Keeney had observed that not only did Bateson not own a vehicle or a dwelling, but he also refused to watch television or read a newspaper or a magazine. In fact, Bateson said he refused to go to his dentist because the waiting room was filled with magazines.

The three of them drove in silence to the dance studio, where they dropped Nora off for her lesson. Along the way, they stopped at a raspberry stand and bought several pints of fresh berries and cream, which they consumed. They then went to a coffee shop about a block away, where they began to chat. As soon as they settled themselves into a booth, Brad began immediately to talk about his frustrations as a university student. "I went to one of the finest institutions in the world, and yet the teachers were so welded to these things called textbooks that were about as interesting as reading a phone book."

Bateson sympathized. He began to complain about all the "stupid people" whom he was forced to interact with. He made a list of those with whom he was frustrated—B. F. Skinner, for one. "And that Buckminster Fuller. He's too damn purposeful. That's why his domes always leak."

Before long, Bateson and his new protégé entered into a kind of collusion, in which they continued to make a list of their mutual nemeses. This reminded the older man of when he had been in charge of propaganda in Southeast Asia during World War II. He had been asked to develop strategies for demoralizing the Japanese, but he refused to follow the standard practices of the time. "Everyone does the same thing. They get on the radio and tell people—who are never listening anyway—a bunch of screwy lies that they wouldn't believe even if they were the truth. Complete waste of time. You tell people to put down their guns, play some popular music, and think that these kamikaze fellows are going to come out of the jungle. Utterly ridiculous."

Instead, Bateson came up with an idea that was later to form the foundation of so many of his theories that led to treatment strategies. He decided that he would tell the enemy exactly what they already believed but would exaggerate by exactly 20%. Not a single iota more or less. In this way, he could confuse people so that they would not know what to believe from their own government and would therefore be more susceptible to other influences.

Keeney looked at Bateson and shook his head, realizing that he was hearing the story of the first therapeutic double bind, even before there was a name for such a thing. Later, Keeney still shook his head as he related this story about his beloved mentor. "Now," he said, "you could see why I love being such a radical because I met this man who was the most radical human being imaginable. I fell in love with his cynical sense of the absurd."

"I'm telling you," Bateson muttered to the younger man, "that things are bad. They are worse than you can possibly imagine."

The two of them commiserated together over coffee. They conspired to join forces. They made a pact, this aging, eccentric scholar and the 23-year-old precocious dropout and jazz pianist.

Bateson ended up clearing his schedule for the next few days so that he and Keeney could spend all their time together talking and comparing notes. Anyone who called was told by the old man that he was sick and was not seeing anyone. The original 5 minutes turned into a long weekend.

On the last day, when Keeney had to depart, he expressed his profound gratitude to Bateson for the time they had spent together. "I so appreciate what you've done for me already, Gregory," Brad said.

Bateson gestured dismissively with his hand, as if this was no big deal.

"Seriously," young, idealistic Keeney insisted, "this has been so important to me, a highlight of my life. This time with you is everything that I had hoped it would be."

Bateson just nodded, clearly embarrassed by all this effusive praise.

"Gregory, I'm just wondering . . . ," Keeney hesitated for a moment, unsure how to ask what he really wanted to ask. He knew he was being presumptuous.

"What is it?" Bateson asked.

"Well," Keeney stammered, "I was just wondering what difference my presence in your life this weekend has meant for you?"

Gregory Bateson, anthropologist and cybernetic
theorist, serving tea during his first meeting with
Brad Keeney. The book under his left arm is
an original edition of William Blake's *Illustrations
for the Book of Job.*

As he nervously asked the question, Keeney imagined all sorts
of ways that his hero might answer him, wishing and hoping that
perhaps, just perhaps, the great man might compliment him in
some way. He held his breath.

Bateson considered the question for the longest time, all the
while staring deep into Keeney's eyes. The silence seemed to go
on so long that Brad wondered if he was going to answer at all.
Then the old man leaned forward and said, "The raspberries."

To Act in Order to Understand

After this initial meeting with his new mentor, Keeney went on to become a devoted student of Bateson's work, designated by the master to carry cybernetics into the next generation. Brad decided to go back to school and eventually wrote his doctoral dissertation about how Bateson's ideas could be articulated and applied to the practice of psychotherapy. This work was to become Keeney's landmark book *Aesthetics of Change,* whose forward was written by another inventor of cybernetics, physicist Heinz von Foerster. He later became a dedicated supporter of Keeney's role in trying to change the academic and therapeutic mind-sets.

"I used to have dreams," Keeney said, "in which I could hear Gregory's voice giving lectures. I ended up writing the book that was my fantasy of all the things that I wished he would say. This is how I began my academic career, as the person to carry on his work."

What this meant was that Keeney set forth the cybernetic ideas with which one could view the world in terms of patterns of men-

Heinz von Foerster, physicist and one of the founders of cybernetics. He is giving a lecture on "recursion" to Keeney's university class at Texas Tech University.

tal processes. Drawing on the tradition that Bateson established of crossing disciplines and blending academic fields, Keeney began looking at the patterns of interaction that organize not only mental health professionals but also dancers and pianists and shamans. Bateson had been as interested in the learning of octopuses and dolphins as he had been in the psychiatric treatment of schizophrenia; in fact, he attempted to find common patterns in *all* these phenomena.

In *Aesthetics of Change,* Keeney talked about a cybernetic and systemic view of therapy based on how we construct the world. This was not anything close to what is now called social constructivism but was more similar to radical constructivism. Instead of proceeding in the usual psychological way, "I must first diagnose the problem in order to treat it," the cybernetic therapist turned things around: "First I must act in order to understand."

This view is perfectly consistent with the epistemology of shamans around the world, whose way of knowing the world is circularly connected to everything else. In the language of cybernetics, this is called the "self-verifying loop" or "recursive connection," but a shaman would just say that it is like the snake swallowing its own tail.

There was a time, in the winter of 1981, early on his shamanic path, when Keeney was talking to a group in Minnesota about some of these ideas, and an Ojibwa medicine man approached him after the lecture. "These things you say," the Indian said, "are the way my people have always seen the world. We see everything as circles and everything as connected. If you would like to visit my people, and see how we live, you are welcome."

Keeney was not yet ready to accept such an invitation, but seeds were first planted that he might abandon his academic robes for those of a shaman. For the time being, however, he first wanted to apply Bateson's theory to the practice of therapy. In order to do that, he needed another mentor who could help him to build these bridges from the theoretical to the practical world.

The Wizard

It was through the cybernetic conceptual lens that Keeney was first exposed to the practice of psychotherapy, by watching a live session of Carl Whitaker at work while a graduate student. If Bateson could have been called an eccentric, then Whitaker gave new meaning to the word—he was provocative, charismatic, goofy, and totally unpredictable.

"I watched him work with a family," Keeney recalled, "and I remember one moment in particular that I have never forgotten to this day. I don't know what they were talking about; it didn't seem very interesting, but I remember Carl appearing to somewhat doze off. The family stopped talking and they just sat there staring at him in silence. Carl sort of kicked his head back, as if startled awake, and looked at the husband. 'What do you know about ice boxes?' Carl asked him.

"The guy looked stunned. 'I'm in the refrigeration business,' he answered. Not only had Whitaker picked up on what the guy did for a living, but he touched on a metaphor that became the whole focus of the session. And he did it while he appeared to be sleeping!"

Keeney was bowled over by this demonstration. He was a student in a master's degree program at the time, and, while trying to figure out a way to make a living, he decided to propose to the university that he would organize workshops and bring in famous speakers; that way, he could pay himself a salary to support his studies. The first person whom he decided to invite to the campus was Carl Whitaker. That was when he first witnessed a session of psychotherapy.

While having dinner together the night after the workshop, Keeney asked Whitaker the same question that now everyone most often asks Keeney: "What is it that you do with people?"

"I don't have the slightest idea," Whitaker shrugged. It was the way he said this, as if he didn't know and didn't care, that really caught Brad's curiosity. This was so different from his mentor, Gregory Bateson, who attempted to explain, understand, and connect everything into a unified theory, in much the same way that Einstein had a generation before.

When Whitaker heard of Keeney's relationship and collaborations with Bateson, he immediately became excited and didn't want to talk about anything else. During this first meeting, they agreed to stay in touch and perhaps to work on some projects together that might join the conceptual work of Bateson with the clinical artistry of Whitaker. "After all," Carl said, as the conversation came to a close, "the difference between being creative and being crazy is figuring out a way to get paid for what you do."

"I followed his advice," Keeney laughed. "And this was what moved me from being a theoretician to a practitioner."

Whitaker and Keeney began a series of correspondences, in which they continued to exchange ideas and compare notes. The older man wanted to learn everything he could about Batesonian ideas, and Brad wanted to study the methods of this amazing wizard who worked such wonderful magic but did not try to explain what he was doing. Whitaker was to become his mentor and father in the field.

The Voice of Cybernetics

Eventually, Whitaker and Keeney figured out a way that they might spend more time together and arranged to meet at the Philadelphia Child Guidance Clinic at the invitation of its director, psychiatrist H. Charles Fishman. This was the absolute height of the growth of the family therapy movement, when some of the most important research in the field was being conducted.

Salvador Minuchin (Minuchin & Fishman, 1974) had been another of the prominent presenters whom Keeney had invited to do a workshop at his university. Their relationship had a very rocky start. Although Minuchin did his usual amazing, theatrical job of putting on a show, Keeney sometimes found his behavior in social situations to be appalling. "He was the rudest man I ever met," Keeney remembered about their dinner together. "I took him to a restaurant with several other people. I was sitting next to him. Once he found out that I had been working with Gregory Bateson, he went on and on about how Bateson didn't have a clue about what was going on in the real world. He had no background as a clinician and no understanding about therapy. But Sal was just goading me.

"Although I was steaming inside, and quite offended, I just calmly got up out of my seat and moved to the other end of the table. I didn't say a word to him. After about 5 minutes, Sal walked over to me and took me outside the restaurant so we could have a chat."

"I want to hire you," Minuchin said.

"Excuse me?" Keeney replied, debating whether he wanted to slug this rude man or just walk away.

"I said I want to hire you. I like the way you work in the flow of social interaction."

And this was typical of the way Minuchin operated, Keeney recalled. He liked people who would stand up to him, especially those who did so by initiating structural changes (as Keeney did, by relocating himself at the table), which was what his method was all about. Don't just talk, *do* something.

Both Whitaker and, later, Minuchin encouraged Keeney to write about Bateson's ideas, specifically to introduce them to the field of therapy. The first place Keeney decided to start was with the current diagnostic scheme in practice, the *Diagnostic and Statistical Manual of Mental Disorders (DSM)*. Rather than pigeon-holing and categorizing people, Keeney wondered how cybernetics could be used to reframe diagnosis so that it became an argument for a different way of knowing. He didn't realize it at the time, but although he thought he was moving toward psychology and family therapy as his home disciplines, he almost always thought like a shaman.

Keeney studied the etiology of the word *diagnosis* and found that it simply meant "to know." It was just a form of epistemology. So, he wondered, what would happen if he introduced a circular epistemology that would be more useful in understanding systemic family processes? In his paper "Ecosystemic Epistemology" (Keeney, 1979), published in a major journal at the time, he launched his career as a family theorist. Within a remarkably short period of time, many of the pioneers in the field sought Keeney out for consultations about how to use cybernetic paradigms to advance their own theoretical constructs. He was approached not only by Minuchin to work at the Philadelphia Child Guidance Clinic, but by Don Bloch (Jones & Bloch, 1993) to work at the Ackerman Institute. He started out as a young man at the Menninger Foundation, where he spent time in residence, writing about how cybernetics could inform clinical practice in creative ways, and then moved to New York City to be director of research for the Ackerman Institute. He chose that institution solely because he wanted to be close to jazz and theater, the great passions of his life.

So Keeney began as a theoretician, a cybernetic epistemologist, who really knew and understood the Batesonian paradigm. Then he moved into the role of cartographer, mapping the concepts in such a way that clinicians might better employ the ideas. Notable figures like Jay Haley, John Weakland, H. Charles Fishman, Olga Silverstein, the Milan Team, and others all sent Keeney their works and asked how these might be translated into cybernetic language. This culminated in his volume on mind in therapy, in which he described ways that cybernetic theory could be used to construct and organize family therapy (Keeney, 1985).

Just at the point when professionals seemed most interested in these ideas, Keeney had decided that there was an unhealthy reverence for this theory, and for theories in general. At this time, he moved to Texas, where he eventually became the head of a doctoral program in family therapy, and people came from all over the world to learn cybernetic-based therapy. Yet Brad was feeling both frustrated and bored, being locked into his assigned role. It was as if the *DSM* had been used to diagnose him as a cybernetic scholar, whose job it was to spend his life teaching Bateson's ideas to the world. This was far too linear a fate for a man who embraced circular thinking, a therapist who did not yet realize that the shamans were calling him.

The Screenwriter and Jazz Player

Keeney believed that a faddish interest in his ideas had developed, almost as if the field had decided that this was the next greatest thing and that everyone should jump on the bandwagon. Oppositional by nature, he invited the critics of cybernetics to his campus and created visiting scholar positions for them. These included Stephen Tyler (1987), a former founder of the field of cognitive anthropology, who had more recently become the most radical postmodern anthropologist in the world. Tyler, holder of an endowed chair at Rice University, came with his colleague, Harvard-bred Tullio Maranhão (1986). Keeney's plan was to create a context for dialogue and formal criticism of exactly the same ideas that students and practitioners were beginning to worship. If that was the intent, to deconstruct, if not to disassemble, the very ideas that formed the foundation of his thinking, then the result was even more unexpected. What is the essence of cybernetics if not improvisation? After all, circularity and feedback were really just about flexibility adjusting behavior in light of new observations and inspirations. And isn't this just what jazz piano and improvisational theater were all about?

Abandoning the posture of the intellectual epistemologist, Keeney became more interested in exploring ways that therapists might work more creatively and improvisationally, in much the same manner as a jazz musician. In fact, he considered therapy to be more of a performing art than anything else. As such, he developed "recursive frame analysis," a way of scripting conversations and therapy sessions that resemble a screenplay, a storyboard, or a musical score (Keeney, 1990).

"I wanted to be able to create a method that would reveal the conversational flow of a therapeutic session, or a whole therapy case. This was analogous to the way you would notate music through a symbolic system of notation. It is based on the structure of a screenplay, where you start by drawing a box or frame that is designated as the beginning (Act I). Then you go to a middle box (Act II), and follow with closure, the ending (Act III). Each frame indicates a theme, and like plays and movies, therapy moves from theme to theme, or frame to frame. However, in conversation and in life in general, themes are more like Chinese boxes, one within the other. They are recursive, in that they don't have a static or fixed beginning or an end. Any theme can change at any moment, transforming itself into either a subplot or a major plot."

We had heard this explanation before and we were confused. We interrupted Brad at this point and asked him to tell us what this recursive framework would look like if he applied it to this conversation.

"Just look in the book *Improvisational Therapy,* and you will see cases scored throughout."

"But Brad, we *have* looked at that book. Maybe you could simplify this for us?"

"It's just a form of notation like a storyboard for a novel or a screenplay. But it is seldom a linear story. Like all great literature, therapeutic conversation operates on multiple levels and can enfold and engulf itself over and over again. The story does not just move backward and forward in time; it moves in circles."

"Can you give us an example?" we pressed again.

Keeney nodded. "Let's go back to chapter 4, about the psychiatrist who wanted to be a priest."

"And the psychologist who wanted to be a shaman," we finished.

"Right."

"Go on," we encouraged him.

"Act one. Scene one. The priest comes in and says: 'Here are all the impossible cases I have had. These people committed suicide. This person was thrown into an institution. I have to deal with all these challenging things. Even my own son has been hospitalized with schizophrenia.'"

"So," we summarized, "rather than using the *DSM* to diagnose a case, you have advocated using this scoring method to get the details down."

"Exactly. The *DSM* keeps you stuck in the opening act. Once you pathologize someone or something, give it a simple name, you lose a whole range of possibilities for intervention."

"What do you mean about staying stuck in Act I?"

"The person says, 'I have a problem.' Then, you give the problem a pseudoscientific name. You concretize it, make it a hardened metaphor, rather than loose street talk that is easier to shift."

"And what are you saying? Say again how you moved the priest-psychiatrist to the next act."

"I asked him if he ever wanted to be a priest. It changes to a different scene—the question of being a priest, instead of being a failure as a father. He went right there and he stayed there. He didn't go back. He might have said, 'Yes, but I failed with my son.' Then he would have come back to the beginning. But then I would have brought him to a new scene in another way."

The simplest scoring of this case would look like:

ACT 1	ACT 2	ACT 3
Theme: Failed father (hospitalized son; list of hopeless patients from the past).	*Theme:* I wanted to be a priest.	*Theme:* You are a secret priest.

Keeney always looks for resources in his clients, rather than dwelling on their problems. He cited another case of a mother who felt like she was failing her marriage and was a failure as a woman. The first thing out of her mouth was that her husband was an alcoholic and that they were going to get a divorce. Not much there to work with if you accept this conception of the situation.

Instead, Keeney shifted the focus to the next act: "But you say you are a good mother, and a good mother is resourceful and creative and doesn't give up." This is a way to stop the complaining from the first act. There is no longer discussion about the husband's drinking, and instead the action moves to a look at how she mothers him. The third act moves to how she can shock her husband, how she can become "the queen of shock" to get his attention in new ways. This is how she moves to a place of empowerment, rather than helplessness.

ACT 1	ACT 2	ACT 3
Theme: Failed marriage	*Theme:* Good mother	*Theme:* Queen of shock

Throughout the session, throughout *any* conversation, the rhetorical shifts and reversals and circles can be mapped and scored. This allows the professional to go back and examine where the best opportunities lie for moving the action to the next scene or act. It also gets the therapist out of the mindframe of diagnosing psychopathology and finding problems, instead of looking at things as a screenwriter would and responding like a jazz musician. So, coming full circle, Keeney moved from being the ultimate intellectual theoretician to the ultimate pragmatic practitioner.

The Spirit of Improvisation

Keeney had been hired by his university in Texas to recruit and train family therapists in cybernetics systems theory, and yet upon arriving on the scene, he had abandoned this framework in favor of improvisation.

"Were the administration and your colleagues a little upset by this change of heart?" we asked him.

Keeney smiled mischievously. We didn't even know half the story. Brad began teaching all his classes and workshops with what might be described as very unusual methods. He would ask students for one line that a client might say: "I thought about killing myself," or "I don't know what to say to my husband." The particular line didn't matter.

"Now," Keeney would tell the students, "I want you to forget that you are learning to be a therapist. I want you to imagine that you are in a school of performing arts. You don't have to care about ethics committees. You don't have to worry about theories. What are all the possible one-liners you might say to a client in response to that opening?"

Keeney would form all the students into two lines, each facing the other. One person would begin with the first line, "I don't know what to do with my life." A person in the other line would respond in some way with another line. Any person in one line could utter anything he or she wanted, and then a person in the other line would respond. This would continue until each side spoke as a single voice.

"And the point of this?" we pressed him.

"I wanted them to learn that there are some things you can say that keep people in the same place, and other things you can say that move them to the next level. This is just the sort of thing they might do in drama school."

Because Keeney was seeing therapy as more and more like a performance, he presented whole class sessions on how to design one's office like a stage. Ordinarily, a therapy office is furnished with the predictable and ordinary "props" of books, diplomas, a few couches and chairs, and a Kleenex box prominently featured. But what if therapy is a performance, and the office is a stage; then how might one construct such an environment for maximum effect?

Keeney advocated that therapists should keep all sorts of things in their offices that they might need to heighten a sense of drama or infuse a spirit of play. An assortment of musical instruments was considered a must, as were any number of other household objects that could be used as props.

Keeping with his goal of teaching improvisation, Keeney began operating more and more like his mentor Carl Whitaker. "For Carl, it was all about the *experience* of therapy, not the theory." And this became the bridge to shamanism. Helping and healing were no longer seen as strategic applications of cybernetics or any other theory: They were improvisations that transformed human experience.

Touching, Instead of Talking

As if cued by the director to enter, stage left, at just this point in the conversation, we saw three figures walking toward us. We were sitting in the meager shade, trying to remain cool in the heat of the day. As they drew closer, we saw that three of the women shamans from the nearby Bushman village had come for a visit. They had come to touch Keeney and to shake with him.

While we shook our own heads in wonderment, Brad joined the three women, who were just tall enough to reach the middle of his chest. The four of them huddled in the sand, squatting on their haunches. Their arms embraced one another, so it was difficult to tell where one person began and the other ended. Their foreheads were touching, and they began to vibrate and shake. We heard moaning, then shaking. The beads of the women were vibrating like rattlesnakes. "Mmmmmmmmm," we heard, deep guttural sounds coming from within their huddle on the ground. From where we were sitting, it looked like the four of them were sharing a contagious convulsion. And in a sense, that was *exactly* what was going on.

We sat there in awe. One minute we were having an intellectual conversation about the conceptual foundations of Keeney's work, and the next he was writhing on the ground with three Bushman healers, sharing their spirits and power. He is the "Big Doctor," the Bushman shaman with the white skin who cannot make the tribal clicking sounds characteristic of the !Kung language.

After 15 minutes or so of being huddled together in their group, shaking, they separated. The three women bowed their heads and clapped their hands as they looked at Keeney. He clapped in return and gave each of them a final hug. As they shuffled off to their village just down the path, Keeney came back to join us. He was red-faced, sweating profusely, and breathing heavily. He tried to speak to us as he settled back in his chair, but he could not catch his breath. He uttered involuntary, guttural moans, gulping air.

We wanted to ask him what the heck that was about, but we waited until he returned to Earth. The muscles in his arms and chest and belly were still rippling.

When Keeney spoke to us again, he completely ignored what had just taken place and resumed our prior discussion. "There is a Zen parable that says it does not matter which raft you take to get across the river. But you must be on a raft. For me, the raft that served my purpose best was the theory of cybernetics. I'm not saying that was the only raft, or the best raft, but it got me across. It got me to here." As he said this, he looked meaningfully toward the path where the three women had just disappeared.

Part II

Shamanic Concepts Applied to Helping and Healing

Chapter Seven

Who Is Not in the Room?

The baobab tree provides continued relief from the desert heat. This is one of the largest such monsters in the world, as big around as a house and as high as a medium-sized office building. Its branches formed a tent of shade to protect our camp from gradual combustion. Yesterday, a deadly poisonous green snake fell off a branch and landed where we were sitting today. The Bushmen shrieked in panic, eventually cornering the critter and beating it to death with sticks.

The heat was so oppressive, we were sitting as still as possible, lazily batting away flies that were seeking the slightest drop of moisture on our skin before it evaporated. We were talking about Keeney's transformation from one kind of a healer to another: What led him to abandon his roots as a psychologist and a teacher, to refashion himself as a shaman? Such a transition had been building for years, only coming to a head on that stage in Brazil, where he not only helped the psychiatrist to realize he was really a frustrated priest but also helped himself to accept that he was a frustrated shaman only pretending to be a therapist.

For some time, Keeney admitted, he had been dissatisfied with his field and its limitations. "Therapy lacks courage," he said. "It lacks love. It operates out of fear."

Kottler, Carlson, and Keeney sitting underneath a baobab tree, discussing what the shamanic healing cultures have to say to psychotherapists.

"Fear of what?" we asked.

"Fear of losing control. Fear of true intimacy. Fear of being hurt economically. Fear of people's judgment. Fear of other things that I have now lost track of because I have had so little interest in new developments."

Keeney smiled apologetically and gestured toward this tree, which may be a thousand years old, perhaps one of the oldest living things in Africa. Thousands of years before this tree was a seedling, the Bushmen who live nearby had been practicing healing rituals that we still think of as primitive.

"Awhile ago," Keeney continued, "I asked a friend what is new in psychology. He said the most important thing was ethics. I thought this was interesting."

"Interesting how?" we asked. It seemed to us the most obvious thing for professionals to talk about. Ethics is about doing the right thing, about maintaining appropriate professional boundaries. Ethics is what keeps us in line.

"To me," Keeney explained, "ethics is not about supposed universal standards written in some sort of code. It is about what you are willing to lose your life for. It is about what you are willing to go to prison for. It is about what you take a stand for.

"To most professionals, all I hear them talk about is how to avoid getting in trouble. That isn't ethics—it's about how to follow the rules so you get to stay inside some elitist guild."

We couldn't help but feel a little defensive. We happen to think that the traditional ethics discussions in our field help to maintain certain consensual standards. They help to protect clients against exploitation. They help to maintain appropriate boundaries.

Keeney maintained that this sort of conventional thinking is so much a part of our culture that we have trouble thinking outside our familiar world. Because he has spent the last decades living and working outside the field, outside the borders of Western values, he has a very different take on the subject.

Keeney finds that helpers and healers in our culture have completely separated themselves from what our counterparts do within indigenous peoples. This talk of boundaries, for instance, of distance between healers and their clients, is all nonsense to a shaman. For that matter, many of the most charismatic historical figures in our field would never be able to work in today's climate.

"What would R. D. Laing or Carl Whitaker or Fritz Perls say about all this talk about boundaries?" Keeney asked. "Whitaker used to take two bottles of milk and hold them on this chest like they were breasts and nurse his patients while they sat on his lap. He would also sit on top of a schizophrenic while the family attempted to push him off. Milton Erickson would invite his patients to hang out at his house."

Keeney laughed as he recalled a recent story he heard from Erickson's daughter, Betty Alice, whom he was interviewing for a retrospective book he was writing about the master hypnotist's life as our field's most notable shaman. "She was telling me how one patient was often at their home, taking care of their garden. That was part of his therapy, and he became an accepted part of their family. These great clinicians enforced few boundaries as we know them. Patients were adopted into their families in much the same way that healers do in other parts of the world. I know this must seem unimaginable to most professionals today."

We nodded our heads, agreeing that this was indeed hard to picture in today's climate. Also, what about protecting clients against lunatics and manipulative quacks? Some practitioners, after all, have done some things of which none of us should be proud.

"It is interesting," Keeney replied, "that people in our field are so obsessed with genitally fucking their clients but don't spend a whole lot of time addressing all the mind-fucking that goes on."

We could muster a whole list of possible responses to this argument and started to do so. Keeney held up his hand to finish his thought. Jon looked beyond the outstretched hand to the baobab branches above, scanning for a venomous snake that might fall in his lap.

A Literary Context for Helping

"Let's stop thinking like psychologists and teachers for a moment," Keeney said. "Think like playwrights and screenwriters. Let go of what you think you know and understand."

"Oh, no," Jeffrey muttered. This was just the sort of thing Keeney liked to do with students—to ask them to imagine the unimaginable. As an ex–practicing cybernetic epistemologist, he loved challenging people's most deeply held assumptions about truth. Now he wanted to take us far beyond what we knew as ethics. What started out as an intellectual discussion to get through the heat of the day had now become a "Keeney experience"—he was beginning to work on *us*. If you don't pay attention, dear reader, you'll find he is now working on you as well.

Keeney asked us to think of a thought we might have that, if known, would have us banned from the profession forever. He mentioned as one example a situation in which a client confessed that he was thinking of killing himself. Picture telling this person to go ahead and do it. You think this is an excellent idea and a much better solution than anything else you could have come up with.

"Then," Keeney said, "create a conversation, a scenario, in which this type of comment might actually be quite therapeutic."

We conceded this point. Indeed, in some circumstances and contexts, almost anything can be helpful, even things we would never ordinarily consider.

"Now imagine another situation, one in which a person confides suicidal intent and you say instead, 'How do you feel about that?' or 'You must be feeling hopeless.' Picture a time when these comments could actually be quite dangerous and threatening."

Okay. Okay. We got the point. It is not what we do but the context in which we do it that matters.

"This is the literary, rather than the psychological, view of things," Keeney said gently, knowing we were struggling with his argument.

Keeney returned once again to the question of safety we'd raised earlier. "All change involves a certain amount of risk—the bigger the change, the bigger the risk. Deep, profound changes involve risking everything. You might lose your house, your marriage, your reputation, your sanity, even your life."

He was talking here about the difference between being a shaman versus the kinds of helping that we practice. The greatest risk that we might face is an unpaid bill or perhaps a malpractice suit. The shaman enters so completely into the spirit world that he or she literally risks death. Jon and I silently wondered whether it was not that unusual during a healing ritual among the Bushmen that even an experienced shaman might pass out, jump into the fire, run screaming into the night, or have a heart attack.

Dualism

Within the cultural healing traditions that Keeney has been operating, there is an expectation on the part of shamans and their clients that they are both taking tremendous risks. The changes they encounter do not take place within a private sanctum but in front of the whole village—and not just the community that is present, but the ancestors and spirits as well!

In this world the shaman is used to dealing with dualisms and paradoxes. Shamans see both good and evil as necessary, embracing them both. They see their roles as both altruistic and selfish. They look at sickness and health as inseparable. These supposedly simple people live with a degree of complexity that we have little tolerance for in our favored theories.

Keeney thought of an example of this with his friend Credo Mutwa, the Zulu shaman and poet we mentioned in an earlier chapter and will talk more about later. When Mutwa works with an apprentice, the person must go through years of training as a *sangoma,* surviving many tests and trials. At the final examination, Mutwa asks the apprentice the question: "What do you do with evil?"

If apprentices should say that their role is to eradicate a feared enemy, to rid the Earth of this blight of ill will, they flunk the test.

If they should say that they pay no attention to it, that they concentrate only on the good in people, they fail as well. The correct answer, the one that demonstrates a deeper wisdom, says that there is no good without evil; they balance one another. It is necessary to stay on middle ground. This sort of paradigm changed the whole way that Keeney thinks about helping and healing.

"It's the complementarity that interpenetrates yin and yang," Keeney explained. "As William Blake insinuated: You are going to have enemies, so just pray that you have damn good ones. Don't destroy your enemies because you will destroy yourself."

Keeney smiled as he said this, but he was quite serious. This is a key reason why he feels that therapy is so limited by comparison and has lost much of its wisdom in the search for simple answers and universal codes. "Stomping out evil under the guise of doing good is the stuff of crusades. And this creates a bloody mess."

Voices of Discontent

It was not Keeney's intention to bash psychotherapy and psychology, but he just finds them so exclusionary and arrogant. He asked us to imagine bringing together in a room all the representatives from our field and providing a forum for open discussion. He had now become quite animated, rising from his chair, his voice dramatic.

We were each trying to remain as still as possible. It had to have been more than 115 degrees Fahrenheit in the Kalahari, perhaps only 100 in the shade. But Brad was energized. He dislikes talking about things in an intellectual way, compared to acting them out improvisationally.

Keeney gestured with his arms in a sweeping motion, asking us to picture that we were sitting in an auditorium, rather than in the most isolated place on Earth outside of the magnetic poles. We grumbled out of our chairs and rearranged the set under the baobab tree as if it were a stage.

"Picture a room full of professionals," Keeney announced. "There are social workers, psychologists, psychiatrists, nurses, psychiatric aids, counselors, any and all of those involved in mental health care in our culture. And they are invited to speak."

As the enactment began, one angry voice was heard from the crowd: "You've been talking crap, Keeney!" Other voices were heard muttering in agreement.

Keeney invited the person to elaborate.

"How can you criticize that which you don't understand?" the person asked him in our fictitious drama. "How can you talk about a field that you left so long ago? You attack our diagnostic system, our ethical codes. You call our theories limited. You glorify and romanticize so-called indigenous shamans, as if *they* have all the answers. So, what do you have to say to *that?*"

Keeney smiled warmly and signaled that it was someone else's turn to speak.

"Harumph!" a voice called out in Keeney's defense. "That's a bunch of right-wing, puritanical, moral majority stuff that has no understanding of the courage that is necessary to operate outside of conventional limitations."

"That's right!" another voice is heard. "Even Emil Krapelin, the man who invented the diagnostic system as we know it, denounced it before he died. Everything in our profession is now medicalized. People want drugs for their troubles. Even psychologists now want prescription privileges."

"But look how much better things have gotten," another voice cried out. "Would you have us return to the days of animal magnetism and lying on a couch? Our treatments are becoming more precise and efficient. The movements of constructivism and social constructionism, and influences from the East, have all helped us find more balance. We have standards now that inform and guide our practices."

"That's true," a supporter agreed. "And look at all the new attention on the psychology of health and happiness."

"Hah!" someone disagreed. "I say, hah again. Psychology's time is over. It is dead. It served its purpose, like other traditions and disciplines. But it has been left behind."

"I am a personal coach," another voice said. "You aren't taking into consideration the ways that the role of helper and healer is changing, morphing into a more flexible conception. Coaching is about doing all the things you say that shamans do—everything except dancing and hallucinating."

The audience laughed, grateful for the comic relief, with all the conflict in the air.

Someone else stood up in the back of the room. "I, too, see myself as more of an educator than a therapist. I see my job as giving people skills they don't have."

"Why must you criticize that which you do not truly understand?" another voice interrupted. Taking up a point raised earlier, she defended the value of science. "We need structures like the *DSM* to give order to our thinking and guide our methods. Some of you people are determined to live in the Stone Age."

"You call yourself a scientist?" someone challenged her. "Social science is hardly a science; it's barely a pseudoscience. The original model for inferential statistics was designed to predict agricultural crop yields; it was never designed for particularizing the stream of human interaction."

"I am a feminist," another voice said. "I take exception to things that have been said here. And I also object to the ways that indigenous healers are being elevated, as if these male hierarchical structures that oppress women should be models for us. They are all based on the traditional patriarchal systems that oppress others who do not have power."

"Yes," a Buddhist voice in the audience agreed, addressing Keeney. "You talk about yourself as not having or coveting such power, and yet you risk perpetuating the very poison you seek to eliminate when you speak about it."

Eventually, there was a pause. Everyone looked around to see who had not yet spoken. They all turned toward one man who stood out from the others because of the rings of multicolored beads he wore around his neck and head. Noticing the attention, he rose from his seat with great dignity.

"I am from far away," he said. "My people are the Guarani from the forests of Paraguay. I have been listening to all of you, and I do not hear anyone say anything about cultures that do not value your science, that do not speak in terms of power, and that do not use your words to say what we do and what it means."

The Guarani shaman looked around the room to see if he was understood. "You talk about feminists. You talk about culture. But you are only speaking of your Western cultures. That is all I have to say." Then he sat down again and lowered his head.

In this imaginary scenario, Keeney nodded his own head in agreement. "Is that everyone?" he asked the assembly. "Have we heard from everyone here?"

The room was silent.

"All the voices, all the possible expressions represented here have been heard?" he asked again.

Everyone looked around the room to see if there was someone present who had not yet spoken.

"Okay, then," he continued. "We can be assured that everyone has had an opportunity to express him- or herself."

Guarani elder, Ava Tape Miri ("Little Seagull Man"), and his daughter, from the lower Amazon basin (Paraguay).

Head nods all around.

"That is the first step. But it is only the first step. It is important for us to honor and respect different voices, whether they speak of the value of Zulu initiation rites or Axis II diagnoses. You may think some of the points of view are naive or misguided or weak; some of them may strike you as frightening. But everyone has the right to be heard, to express his or her opinion."

"Isn't that a sign of our evolution?" someone asked. "Here we tolerate the views of all those present."

"That is true," Keeney answered. *"But what about those who are not here?"*

Voices Yet Unheard

"I ask you," Keeney raised his voice, "Who is *not* in the room with us today?"

There were looks of puzzlement in the crowd. They *were* all present, representatives from every point of view. There were psychoanalysts and constructivists and cognitive behaviorists, two by two, as if from Noah's ark. There were feminists, humanists, nihilists, chaos theorists, mystics, phenomenologists, and empiricists. What the hell was Keeney talking about now?

"I would submit to you that many voices have not yet been heard. There is not a Kalahari Bushman among us. There is no country preacher here from a rural African American church in Louisiana. Where are the healers from Mexico or Jamaica or the Aboriginal communities or the Native Americans? Where are the people without money or without the means to travel? They are not represented here. Their voices have not been heard. Helping or healing in our culture is run mostly by guilds of the privileged and the upper middle class."

"Even the whole idea of therapy is based on helping the privileged," a sympathetic voice said.

"Indeed," the Guarani shaman agreed. "Where I live, we cannot imagine that it is possible for one person or one family to 'buy' the time of a healer for private sessions."

"So," Keeney said, "what we all have in common in this room is that we represent the privileged. We are educated. We have food and shelter."

"We should apologize for this?" someone asked.

"No," Keeney shook his head. "But we should acknowledge this. You may not respect or value the traditions of other cultures, but arrogance can sometimes get in the way of realizing what these ancient practices have to offer us. These are cultures that have developed wisdom over thousands of years, not mere decades or centuries."

"Big deal," someone said. "We have computers and cell phones and airplanes. These people have nothing. They die before they are 30 years old. They are starving to death. They can't even take care of themselves without our help. These are the people whom we should emulate?"

"What you have just said unmasks the central paradox of our time," Keeney countered. "It is true that many of these indigenous peoples have very little in the way of luxuries; they do not *own* things. They are hungry and often sleep in the dirt. But they know a kind of peace and happiness that we can only dream about. Some of them work 3 hours a day, maximum. The rest of the time they spend playing with their children and talking with their friends. There are things we can learn from them."

The audience quieted. More than a few professionals who were present personified the rat race that had become their lives, with mortgage payments, taxes, promotion worries, social obligations, stress disorders, and the like. Many of them (including us) worked 50, even 60 or more hours per week. They had trouble sleeping at night.

"I am asking us to humble ourselves by seeing how relatively young our culture and our profession are compared to other traditions that have been practicing for over 10,000 years. I am just asking that we make a place in this room for these voices that have been forgotten or ignored. I am asking that we invite these healers to tell us about their traditions. This means, however, that we become smaller when we invite the unheard and the unseen."

Global Voices

Keeney is the first to acknowledge that there is hardly agreement or consensus among the healers of a single tribe, much less among a people. Shamans disagree among themselves and express just as many different voices as were heard in the imaginary room we created. Some healers think that the tribe should dance once a week; others two or three times. Some say that they should dance at night, others during the day. Some call the spirit in the belly *thorns,* from the old days; others prefer the name *arrows* or *nails.* It is just like the types of disagreements we might have about diagnostic schemes or preferred jargon.

"The big question, though," Keeney asked, "is why we would want to listen to these voices?"

One answer is based on the realization that helping and healing in our culture represent such a narrow segment of practices that have been used since the beginning of time and are still being used throughout the world. There is no doubt that the technologies that spawned MRI and CAT scans, laser surgery, and pharmacology are wonderful contributions. But indigenous cultures have been using other methods of diagnosis and treatment that are just as miraculous, even if we can't explain how and why they work.

In the chapters that follow, we introduce you to some of the main concepts derived from shamanic practices throughout the world and talk about how we might use them in our own work as helpers and healers. It begins with inviting other voices into the room.

Chapter Eight

The Value of Play

Although helping and healing are serious businesses in our culture, shamans have great reverence for play. They are irreverent pranksters and sacred clowns.

Because it would be grossly incongruent to *tell* you about this idea, we would like to *show* you instead. We would like you to imagine that we have the power to hypnotize you through the words on this page and through the voice you can hear reading them in your head. Pretend that this trance state is so powerful, you have the experience of being able to play with chronological time. Rather than being in the middle of this book, imagine that you have already completed it. You have read the ideas carefully and have taken them into your heart in such a way that they feel part of you. This would be similar to having just attended a 3-day workshop on the applications of shamanism to helping and healing, and we are now in the final few minutes of the program.

Once you can imagine placing yourself at the end (rather than in the middle) of this journey, we would like you to select a word, a single word, that best captures the essence of what you learned. This should be a word that represents the best possible metaphor for what has been most meaningful to you. This might have been something you knew all along, or perhaps you heard ideas expressed in a more useful way with this term.

Now, imagine that you are sitting in a room with other readers who have also transported themselves to the end of the book (even though they are also on this page, in the middle).

"What is the word that stands out for you?" Keeney asks.

"Love," a voice says.

"Light," says another.

"Transformation."

"Shaman."

"Circle."

"Home."

"Tired."

"Heart."

"Imagination."

"Play."

Other voices call out their favorites, each a single word.

"That's fine," Keeney reassures you with a smile. "Is that everyone?"

There are a few more nominations, but they are variations of what was heard before.

"Now, I'd like three volunteers to say out loud any other word that comes to mind. Any word at all will do."

"Alfalfa," a voice says.

"Dirt."

"Tire," says the third."

Keeney writes them on the board. "Okay, we have a list of words now. Each of these words represents the essential experience of everyone who is present with us now. Plus, we have added to the list three 'wildcards,' three random words, just to make it interesting."

Keeney turns his back to the audience. "Now I'm going to go into a trance. When I turn around, I'm going to look at each word on the list sequentially and create a lecture based on their cues."

Keeney bows his head and can be seen taking deep breaths. His feet are shuffling and his shoulders and back seem to be shaking a little. Finally, he raises his head, turns back to the crowd. He focuses his attention on the word list written on the board.

"In the beginning, there was *love*," Keeney says. "It gave birth to *light* that created that which we sought for personal *transformation*. This brought forth the shamans. The *shaman* knew that all was connected as a *circle*. A circle is as simple as a *tire* on every car that passes you every day as you move to work and every day that you take your kids *home*. The circle never gets *tired*. Circles are present throughout every part of your life. They are within the therapist's *imagination* and within the therapist's respect for *play*. They circle about like eagles high in the sky. This applies to all fields—not just to professions, but to corn, *alfalfa*, and other crops grown in *dirt*. The foundation of them all is Mother Earth."

The audience laughs in appreciation.

"So you see," Keeney says, "everything can be linked together—even words that seemingly have no connection."

"That's very clever," a reader says from the audience, "but what does this have to do with helping people?"

"I'm so glad you asked. You could say that this exercise is a perfect metaphor for how you can be with people. In a shamanic way, you are asking people for their list of essential metaphors and ideas, and you are doing so without the long, laborious process of hearing the whole story."

Keeney has been known to ask a client in the first minutes of a session to imagine that they have been working together for years. "Imagine we have spent thousands of hours together in intense sharing. Picture that we have talked about everything that is meaningful and important in your life. Now, describe one sentence that best summarizes everything we have said and done together."

After the client does this, Keeney might ask again, "Now, pick just one *word* that summarizes the essence of the sentence that represents the whole of your life story."

Now here is where Keeney, the shaman, might become *very* playful. "So this single word is the seed from which everything else in your life has grown."

It is at this point that Keeney might ask the client to write the word down on a small piece of paper . . . and then to eat it, or burn it, or fold it and put it on the bottom of his shoe, or bury it beneath a tree, or give it a formal burial, or break it into small pieces and sprinkle on breakfast cereal, or throw it to the winds, or wrap it as a present to give to a stranger, or . . . anything is possible as long as it is done within a spirit of play.

To Keeney, the essence of helping and healing is not about prescribed techniques or formalized strategies but about improvisation. This is not an entirely rational process; in fact, it is often quite irrational and nonsensical. For Keeney, operating as a shaman means accessing a deeper level of primary process, one that he cannot explain.

Although this may bother those among us who got into this field in the first place because we hunger for understanding, Keeney has surrendered this myth. "I don't believe that I can ever understand anyone, nor can they ever understand themselves."

"So, you are not exactly a narrative therapist then?"

"I am an *anti*-narrative therapist," he says. "People are not their narratives. They are not stories. They walk around with story fragments that change constantly, depending on the context. All I'm saying is that the shaman attempts to play with these fragments with no expectation that they will mean anything. It is through the spirit of play that we get to the essence of things."

The Sad Town

When we asked about an example of this in action, how play could be used to move people along in constructive directions, Keeney recalled a husband and wife who complained a lot of having too much sadness and disappointment in their lives. One story after another was a tale of woe and grief.

"Do the two of you ever laugh together?" Keeney asked the couple.

"What's to laugh about?" the husband responded. "It's been so long, I don't know if we could even remember how to laugh."

Keeney nodded, an idea forming in his head. "I think I have something in mind for you that would be just what you need."

For the first time, both the husband and the wife seemed alert at the same time. Throughout their time together, they appeared to take turns becoming mildly activated—while the husband would speak, the wife would look like she was nodding off; then when she would speak, the husband would drop his head and remain perfectly still. In truth, Keeney did have a hard time imagining them having any fun together.

"Before I give you this assignment, I'm not sure that you have the energy to follow through." He was teasing them, of course, soliciting their cooperation.

"No, Doctor," the husband protested. "We'll do whatever you say."

Keeney looked to the wife for confirmation, and she nodded.

"Okay, then," he said to the couple. "What I'm going to ask you to do will take a full day, and you must do it together."

They both nodded solemnly.

"I want you to get out your state map and choose three small towns you have never visited."

"Any towns?" the husband asked. He was a most diligent man and wanted the most precise instructions possible.

"Any towns," Keeney said. "As long as you haven't been there before. I want you to drive to each of these places and get a feel for the town. Walk around a little. Observe what is going on—the people and the atmosphere. I want the two of you together to determine which of the three towns is the saddest."

"The saddest?" the husband interrupted.

"Exactly. I don't care how you figure this out, as long as both of you agree on your choice. Will you determine whether the buildings on the main street create a feeling of sadness? Or perhaps you will examine how people look in that town, the dress and manner. Or the color of clothes and jewelry they choose to wear. Maybe you assess the sadness of their landscaping, the bumper stickers on their cars, the sermons advertised at their churches, the items on the local diner's menu, or the mascot of their high school. It's up to both of you to make the rules for this contest."

The partners nodded that they understood, even if they did seem quite confused by the task. The truth of the matter was that they were both so desperate, they were willing to try almost anything.

"Once you select the saddest town among the three, I want you to do the following." Keeney stopped for a moment and looked directly at the husband, who was straining to remember everything. "You might want to write this down."

Dutifully, the husband removed a notebook and a pen from the inside pocket of his jacket, which he kept expressly for this purpose. Keeney gave him a minute to write down the instructions thus far.

"Good. Now, once you identify the saddest town, I want you to bring with you copies of many cartoons that you both agree are particularly amusing and clever. These could be from magazines like the *New Yorker* or even the 'funnies' section of your newspaper. What I'd like you to do is to 'invade' this town with these cartoons, placing them strategically where you think they might do the most good. You might post one on a bulletin board in the market or a church or a school. You could leave one underneath the windshield wiper of a sad-looking car. Insert one in-between the pages of a brochure at a doctor's office. It doesn't matter where you put them, as long as you sprinkle them around the town."

Before the next session, Keeney received a phone call from the husband, who said that they had completed their assignment. In fact, they couldn't wait to tell him about what had happened. Keeney said he could schedule them in for the next morning, to hear their update.

"So," Keeney prompted the couple, "how did you choose the town?"

Although it could not be quite classified as a laugh, or even a giggle, the couple looked at one another with what could only be described as a restrained smile. "Well," the wife said, "we were driving down the main street of _____. I think it was the second place we visited. We were driving kind of slow, I guess, because this car behind us started honking at us. Such rude people, we thought."

The husband made a disgusted sound, signaling his complete agreement with his wife's assessment.

"That was just the first signal," the husband continued the story. "There was something about the whole place that seemed so . . . I don't know . . . so angry. We attacked that town with a great sense of purpose, wanting to get back at those impatient drivers. I guess we forgot that we were supposed to attack a sad town. We just went after the town that upset us. Armed with our 'cartoon missiles,' we went into three diners, the post office, a feed store, a drug store, and a grocery store. But wherever we went, we each found, to our great surprise, that our funny bone had been tickled. We couldn't stop laughing. When people stared at us in shock, wondering what was going on, we would get even more tickled. Once, my wife fell to the floor with laughter. I've never seen her laugh that hard in my entire life. Several times, people asked what we were laughing about, and we simply handed them a cartoon bomb and ran out of the room, giggling our heads off. Boy, Doctor, that was some medicine you prescribed! We want to do it again. Would that be okay?"

Indeed, it was.

The Ghost and the Box

The shaman does not believe that it is possible to understand another person's problem or even to determine its origin and etiology. The world and the creatures within it are far too complex for anyone to ever comprehend them. Futhermore, the world of spirits is considered sacred, not ever to be understood but to be honored.

This reminded Keeney of another story that involved Credo Mutwa, the Zulu *sangoma*. As we mentioned before, Mutwa is considered one of the most prominent shamans and writers in all of Africa. Because of this reputation, he was approached by a community that was struggling because of the presence of a ghost in one of its dwellings.

First, the family invited a Christian priest to come to the home. He sprinkled blessed water on the doorstep, attempted an exorcism, and screamed at the demonic force to leave the premises immediately. It seems that the ghost dug itself even more deeply into the home, refusing to depart under any circumstances.

It was at this point of desperation that they called upon Credo Mutwa to intervene. As soon as he arrived in the village, the noted witchdoctor asked everyone in the community to assemble near the haunted hut.

"I would like to have some words with this ghost," Credo began his address. "I wish to say in front of all the witnesses here that this ghost cannot possibly be happy here. All this commotion and distress tell me that you are not happy and want some help. I want to be your ally and help you get what you want. I am certain that is not to be found in this place."

Credo next addressed the family members, who were standing just outside their home, waiting with trepidation. "What do you think would make this ghost feel more comfortable?" he asked them. "How can we help this ghost feel courageous enough to decide on its own to find a more comfortable place?"

The family members looked at one another and shrugged. They hadn't a clue what to do.

"Let me ask you, then," Credo said. "How might you make your home an even more welcome place for this ghost, instead of trying to chase it away?"

While the family members considered this strange request, other people in the community called out their own ideas. Perhaps they could leave the doors and the windows open so that the ghost might pass through much easier, without having to negotiate through solid walls. They could leave food out for the ghost, and they wondered what he preferred to eat.

"This is good," Credo told them. "Now, I want us also to consider other places where this ghost might reside." He then pulled out a map of the area and marked a number of alternative residences for an orphan ghost to live.

"Among the places I have selected on this map," Credo said to the family and the community, "I want you to spend the next few days considering where the ghost might go next. Where do you think he might be most content and comfortable?"

Some said that they thought the forest would be best. Others mentioned the mountains.

"That is fine," he reassured them. "There is no need to decide this moment. Let us give this some thought about how to make your village friendlier to the ghost, rather than trying to frighten and threaten him. I will come back in a few days and hear what you have decided."

When Credo returned, the family and the other villagers reported that they had done as he had suggested. They left food and water for the ghost. They spoke to this spirit in more inviting ways. They left the map in the hut with the alternative residences prominently circled in the mountains and the forest and even a nearby cave. They had all decided that the happiest place for a ghost was clearly the cave, so that is what they talked to the ghost about.

"Well, then," Credo announced, "let us take the ghost to the cave, if you think that would be the best place for him. Let us ask him if he could be happy there and see if he shows us a sign of agreement to leave and go there."

Credo sang a song to the ghost. Then everyone remained perfectly still and quiet. Nothing was seen and nothing was heard.

"This is good," Credo said. "The ghost has had the opportunity to express his displeasure if he was not satisfied with this plan. It is clear that it would be happier in a cave, rather than in this meager hut that is crowded with other people. But I sense that the main problem is that it does not know how to transport itself to this cave."

The villagers nodded, as this made perfect sense to them.

"Tomorrow I will bring a box for the ghost. I will place it in the hut and then we will give the ghost time to jump inside. We will then carry this container to the cave and free the ghost there. It will be out of your lives forever."

The point of this story was not just to show how creative and playful a shaman can be in solving a problem (although this was certainly the case), but rather to demonstrate that Credo had no interest in getting at the root of the conflict or in understanding why it had developed. There was no attention directed to understanding why the ghost had decided to haunt this particular family or community. There was no history taken about the prevalence of previous ghosts in the area. There was no effort expended trying to figure out the deeper meanings and metaphors of the ghost's presence or even to identify whose spirit it represented.

But What about Understanding?

This is certainly a cute story, which demonstrates the value of non-oppositional interventions. And there are lessons here reminiscent of the work of Milton Erickson, Jay Haley, or some of the other strategy, problem-, and solution-focused therapists, but what about those clients and helpers who *want* to understand the source of their problems?

"I am intrigued and amused and respectful of the work that you do," Jeffrey said to Brad. "I think this is wonderful stuff—for you and the people you help."

Keeney smiled, knowing that there was more.

"But I have my own strong beliefs—some of which I am willing to challenge. I happen to think that it is important to understand the reasons behind what we do. I think there is value in developing insight, in coming to terms with the legacies of the past, and in understanding the ongoing patterns of our lives. Moreover, I have a number of people who come to me, not because they want to rid themselves of ghosts but because they want to understand their deeper meanings."

"What is an example of this?" Keeney asked.

"Well, someone might come in and say that she has been involved in a series of unsatisfying relationships, all of which end in the same way. She says that she does not just want to fix this problem, but she wants to understand why this is so. This is important to her—so it is important to me."

Keeney nodded. "I think the largest obstacle to finding meaning is understanding."

"Huh?"

"Meaning doesn't necessarily mean the same thing as understanding," Keeney clarified. "Finding meaning has many, many levels on the healing journey. This could be called enlightenment in the Buddhist tradition or *satori* in Zen practices. As you move toward greater meaning, there is less and less understanding."

Jon and I looked puzzled, clearly not understanding the distinction.

"Look," Keeney tried again. "When you say that people want to hold on to understanding, and that understanding is important to them, I say that is expected. However, in our culture, understanding is the greatest addiction in our time. Part of this is based on the delusion that understanding will help us to find the meaning we so desperately seek."

"So, what are you saying?"

"I'm saying that sometimes we have to create the illusion of meaning with our clients. But this does not mean that you ever understand them or come to any sense of truth about what things in their lives mean."

"So," Jon said, "you are saying that understanding can be fun and interesting and familiar to those of us with an academic background, but is not really central to the core of what change is all about."

"I would say this," Keeney answered. "For those who cherish the idea that understanding is an important aspect of human life, then I would suggest that there is a greater understanding that they can have for themselves, as well as for others, when that understanding holds a great amount of respect for that which can't be understood."

"Jeez, Brad," Jeffrey responded. "You've lost me now. I have no idea what you're talking about."

Keeney smiled. "Then now you understand."

Finding the Central Metaphors

"Maybe you could give us an example of what you are talking about?"

Keeney agreed. He asked us to imagine that someone came in with a problem and said, "I am depressed."

Rather than asking, "Why are you depressed?" as a psychologist might, Keeney, in his shaman role, might say, "If we were to spend a great amount of time together to get to know each other so that I fully knew your story and you felt completely comfortable with me, and felt fully understood by me, what would you tell me best summarizes the essence of your experience?"

The client thinks for a moment. "I am lost," he says.

Keeney asks us to consider what the client would say if we asked the question again. And again. And again. "The more times, and the more different ways you ask, the more information you get. But the real question is: How much information do you need? The shaman is just not interested in such questions of understanding."

With the previously mentioned client, Keeney might ask him for a single word that acts as a metaphor for his troubles.

"Misunderstanding," the client says.

"What's another one?" Keeney asked

"Abandonment."

"And a third?"

"Ah, how about love."

According to Keeney, that is plenty of information. Those three words hold whatever the client is most attached to. All of the meanings, submeanings, stratas, consistencies, and contradictions are found in those three metaphors for this person. "There might be more," Keeney said, "much more. But that is enough to work with. Besides, we can never be clever enough, or patient enough, to sort out all the complexities that make up a person's experience."

In a case Keeney presented in an earlier book, he talked about a medicine man who consulted him because he'd never had a vision. He came to Keeney for help because he was too embarrassed to admit this failing to another member of his tribe. He trusted Brad as a medicine man who would work in the Indian way. Keeney's intervention involved asking the medicine man to go into the forest and gather twigs, which were to be arranged in a circle under his bed, right beneath his heart. This intervention, accompanied by much praying and chanting, did produce the desired result: The medicine man had his first vision and was blown away by the power of this healing magic.

When we asked Keeney what happened, how he could possibly explain this phenomenon, he just shrugged. "When I look at a beautiful fire, I could reach in and pull out a burning log to study and examine it until it cools. But I would much rather just watch the fire burn."

And this is the shaman's way. To Keeney, the burning logs are the metaphors that he works with. He does not try to understand what they mean but merely wants to play with them in a way that has particular meaning for the person he is helping

Yet Keeney does not rely on language and words and stories the way therapists do. Instead, he merely invites the client to select the hottest logs to play with. If one log says, "abandonment," another "misunderstanding," and a third "love," then those are the burning logs that he builds with. The three can be mixed together playfully in an infinite number of ways, just the way an improvisational jazz musician might play a tune that has never been played before.

Finding the Burning Logs

"I'm here because of the court," the young man said with a sneer.

"The court?" Keeney answered.

"Yeah, the judge. He told me I had to come here."

We are reviewing the case of a resistant client to see how Keeney would apply this shamanic method of looking for burning logs to play with.

"So, what do you want to do?"

"Nothing. There's nothing you can say that can help me, and nothing you can do to make me talk."

"Okay," Keeney agreed. "You don't want to be here with me. And guess what? I don't want to be here with you, either."

This sparked some interest in the young man, who looked a little less surly.

"So, we are stuck here together. I have to be here and you have to be here. I wonder what we could both do together that might be interesting for each of us?"

"What do you mean?" the boy asked suspiciously.

"Just that there are other people I'd rather be seeing than you right now and other things I'd rather be doing. You feel the same way about me. And that gives us a place to start."

Keeney explained that he would take this young man's resistance and accept that as the first burning log to play with. "You just accept wherever the person is at as a particular theme that has been offered."

In one sense, by not pursuing understanding, by avoiding asking the person why he does not want to talk, or by not trying to

The metaphor of fire is central to shamanic practices. Pictured here
is the "healing Giraffe dance" with Keeney and Kalahari Bushmen.
When the spirits are strong, the shaman might actually dance in the fire
without feeling the heat or becoming burned.

figure out what is wrong with his life that resulted in his ending
up in court, you actually create a deeper-level meaning. If you
find the most salient burning logs (and the client will tell you what
they are, if you only ask), and you play with them and connect
them in a meaningful way, the person will feel understood. The
conversations that take place between a shaman and a client are
really just the search for logs that are hot enough to play with.

As another example, imagine that a client seeks help for a problem in his marriage but is very resistant to the process.

"What would you like to speak about?" Keeney begins.

The man shakes his head. "There is nothing you can say to me
that is helpful. I am only here because my wife has been nagging
me to come. So here I am."

"There's nothing I could possibly say that would impact you?"
Keeney asks with a mischievous grin. He loves these sorts of
challenges.

The man just shakes his head again and crosses his arms.

"What if there was an accident of some kind and I said something to surprise you?"

"Couldn't happen," the man insists.

"Okay. I accept that," Keeney says. "But what if I could somehow surprise you by offering you something helpful? Purely as an accident. Would that please you or upset you?"

The man shrugs. "I don't know. Maybe please me. Depends what it was."

"So it is possible?"

He shrugs.

"What if I got a phone call in the middle of our session? I pick up the phone but it's a wrong number. But the person said something that confused me and I shared it with you. Although the comment made no sense to me, it impacted you profoundly."

The man looks at Keeney as if he is crazy. What the hell is he talking about? A phone call from a stranger? A wrong number?

"We are talking about impossibilities anyway, right?" Keeney asks him, seeing (and enjoying) his puzzlement.

"Hey, whatever floats your boat," the man responds, looking at his watch. "I gotta stay here for the full hour anyway or my wife will be mad."

"Let's make an agreement, then," Keeney says in a conspiratorial whisper.

The man finds himself nodding.

"Look, I won't do all that dumbass stuff that most therapists do because I know you are not the kind of person who is going to be impressed by that."

The man nods again in agreement.

It is at this point that Keeney knows that this man has joined him in the play. Now it is a matter of engaging him on a deeper level.

"Well," Keeney continues, "I can see you are a man whose time is valuable. You don't like wasting your time, even if it is just to make your wife happy. And I don't like to be bored, either. So we might as well create something together so we don't bore the hell out of one another."

"What do you mean?" The man actually leans toward Keeney as he asks this.

"Let's create some sort of surprise. You admitted earlier that you'd enjoy a surprise of some sort. So my question for you is this: Would you rather create a surprise for yourself or for your wife?"

It is at this point that no matter which way the man goes, he has joined Keeney in improvisational play. Keeney will not oppose a client but will go with whatever he or she brings to the conversation.

"If the man said he didn't want any surprise," Keeney explained, "then I'd go with that instead. Whatever burning log he pulls out of the fire, that's the one we play with. If it's not hot enough, then we just blow on it enough until it flames."

The main operating premise that guides Keeney's work is to do what is unexpected, to shock and surprise the client as much as possible. The shaman's main goal is to engage the client in the sort of play that leads to transformation. This does not happen through talk alone or through gathering a relevant history. There is no intent to name the burning logs or to understand their origins and deeper meanings—merely to arrange them in such a way that they stoke the fire.

Chapter Nine

Evoking the Sacred

In the previous chapter, when we talked about focusing less on insight and understanding when we engage in helping and healing, this begged the question: Then focus more on what?

Rather than seeking clarity and understanding, the shaman actually aims for greater mystery. This is a 180-degree rotation from what therapists usually do when they help people. Clients often come to us in a fog—confused, dazed, disoriented, and reeling. Therapists usually conceptualize their role as helping people clear up this mess. This might take the form of promoting any number of insights, depending on one's preferred theoretical orientation: (1) understanding how the templates of our past control our present behavior (psychodynamic), (2) increasing awareness of unexpressed feelings (person-centered), (3) exploring core issues that give life meaning (existential), (4) identifying irrational beliefs (cognitive behavioral), (5) examining how issues of power and gender roles limit and expand choices (feminist), (6) exploring lifelong narratives (constructivist), and so on. In other words, we start out promoting some degree of better understanding of the situation, helping clients to get a firmer handle on how they ended up in this predicament, how this may reflect ongoing patterns from their past, and by implication, how they might use this knowledge to make alternative decisions.

The Dance

Mystery is that which you cannot understand. Mystery is, by definition, that which is beyond understanding. It cannot be held. And this is the posture favored by shamans around the world, who have great reverence and respect for such states. Rather than trying to clear up confusion and disorientation, they might be more inclined to encourage it.

Brad reached over and put a hand on Jeffrey's shoulder, then asked, "Remember at the dance last night?"

"Ah," Jeffrey stammered. "Not exactly."

In truth, it was more than a little foggy. We had traveled down the well-worn path from our camp under the baobab tree to the Bushmen's village, where they had scheduled a healing dance for the evening. This was a rare occurrence indeed, for it would be the women's dance, a ritual that has rarely been witnessed by outsiders—and almost never joined by visitors.

We were sitting outside the circle, watching Keeney dance and shake and writhe with three of the women healers—Texae =oma, Lesua /hun, and Tcqoe lui. These were the elders of the village, adorned in colorfully beaded ropes that encircled their necks and adorned their heads. We had spent the day talking to them through an interpreter and communicating through a combination of smiles, hugs, clapped hands, and raised thumbs.

"I am old now," Texae told us. It was impossible to tell just how old she was, as the Bushmen do not know when they were born, nor do they celebrate their birthdays. She looked like she might have been in her sixties but actually could have been younger than we were—the life expectancy of the Bushmen is among the lowest in the world.

"When I dance," she said, "it becomes so strong that sometimes I fall down."

We nodded our heads in understanding.

"My mother taught me how to move my arms and my body in the dance. She showed me the way of moving that helps the power to get stronger. She told me that I must always use the dance to keep myself well and that I must help other people who are sick."

Texae consulted with the other women for a minute in that amazing clicking language that distinguishes their speech. After some time, they began laughing, and we asked what was so funny.

Tcqoe lui, who had a glorious smile and a gentle, regal bearing befitting the wife of the chief, giggled. "We women like to dance longer than the men. They say they are tired after a time. But we have more energy to continue. Our secret is that we are stronger than the men. We like to dance all night."

As we sat on the edge of the circle, these words came back to us. We were settling in for a long night. The fire had been stoked so that the flames lit up the area. The drums were pounding, answered at times by a hyena encircling the village. There was a chill in the desert air and a sky so clear that the ceiling of stars looked like it might collapse on top of us.

"No way I'm going in that circle," Jeffrey whispered to Jon.

"Me neither," Jon agreed.

"Good, then," Jeffrey said. "We've got a deal." He was convincing himself as much as he was Jon. Earlier in the day, when we had been talking to the women and the men shamans, Brad had announced that Jeffrey and Jon were also shamans from their country and would be joining the dance that night.

Before Jon and Jeffrey could protest or make excuses, the elders clapped in appreciation and gave both of them Bushman names so that they would feel more related to the tribe.

"So, Cgunta," Jon teased him, "chickening out, huh?"

"Damn right! No way I'm getting in that circle."

Things did look a bit treacherous out there. This was not the classic, graceful African dance, but rather looked like a bunch of people in the throes of convulsions.

"How about a few beers?" Jon proposed. "Just to keep the chill out."

"Sure," Jeffrey agreed, but just then Brad danced over to the spot from which we were observing. He draped himself over Jeffrey's body and began to moan, shake, and dig his fingers into Jeffrey's ribs. Jeffrey rose from the ground, as if levitating, embraced in this shaking bear hug. He was half dragged, half carried, half danced toward the fire, literally dragging his feet along the way.

"I don't think I want to be doing this," he said to himself. "I was going to wait this dance out."

Keeney was now supporting Jeffrey from behind, holding Jeffrey with his hands around Jeffrey's belly. At that moment, Jeffrey leaned back into the embrace and looked up at the sky filled with stars. There was Orion and the Southern Cross, he was sure, not that he could recognize them. But he was amazed by the beauty of it all, the fires spread across the horizon of the village, the stars lit up. It was then that a shooting star sailed across the sky.

Jeffrey doesn't believe in signs. He doesn't believe in anything he can't understand or explain. But for some reason, at that point he began to move and shake as if energy were filling up his body. His feet were planted in the soft sand, and his legs began to shake of their own accord, rippling from his calves to his thighs and lower belly. He heard the chanting, the clapping, and the drumbeats. And then the women were on him.

By now, they had removed their tops and many of their clothes that had restricted movement. They were covered in sweat from the fire and the dance. Jeffrey could not actually see them because his eyes were squeezed shut, and he was afraid of the weird things happening in his body. But he felt them. Hands were touching him everywhere, but mostly digging into his stomach, sides, back, and chest. He doubled over in a crouch, his stomach contracting. And then he passed out and fell to the ground. He felt hands massaging him, and he realized they were "cooling" him down. The hands gently lifted him and deposited him back on the spot where he had originally been sitting.

"So," Jon said to the prone, still body lying next to him. "I thought you weren't going to dance."

Jeffrey just moaned.

"Tough night, huh?"

Indistinct mumble.

"So, what happened out there?" Jon asked him.

Jeffrey slowly rose to a sitting position. He brushed himself off, covered in sweat, sand, and ash from the fire. "I don't know," he answered. "I have no idea what happened. But they tell me I've had my first lesson as a Bushman shaman."

About Last Night

"Let's talk about last night," Keeney prompted again.

"Yeah," Jon teased. "I want to hear how you explain to your wife that you were writhing on the ground with three half-naked women."

"When you were in the dance last night," Keeney continued, "and the women elders began to rub their hands along the sides of your abdomen and to vibrate your hands, you began to exhibit some pretty unusual postures and movements."

Jeffrey nodded but was still unable to speak about what happened. It was as if by talking about the dance, making sense of it, trying to understand what had taken place, it would lose its power.

"Last night," Keeney said, "when you were asked what happened, do you remember what you said?"

Jeffrey shook his head. "I don't know. I don't remember much of what happened."

"Yes! Exactly! That is just what you said last night as well! At that moment you were beholding the mystery of life. You had no idea what was happening to you. And most important: You didn't care to know. You didn't even know what it was to understand."

"So, that's mystery, huh?"

"Yes, it is," Keeney answered. "I marvel, I shudder, at things that are far beyond my capacity to ever fully know what is happening. I have learned to stop trying to make sense of things and just to appreciate them. That is the shaman's way."

This is another reason why Keeney abandoned the posture of helping and healing in our culture: because it destroys the mystery in things. The social sciences always seek to explain things, define things, measure things, understand things—to create theories that postulate and hypothesize about things. And it is through such scientific efforts that mystery is obliterated and that academics entertain the illusion that they have things under control. Mystery is terrifying to people, so we attempt to explain it away.

Dream, Hallucination, or Mystery?

As one example of this, just prior to our trip to the Kalahari, Keeney had been in Oaxaca, Mexico, working with some *curanderos* (traditional healers), when he received an e-mail from his wife, Mev. She reported being awakened in their Tucson home at 2:44 A.M. by the sound of Bushmen singing at a dance. She said that the singing was loud enough to wake her up, and it continued while she walked through the house. It also puzzled her that rather than feeling alarmed by possible "auditory hallucinations," she was quite intrigued and engaged by this sensory mystery.

Keeney kept a copy of her message and showed it to us. Here is an excerpt of Mev's report:

> It startled me and sounded like it was coming from my right side, either from the guest room or outside our bedroom window. At first I thought it was some neighborhood party going on but then it dawned on me that it was unlikely that our neighbors would be partying to the Bushmen beat. Then I collected my thoughts and assumed that my friend, Deb (who's been staying with me while you're gone), must have awakened in the middle of the night and was listening to one of the Bushman tapes in my guest room. But then I realized she would have no idea where to locate it. Besides, there's no CD player in there.
>
> I stayed in bed trying to figure out where the singing was coming from. Then I got up and listened through her door and subsequently walked to the family room and the singing slowly began to fade. It sounded exactly like being at the dance in the Kalahari. I don't recall if I had been dreaming before the singing woke me up, and I don't remember any of my dreams last night. Just the singing. Amazing. It was so real. I really did hear it somehow.

Now, a psychotherapist in our culture would readily deconstruct what was going on (and perhaps would suggest therapy or even medication, if other "hallucinations" were to take place).

Or, perhaps this meant that Mev missed her husband, and her unconscious was bringing back memories of their time together with the Bushmen. Of course, that hypothesis, framed in scientific terms and delivered with a pedantic voice, is still entirely made up; it is no more valid than a host of other explanations, even if the therapist were to pretend that this really *was* going on. If the therapist believed that it was anything other than that, it might destabilize his or her own experiential reality. Then the therapist would need therapy!

Our cultural reflex is to respond to mystery by making it go away. It is as if we can't tolerate, for a single moment, the very idea that some things are beyond our comprehension, beyond our scientific explanations, beyond our grasp. And even when we are clueless as to what might be going on, rather than admitting our ignorance, we just make something up that is couched in scientific-sounding terms.

It is one of the great secrets of the therapy profession that much of the time we have no idea what is going on with our clients. They come in confused and disoriented. They present a particular configuration of symptoms. They bring a unique set of experiences and an individualized history. They feel desperate for some explanation to account for their suffering. Then, after a forty-five-minute song and dance, they fully expect us to tell them what the heck is going on and, furthermore, what needs to be done to fix it. Then the really amazing thing is that we actually attempt to do just that! As soon as the client leaves the office, we immediately pronounce some diagnostic entity on the treatment summary, filling in five different axis spaces on the form, and then prescribe a treatment plan.

But the greater truth of the matter is that human beings are far too complex to ever understand anyone else. (After all, how well can you really ever understand *yourself?*) When a new client walks in and presents the initial complaints, therapists may have some ideas about what *might* be going on, but these are only guesses, based on past experiences. And they certainly don't justify the level of authority and confidence we pretend to demonstrate. It is difficult to admit this, but even though our clients, and the public, expect us to behave as if we know what is going on with people and to know exactly what we are doing and where things are going, it is really all a mystery. We could never truly understand any person's experience, much less his or her life context, in a lifetime. A whole herd of doctoral students could write dissertations on any single session in therapy and still not grasp all the complexities and the intricacies of what took place. And when things go wrong or go spectacularly well, we may have our explanations about what occurred, but we actually don't really know what happened. It is a mystery that we pretend has a definitive answer.

If Mev asked the Bushmen (or many other indigenous healers) about what she had experienced, she would assuredly not get an answer to clear up the mystery of what happened. They would say that what took place was not a dream; in fact, what she reported is quite different from any dream, in that it had a lingering

Mev Jenson with Bushman friends in the Kalahari

emotional impact and, in some ways, felt more "real" than every-day reality. The Bushmen would call her experience a "visitation," a visit from the spirit world. Furthermore, they would see it as a great gift, something more important than winning a multimil-lion-dollar lottery. For the Bushmen, Mev received the song of their healing dance and an official invitation to be a member of it. They would hold a dance upon hearing her report. Its mystery would be honored and deepened.

Incidentally, after receiving her e-mail message, Brad wrote back to Mev:

> That's fantastic dear. There is something you should know. Before I left town, I took a jar of sand I had collected many years ago in the Kalahari. It was sand from my first dance with the Bushmen. I sprinkled all of the sand around the house as a way of encircling our home under the spiritual custody of the Bushman culture.

Brad and Mev chose to respect the mystery of her experience and to allow it to make a deep impact on their lives.

Some Things Defy Explanation

"So, let me ask you again," Jon directed toward Jeffrey. "What is the reaction to the mystery of what happened to you last night at the dance? Do you need to understand what took place?"

"Well, I probably could make something up, but I'm still vibrating. I suppose there will come a time when I will think about things and consider possibilities. I think it had something to do with Brad's approval and not wanting to let him down or embarrass him in front of his Bushmen friends. . . ."

"My gosh," Keeney said, "the gods gave you the gift of psychobabble. You are trying to rationalize what happened and what moved you to the dance. You are using the language that is most familiar to you."

"Sure, but . . ."

"Hey, that's fine! Use what works for you. Understanding can be a very good thing, unless it is used to excess. Just don't let it destroy the mystery of the sacred."

"What are you grinning about?" Jeffrey turned to Jon.

"Just that you aren't hearing what Brad is saying. He is teaching you about how trying to understand things can destroy them in the process. He is telling you to value mystery and let it be."

Keeney nodded in agreement. "On the other hand, I would not want you to throw away psychology because this is what led you to join the dance. In that sense you could think of creating a ritual that, for you, enacts how you can separate psychology into something that delivers you into the greater meanings, as opposed to killing the greater mysteries. You never want to take away what a person already has; instead, you want to allow those existing resources to bring forth movement toward deeper meaning."

Let's Get Practical

"Okay," Jeffrey said, abruptly changing the subject, "let's assume that moving toward greater mystery, rather than toward understanding, is a good thing to do. How can helpers and healers use this shamanic idea in their work?"

"Did you think we wouldn't notice that you are taking the focus off yourself?" Jon pointed out.

Ignoring the barb, Jeffrey mentioned that he has seen two kinds of clients. There are those who come in and say, "I have a problem. Fix it." And there are those who say things like: "I don't know what my problem is and I want to understand that." Or: "I do know what my problem is and I want to understand why I get myself in the same trouble over and over again." Or the ones who say: "I don't really have a problem, but I just want to understand myself better."

"Now, I can help the ones who just want to fix things. But the kind of work I enjoy the most is the journey to help people develop greater awareness and understanding of themselves and the world."

"Do you think that is the difference between a psychologist and a shaman?" Keeney asked.

"Maybe so. Maybe this is about my own needs to make sense of my life. I enjoy the process, as well as the outcome."

Jon laughed. "Given the choice between going to heaven or having a discussion about heaven, you would prefer having the discussion."

"Well, I wouldn't mind going to heaven, but I still would like to talk about it first."

"You can't have it both ways," Jon challenged him.

"Sure, I can."

"Brad just said you can't."

"So, who the hell cares . . ."

"Okay, fellows," Brad intervened. "I haven't said anything yet."

Keeney explained that this was not really an either/or polarity—either preserve mystery or go for understanding. Shamanism simply brings a widening of the field of understanding, a broadening of the boundaries, to embrace alternatives that bypass intellectual understanding.

"The problem is not understanding," Keeney continued. "The problem is *limited* understanding. We think that understanding is sufficient and satisfactory, as if when things are understood, they can be washed away. This takes away wonderment. We need the sort of understanding that can hold that which we don't understand. We need more reverence and awe."

"But what you are advocating so passionately about not understanding for its own sake completely negates the academic books you wrote in your previous life. These books were about understanding to the nth degree, to such a level that nobody understands them."

"That is precisely what I am talking about," Keeney agreed. "It is about pushing the boundaries of understanding to the point that they bankrupt the capacity for knowing."

"So then, anyone who claims to understand this aesthetics of change epistemology and recursive frame analysis stuff you developed you know is full of crap."

"Probably so. But I would say that for any theory. Between the two of you, you guys have written more books than anyone else I know. You've had that experience where someone comes up to you and tells you what your books are really about."

"And you have no idea what they're talking about!"

"Yes! You didn't realize that you said that at all. In fact, what the reader came up with is far more interesting than what you had in mind. The readers rewrote the book as they were reading it."

"Just as they are doing right now."

"In a good book, all the readers are coauthors. It is the same with good jazz. The audience joins the music."

Shamanic Rituals That Bring Mystery to the Dance

Now we come to the more practical side of ways to evoke the sacred in helping work. For Keeney, the rituals of the shaman bring a person into a context that invites mystery. That is why shamans do not limit themselves to talking to the people they are helping; they may also dance with them, pray with them, sing with them, or tell them stories. There is almost always a connection between the present predicament and the ancestral spirits. This is not unlike a psychodynamic conception, except that the goal is not to understand these spirits but to connect with them.

Keeney believes that our own helping rituals and traditions have turned themselves inside out; they are used for creating routines of what used to be holy. They have become diluted, in the same way that the Catholic Mass moved from Latin to English, or the sacrament in the Church changed from wine to grape juice.

Sacred ceremony does not just have to be about religious rituals but can include any sort of communion with the divine. "This can be as simple as asking someone to go into her backyard and examine ten separate blades of grass with a magnifying glass. Or partners can be asked to talk to one another while looking through separate ends of a pair of binoculars. It's all about looking at the world through new eyes. Any assigned task that creates a greater sense of wonder constitutes an appreciation for the sacred. The first step is acknowledging there is more here than what meets the eye."

One way that indigenous cultures are still so far ahead of us is in their traditions that create altered states of enhanced awareness. We are not talking about those induced through hallucinogenic drugs but those using movement, prayer, meditation, and music. They don't need to use artificial substances like alcohol and drugs to produce euphoria.

"When we are in the Kalahari," Keeney said, "it is easy to access sacred rituals because the Bushmen have a community structure already in place. I am not suggesting that therapists and teachers invite groups to build bonfires and dance all night and shake. I am not suggesting that they jump up and down. I am not saying that we transplant the ceremonies from other cultures into our own."

What Keeney is saying is that helpers and healers who are informed by shamanic processes could create for their clients certain rituals that evoke and expand their sense of awe, wonder, and surprise. This can take place on any level and can involve daily rituals. In his book *Everyday Soul,* written to help people awaken the spirit of everyday life, Keeney (1996) catalogued a number of examples of how to activate and nourish the sense of mystery.

1. Introduce more rhythm into your life.
2. Learn to gently (and sometimes wildly) rock your body.
3. Dance, think, and pray in the dark.
4. Bring on the music.
5. Faithfully write down a request for guidance, and carry this invitation with you throughout the day.
6. Bring more absurdity into your daily rituals.
7. Be irreverent with the "why" questions in your life.
8. Remind yourself, constantly, that you will never understand the big things in life.

These are just examples of the sorts of rituals that are part of shamanic traditions. Keeney is not saying there is an absence of rituals in our lives, just that they have become so much of a routine (brushing your teeth, saying the "Pledge of Allegiance," repeating stock prayers) that they have lost their capacity for wonder. They do not evoke powerful dreams. They do not hit you in the belly.

Operating shamanically, we would want to interrupt people's current rituals, to stop them from doing what is already familiar, so that it might be possible to create more enchantment and magic. Keeney believes that helping and healing ought to be more centered on creating possibilities for extraordinary and unexpected surprises. In order to do this, however, it is necessary to pry loose the glue of habituated rituals that prevents the possibility of something unexpected.

Again, Keeney makes the point that the goal is not to import rituals from Africa, South America, or Asia. "We must find what works for us and for each of our clients. This can involve a special way of taking out the trash or watching a television show."

Keeney (1994) has written a whole book on rituals for watching *The David Letterman Show* that involve such wacky suggestions as: (1) tying a string from the television set to a pair of cheap sunglasses from which you have removed the lenses, (2) watching the show from a different place in the house every night until you find the "funniest" spot, (3) cutting out a piece of cardboard to fit over the television screen with a hole removed exactly where Letterman's face first appears on the screen. Well, you get the point. You *do* get the point, don't you?

Let's take another example. Ask yourself what you believe would bring forth the deepest bliss in your life, that which would move you and satisfy you the most beyond all other experiences. Is it singing a song with such musical purity that it lifts you into the clouds? Does your bliss have to do with the sound of your children laughing and giggling? Does it involve being on a voyage, working in the garden, cooking a meal, or perhaps being in bed with your lover?

Whatever you believe constitutes a definition of your bliss, write it down on a piece of white paper. Cut this paper into an oval shape so that it resembles an egg. Carefully place this egg under your bed, directly underneath where your heart resides when you sleep. Tonight when you go to sleep, see yourself as a mother (or father) hen resting over an egg, waiting for it to hatch. Know that the clues may be born into your imagination while you sleep, directing you to take significant steps toward finding more of your bliss. This hatching may take place in your dreams, where you'll be told or shown something about moving toward your bliss. Or, it may pop into your mind unexpectedly during the forthcoming days. Be mindful of trying to hatch your egg, and wonder when the miracle of birth will take place. Anticipate the hatching of your bliss as a major spiritual blessing in your life. Prepare for it in the same way you would any new arrival in your life.

This exercise (if you actually do it) represents a powerful bridge for entering the deepest part of your imagination, the well of mystery that inspires all the answers and the direction toward what you desire most. It can be used to help bring forth the dreams that will move you into the heart of mystical bliss and more soulful living. Will it work? That's up to you. If it does promote dramatic movement, what explanation could you offer to account for this transformation? We urge you to resist the impulse to deconstruct, analyze, and make sense of the underlying structure of this idea; instead, we invite you to take on the mind and the spirit of the Bushmen and to honor the mystery, rather than trying to clear it up.

What Keeney, or any self-respecting shaman, tries to do is get people to abandon their usual ways of doing things so as to create a greater sense of mystery and awe for everyday activities (even for watching a late-night talk show). It is the shaman's (or the therapist's, the teacher's, or the parent's) job to juggle and toss things around in such a way that sacred moments become possible. We don't do this through the usual channels of organizing things for people but through *dis*organizing them. We must create the possibility of surprise. It can be through a dream, a sudden discovery, or an impulse. The overriding goal is to bring mystery and magic to people's lives.

Keeney sees his shamanic work as a movement between four kinds of experience: (1) stimulation of the client to have an ecstatic experience, which serves to open the gate to imagination, whether through provocative suggestions, improvisational movement, or modeling surprise and unpredictability; (2) working with spiritual dreams, those with little psychological content, that deeply touch the heart of the recipient; doing so through both incubating dreams (making suggestions and rituals that unconsciously seed them) and transforming them when they are shared (improvising a word play with the dream's most important metaphors); (3) encouraging creative expression, particularly in the context of making something concrete, based on what was dreamed; and (4) administering heavy doses of absurdity that help undo any overserious-

ness or inappropriate concretizing of the visionary and the shamanic metaphors.

Moving back and forth between these different aspects of
shamanic experience helps keep us in the here and now, existentially engaged, and filled with the desire to live more coura-
geously, imaginatively, and playfully. A visionary experience can
become as dead as a boring textbook if it is not transformed and
played with. In this shamanic dance of Shiva, metaphors and fantasies bring inspiration to action, and heightened experience
opens the channels for different ways of knowing the world, including one's self and others. And without a continuous infusion
of comic relief and absurd enactments, we'd take ourselves too
seriously, and any presence of mystery would quickly evaporate.

Comfort with Confusion

One of the challenges for therapists and other helpers is that because we have trained specifically to clear up confusion and supply answers to questions that plague us and others, it is difficult
for us to also honor mystery. We have less tolerance for ambiguity
and complexity than we pretend and less comfort for that which is
unexplained. We often see our jobs in terms of reducing mystery,
rather than embracing it.

Many therapists and helpers went into this profession in the
first place because of feelings of helplessness and powerlessness
that we suffered early in life or may still be struggling with. We
yearned for answers to questions that haunted us and believed
that through advanced training, we could become the sort of wise
sages who Knew Things. Mystery and unaccounted phenomena
were seen as the enemy to be defeated. If only we studied more,
read more books, attended more workshops, accumulated higher
degrees, sought supervision and mentors, then finally we could
attain the sought-after position of "expert"—someone who can
make sense of the world.

Of course, the shaman has no interest in making sense of the
world, much less of any phenomenon within it. Not only is this enterprise seen as futile, but it also is not particularly useful. Perhaps it is not that we wish to diminish the power of insight,
self-awareness, and understanding in the search for meaning in

our lives, but rather that we want to introduce an alternative paradigm that can often produce breakthroughs when intellect fails us.

A Hasidic Tale

It was a dark night in the Kalahari, and we were all getting ready to retire. As we collected our flashlights to make our way back to our tents, Jon told us an old Hasidic tale about a famous rabbi who was on his way to teach a village that was very interested in his ideas. This was going to be a very big event, and each Jew in the community made great preparations, pondering what question he or she might ask the wise man.

The rabbi finally arrived and, after the initial welcome, he was taken to a large room where people gathered to ask their questions. There was tremendous anticipation and excitement all around.

The rabbi walked silently around the room and then began to hum a Hasidic tune. Before long, everyone started humming along with his soft voice. As people became comfortable with his song, the rabbi started to dance. He danced everywhere in the room, and, one by one, every person danced with him. Soon everyone in the whole community was dancing wildly together. Each person's soul was healed by the dance, and everyone experienced a personal transformation.

Later in the night, the rabbi gradually slowed the dance and eventually brought it to a stop. He looked into everyone's eyes and said gently, "I trust that I have answered all of your questions."

Chapter Ten

Multiple Modalities

Psychologist. Teacher. Priest. Physical therapist. Physician. Musician. Theologian. Philosopher. Dancer. These occupations are all specialized in our culture, requiring years of devoted training in one focused area or another. Among indigenous peoples and ancient traditions, many of these discrete jobs are integrated into the single role of shaman, a person who is expected to have a working knowledge of botany, physiology, theology, and performing arts, as well as in social work, psychiatry, and counseling.

The shaman is as much a stand-up comic and an entertainer as he or she might be a practicing healer. There are few boundaries and constraints on specialization, as there are in our own world, where a helper concentrates only on a small, narrow slice of human experience—a special education teacher who works only with attention deficit disorders, a physiatrist who specializes only in rehabilitation medicine of stroke victims, a sports psychologist who improves the performance of athletes. We have music therapists, family therapists, play therapists, dance therapists, art therapists, group therapists, individual therapists, and personal coaches. We have expressive therapists, body therapists, yoga teachers, and personal trainers. Each of these disciplines is licensed and regulated.

The shaman is all of these things, and none of them. The shaman goes through training by ordeal—a series of pains and sufferings and self-deprivations that is intended to make him or her into an empty vessel. This is not intended for the purpose of increasing power but rather to silence the self-absorbed mind, awaken one's heart, and improve one's receptivity to the spirit world. Throughout the world, the shaman's highest purpose is to receive music.

"No song," Keeney said emphatically, "no shaman. There is less concern with saying or doing the right thing, but a strong emphasis upon receiving sacred music. Songs hold the rhythm. Rhythm is what invites the body movements, the dance. The language of the gods is music."

A Song Is Born

When Keeney was a boy, he used to play the piano at his grandfather's and father's summer revival meetings. They were country preachers who loved to tell the story of how the gospel hymn "Precious Lord" was created. Thomas A. Dorsey, a pianist who had accompanied the great blues singer, Ma Rainey, got religion and brought the rhythms of the blues into the Black Church. That's how he became known as the father of gospel music.

One night Dorsey was away from home, conducting the music for a revival service. In the middle of the religious meeting, a Western Union messenger arrived, carrying a telegram. Standing in front of the congregation, Dorsey was informed that his young wife had died while giving birth to their daughter.

Dorsey was stricken by grief, and the deacons of the church gathered around him and tried to console him. Within the next hour, another telegram was delivered, announcing that Dorsey's baby had also died.

"What can I do?" Dorsey cried out. He was sobbing, unable to contain himself.

There was silence in the audience for a moment, before one of the deacons called out, "Say Precious Lord."

At that exact moment, the song came to him. Without any hesitation, he began the soulful song that has become the hallmark of gospel music: "Precious Lord, take my hand. Lead me on. Help me stand. I am tired. I am weak. I am worn . . ."

Keeney sees this story as a perfect example of what shamanism is all about. When the trials and tribulations of life get to the place

Keeney family photo taken in grandfather's Church.
From left to right: Reverend W. P. Keeney, Brad,
Reverend W. L. Keeney, Virginia, Phyllis, and Jan.

where your mind bankrupts its ability to deliver a single thought or course of action, your heart takes over and reaches out. If it is done sincerely, with the fire of deep longing, a song may be born. These are the songs that bridge us to spirit.

In Keeney's own life, he has tried to follow this path first shown to him in the church of his grandfather, then as a member of the Black Church. It was during a time of great suffering, while going through a painful divorce and separated from his son, that a gospel song came to him, "Precious Is His Love." It has since been recorded and performed by a New Orleans jazz band and is still one of the most treasured credentials that Keeney lays claim to as a practicing shaman. To those familiar with Eric Clapton's ode to the tragic loss of his son, "Tears of Heaven," one can readily see the ways that music plays an important part of healing catastrophic losses. In Clapton's own words: "The blues are what I've turned to, what has given me inspiration and relief in all of the trials of my life."

Sensory Modalities

A shaman takes on the roles of a dancer, a composer, a singer, an actor, a choreographer, a director, a poet, a rabbi, and a trickster. In each of these ways of being comes a particular sensory modality.

"What of the song?" we asked.

"The shaman's song not only brings forth an expression of heartfelt contact with the gods and spirits but touches the presence of all the others who are in attendance, including the whole community. This is when all the people begin to move and dance."

Keeney mentioned that shamans not only are proficient in the performing arts but also are exquisitely sensitive in other modalities. They are particularly tuned to the scent of sweat that accompanies the dance.

"Sweat?"

"Yeah. The shaman knows intimately the smell of his own body, as well as of everyone else in the village. And that's not all: Taste plays an important part."

"Tasting the sweat?"

"Yes, indeed," Keeney said with a smile. "Some shamans will lick the skin of others to get a sense of the body's condition."

We were just imagining a doctor or a therapist in our culture sticking out his or her tongue to lick a patient as part of the diagnostic regimen.

"I'm serious about this," Keeney said, seeing our skepticism. "If you ask a Bushman shaman how she knows if someone is sick, she will tell you that she can smell it. And when she says smell it, she also means taste it and hear it as well."

A good shaman, like a fine therapist or teacher or healer, has an enhanced state of awareness and sensitivity to others. It is just that shamans do not rely only on their eyes and ears but also on their "second eyes," which are really all the other senses that we neglect or ignore.

Then there is the state of synesthesia, in which sensory states are blended and combined in unusual ways into a unified perception. This is a condition that children have early in life but eventually outgrow because it does not conform to adult reality. Still, some people in our culture retain their synesthetic abilities—when they hear music, they also "see" the music as visual imagery. With particular chords, notes, or rhythms, they might see glowing lights as an accompaniment. Most of us have such a joined sensation when we hear the sound of a fingernail scratching across a chalkboard and feel our skin being touched at the same time. The shaman merges these sorts of sensory modalities during ceremonial time, and this is what allows him or her to smell, taste, and feel sickness in others.

It is as if we have blinders on that limit the possibilities of what we might intuit and sense in others. Because not only do we compartmentalize the various helping specialties into artificially created boundaries, we also do the same with our senses. We either listen to someone or watch him, but never would we consider combining these perceptions into one unified sensation. And, of course, smelling and tasting are out of the question.

A Secret Shaman

We live in an age in which professional scope of practice is limited by licensure and certification. There are ethical codes, standards of practice, as well as state and federal laws, that tell us what we may and may not do as part of our jobs. Counselors are not allowed to use projective tests. Ministers are not supposed to do long-term therapy. Psychologists may not prescribe medications. Teachers may not use hypnosis. Psychiatrists may not do surgery.

Keeney clarified that he was not suggesting that we should all transform our work into that of the Kalahari Bushman or the Amazonian medicine person, although it would greatly amuse him to hear a therapist say to a patient, "Next week we will meet in the field behind the office and dance around the bonfire."

What he is advocating, however, is that we could all be a lot more resourceful and creative than we learned to be in school. And we don't have to do this under the guise of anything that resembles what shamans do on the surface. We can mobilize the resources of a shaman without colleagues, or even clients, knowing what we are doing. Keeney is simply inviting helpers and healers to be more expansive in the ways we work. And all this can be done in camouflage.

We asked for an example of this, and Keeney mentioned one of his own private rituals that he borrowed from the shamans he has known. Prior to any therapeutic performance, whether on stage before 10,000 people at an arena, in a workshop demonstration, at a media appearance, in a lecture, or in a therapy session, Keeney spends a few minutes preparing himself the same way he would before joining a dance in Africa or the Amazon.

"I stand backstage, or find a private place to be alone. Most performers in such a situation try to calm their nerves, settle themselves down. They take a deep breath. They try to relax."

"But you do just the opposite," we guess, remembering the ways that shamans seek arousal, rather than tranquility, to maximize performance.

"Exactly. Prior to seeing a client or a family, or going on stage, I activate my nails."

Keeney is describing the Bushman practice of heating up the nails in his belly. He begins to vibrate his belly. He shakes himself from his legs, up his thighs, deep into his belly. He creates spontaneous movements, even to the point of doing a small dance in the space. By the time he greets his audience or client, he can feel his whole body vibrating and all his senses heightened. This, he believes, is the source of his extraordinary creativity and intuition.

This is so disorienting that we can barely hold on to the idea—that when faced with stressful situations when we are called on to perform under pressure, rather than calming ourselves down, we might instead arouse ourselves further. Of course, Keeney doesn't mean that we should cloud our minds with self-critical, anticipatory thoughts. Quite the contrary, he is talking about shutting our minds down completely and instead accessing the wisdom of the body.

"This is essentially what clinical acumen is," Keeney explained. "It is like when you can feel something in your bones. You can smell trouble. You can sense that there is a grandparent in the closet who is causing some trouble in this marriage. You can feel the ghosts. The problem is that we have no language to describe these senses."

What Keeney means is that unless we can define something, unless we can measure it, we don't acknowledge that it exists. That is why intuition is relegated to an afterthought, a sort of ethereal garbage bin that captures anything the least bit mysterious or flaky.

To Sing a Song

"La dee dah. Lee dah do. Dum dee dum da . . ."

"Excuse me," the client interrupts. "But what the heck are you doing?"

"Why, what does it sound like?" the therapist answers. "I'm singing a song."

"Yeah. I hear that. But why on earth are you doing that?"

The therapist shrugs. "I don't know. I just feel like it."

"You just feel like it?" the client asks again.

"Yes. It's just something I needed to do."

Keeney used this example as just one way that therapists might merge their multiple roles.

"But isn't that self-indulgent?" we wondered. "Aren't you meeting your own needs, instead of those of your clients?"

Keeney laughed. "I remember Carl Whitaker once being asked why he became a therapist, and he said for his own growth, for his own amusement."

"That's all very fine for Whitaker, whom some conservative professionals don't have the highest respect for. The traditional posture that we have taken is the idea that our helping is not about us, but it is about and for those we help. It is about them and taking care of *their* needs, not our own. This is a place for others to come, where we are not going to do anything to meet our own needs."

"Sure," Keeney agreed.

"As you know, our field attracts more than its fair share of narcissists—self-involved, self-indulgent, manipulative people. What you are proposing—singing a song because the spirit moves you to do so—could be taken as a license for professionals to redefine therapy as doing whatever the hell they feel like. This is all about me, not about you; as long as I am amused and entertained and informed, then things are fine."

Keeney nodded in agreement. "The shaman starts with a very different premise than that which you present. I am not saying this fits for what you do or for what therapists and teachers do, but it presents an alternative view of things. The shaman embraces his own humility. He comes into the encounter with the assumption that he has as much madness, neurosis, and sickness as anyone he would attempt to heal."

Keeney recalled a conference from the 1960s in New York called "Beyond the Double Bind." There was a big argument on the floor about whether there was any such thing as schizophrenia. All the biggest, most provocative voices were represented—Thomas Szasz, Jay Haley, Carl Whitaker, and others. During one panel discussion, Haley claimed defiantly that he had never seen a schizophrenic in his life, that there was no such thing as schizophrenic. It was all a figment of one's imagination.

Carl Whitaker asked for the microphone. "I've never met any-one who was *not* a schizophrenic," he said, dead seriously.

Relating this story, Keeney said that both of these mavericks were really saying the same thing. A shaman does not enter a re-lationship with someone believing that he is somehow more healthy, more evolved, or less sinful or bad than the other. The shaman submits himself to the healing process in such a way that both he and his clients will be helped. They will touch one another and be touched by God.

Therapy or teaching, shamanic style, creates a context in which the partners in the process grow together. "As I grow," the shaman says by her behavior, "so, too, will you grow."

Supervision Reconfigured

For mutual and reciprocal growth to take place, therapists must confront their own issues, as well as those of the people whom we are trying to assist. In cybernetic terms, because the interaction between doctor and patient (or between any helper and client) takes primacy over any individual side of the relationship, chang-ing either side produces a similar result. This has interesting im-plications for supervision. Whereas a lot of "live" (as opposed to after-the-event) supervision of the clinician takes place with the supervisor behind a one-way mirror, directing the discourse of the trainee through phone contact, Keeney is more inclined to actually enter the room and speak to both participants in the process. His reasoning is that it is not just the therapist (or the teacher) who needs guidance when stuck—the clients, as well, need help work-ing through the impasse. In this sense, supervision is not solely di-rected to the professional but rather to the relationship.

"What could you say to your therapist that would help her be more surprising to you?" Keeney would ask the client. "What would be the most unexpected thing she could ask you right now? If you had a chance to discuss your therapist with another thera-pist, what would you say needs to happen to change what your therapist is doing with you right now?"

In this model, phone consultations can be directed not only to the therapist ("Please tell the client that the supervisor behind the one-way mirror is bored and wants us to be more interesting") but also to the client ("Your supervisor wants me to ask you to move to another chair. He said that might give you a different view of my situation.") And if the therapist (or the client) should become confused, *either one* could step out of the room to have a consultation. In this model, similar to shamanic ideals, the helper is no more of an expert than is the client: Both are seen as partners in the process.

The Making of a Shaman

The sort of humility that underlies such an attitude is nurtured in ways that are quite different from our own training models. When you look at the ways that shamans are prepared, what is most critical is not developing so-called expertise but having the kind of life experience that comes with surviving ordeals. The apprentice becomes more and more aware of how he is no different from anyone he might attempt to assist. He or she is no more important, no less despicable, and just as much an outcast. In fact, the most common training ordeal is one in which the apprentice must first undergo destruction before he or she can be reborn.

"Shamanic initiation involves the radical deconstruction of one's self through the processes and rituals of ordeal and self-negation. They bring you to your knees."

We're not sure if we heard right or, at the very least, what Keeney means.

"The island of St. Vincent in the Caribbean has a special ceremony called "mourning." If you have a dream about a certain kind of person who is called a 'pointer,' you are supposed to go to that person and ask for guidance, to ask that person to point you in the right direction of the spirit world."

As usual, Keeney spoke from personal experience. While in St. Vincent, he dreamed of a man named Cosmore Pompey, who told him in the dream, "I have God's number." A spiritual elder advised Keeney that this meant he was to go to this man and ask him to direct him in a mourning ceremony. So he hired a guide and went to the northern end of the island.

"I don't know what this means," Keeney told the man when he found him. "But I was told to come to you because you appeared in my dream. I was told that you have God's number, an actual telephone number, and this allows you to have a more direct connection to the spirit world."

Archbishop Cosmore Pompey and Mother Pompey
of the St. Mary's Spiritual Baptist Cathedral,
St. Vincent (an island in the Caribbean)

"This dream is true," the man said. "I do have God's number."
Keeney was invited to participate in the shamanic ceremony
that involved being wrapped in many bands around his eyes.
Each band was represented by a different color that would appear in the dream, and each one was decorated in wax drippings
that were considered symbols of the spirit world.

Keeney was then led into a tiny room that was barely large enough for him to lie down. He received neither food nor water for an indeterminate period of time, during which people continuously visited him and prayed over him. In the evenings he was required to privately critique and "mourn" every detail of his life, particularly those that he had previously avoided or ignored (even after years as a clinician). Particular emphasis was placed on his most shameful behaviors, those that he was most anxious to deny or hide. The purpose of this exercise was for the apprentice to come to grips with the reality that he is just as full of crap as anyone else. This is designed to leech out of the neophyte any remnants of arrogance and any illusions of superiority. Rather than the training designed to increase one's confidence as a healer, it is instead structured around breaking one down to the lowest possible element.

All the while he confessed, the villagers and shamans present moaned, chanted, and sang over him. They guided him to the point where he felt nothing but despair, as if he were dying. He was hallucinating anyway, because of the food and water deprivation, but was also suffering terrible pain. He had stomach aches and headaches. It felt like a terrible flu had penetrated his bones. At one point, he didn't think he could stand any further deprivations; he cried out for God to just take his life and be done with it. It felt like his whole life had been wasted, that he had spent so many years pursuing knowledge that had nothing to do with wisdom. He had been attracted to the abstract and the intellectual and found that it gave him feelings of specialness and superiority to understand things that others could not grasp. It felt as if his being a therapist and a theoretician all those years had fed his narcissism, and now all that had been stripped away, leaving only darkness and despair.

"I began to see that my greatest weakness was in a piety and pride that I had accused in others but which was fully present in my own being. I went through this deconstruction of myself and finally didn't want to live that kind of life any longer. I begged God to remake me, or take me. I couldn't live with myself a moment longer."

This feeling of hitting bottom, which is so often described as part of the recovery process of substance abusers, is also a significant part of the apprentice shaman's journey. You must surren-

Keeney undergoing a "mourning ceremony" with the
St. Vincent Shakers. The bands around his head
hold special wax drippings that symbolize visionary
journeys he was sent on during a week-long fast.
Candles are held while people are praying
and dancing with the community.

der the search for validation and power and the need for approval. What is left is a strong identification with the oppressed—
without judgment.

"At that moment," Keeney recalled, "I no longer wanted to
carry a business card that said I was a cybernetic epistemologist,

or a psychotherapist, or an anthropologist. These things were not important at all. I would rather have had no card at all. I would rather find the value in people who have never been seen. I found at that point my world completely changing."

It was then that Keeney decided to choose as his teachers not the academics and scholars but the often-illiterate holders of ancient wisdom traditions. Most of them had never seen a book before in their lives. But they lived their lives with an integrity that Keeney could only dream about. He realized that before he could learn what the shamans had to teach, he first had to unlearn most of what he had already been taught. When this week of fasting ended, not surprisingly, he was transformed. He had died and been reborn.

The Amos Quotient

One of the greatest spiritual teachers Keeney ever knew had no university degree, if he had any education at all. He grew up in a small town in Louisiana and became the senior deacon of a small Black church. Amos doesn't have a judgmental bone in his body. He accepts every person as equal, whether he or she is a Nobel Prize winner or a convict on death row. Amos believes in and practices God's grace and forgives everyone he ever meets for whatever crimes or misdeeds they may have committed or thought about doing. He is a pure saint. An unqualified love flows out of Amos's being that Keeney holds as his own moral compass. Keeney even has a name for this: "AQ," which stands for the "Amos Quotient." This is a measure by which to assess the quality of love in other spiritual healers.

There are many famous spiritual leaders around the world, dressed in colored robes and wearing all kinds of fancy hats and caps, beads and feathers, but no one has touched Keeney more deeply than the easy-to-hug and quick-to-smile Amos. He is a love-being who radiates egoless affirmation upon all those who are lucky enough to be in his presence.

Paying a Price

Keeney finds it amusing that students today who are learning to be helpers and healers complain about the ordeals they must suffer: final exams and papers to write, lectures to attend, internship hours to log. "This is nothing compared to the sort of journeys that an apprentice shaman must undergo, tasks that are designed specifically to take the person to the edge of spiritual, if not physical, death. This is the paradox of learning to be a shaman: that you must relinquish all power to have any chance of healing others. You must be willing to give up everything you want in order to get what you want. You have to know what it feels like to be sick, bad, and mad. You must go all the way to the bottom of human despair and fraility. You have to pay a dear price."

"This reminds me of another sermon," Jeffrey interrupted. "We have all heard these kinds of talks by preachers or rabbis or ministers or other holy people. We yell out, 'Amen, or 'Hallelujah,' or 'Praise the Lord,' or 'Praise Allah.' And yet I don't have the slightest confidence that these scoldings or sermons will have the slightest lasting effect—either on those in the congregation or on readers who are viewing these words. They have no lasting impact. So, how on earth can we touch the reader's soul? How do we get these ideas across so it doesn't sound so much like church?"

"But it *is* church. Remember that shamans don't make these artificial distinctions that we do between the rabbi, the priest, or the minister and the psychologist and the doctor. It all depends on what kind of church you attend. Unless you are prepared to get on your knees and reckon with the relative unimportance of your life, all your education and training are worthless. There just is no easy, organized, sequential path to being a shaman. You must first be broken before you can be delivered into peace. If you're not there, then, to paraphrase some biblical scripture, "Go sin boldly and get yourself at the starting gate."

We are nodding our heads, but still with little intention that we would ever choose this path, at least on purpose. Yet here we are in a most inhospitable place. We have our comforts, but they are only illusions that prevent us from looking deeper. We suppose all we are really talking about that distinguishes the shaman from a therapist is that the former practices genuine humility, the kind that only comes from authentic confrontation with our own powerlessness.

"I would tell readers," Keeney said by way of summary, "that unless they can get to their tears and allow themselves to be overcome by the misery and suffering that are already present in their lives, they can't ever begin the journey. Unless you are prepared to go through the most severe ordeals, you will never find your unique place or articulate your own voice."

Most of the world's great spiritual teachers have taught that we learn and grow from the suffering and pain that life brings us. Life too easily becomes shallow when we aim to remove ourselves from risk and overly protect ourselves from harm. Being insulated from others means that we are ensuring that we won't be touched by anyone or anything. To know joy requires embracing, rather than running away from, the suffering in the world. This paradox is at the heart of many religions. Accepting and working with the complementarity, or the inseparable relationship between suffering and joy, comprises the heart of the wisdom carried by the grand religious traditions. Unfortunately, this is typically a blind spot for many secular helpers of our time.

Our culture is dominated by the search for ways to avoid, minimize, and dull pain at all costs. We medicate ourselves at the slightest indication of discomfort. We use alcohol, drugs, and other means to escape that which we find uncomfortable. Even therapy or self-education takes too damn long; it's much easier to take a pill.

The wisdom of the world's religions, as well as the practices of indigenous healing, teach us to embrace pain and suffering as partners in an adventure into learning and growth. Without them, you get nowhere. When suffering is wed with ecstatic experience, that is when the real transformative action begins. It is at the intersection of bliss and suffering that we may find compassion, love, and wisdom.

Chapter Eleven

Arousal

"Calm down."

"Whadya mean, calm down! I can't believe that all this crap is happening at the same time. It's outta control."

"Lower your voice. Then begin again."

"I'm trying to calm down, I tell you, but it ain't easy."

"Okay, then, what I'd like you to do is close your eyes for a moment. You're overexcited and not thinking clearly. Take a deep breath."

"I can't seem to catch my breath. I feel so anxious, I don't know what to do."

"Okay, then, I understand. Maybe a prescription for Xanax would help. It will take the edge off your overanxiousness."

"Whatever you say, Doc."

Typically, what helpers and healers do in our culture is encourage people who are troubled to calm down. Therapists teach people relaxation training. They use hypnosis to reduce tension. They prescribe meditation or yoga for calming states. They suggest taking hot baths to soothe tensions. They use their smoothest, silkiest voices to instill a sense of peace and tranquillity. And if all else fails, then they often recommend drugs to do the job.

These strategies are in marked contrast to some indigenous contexts, where they do the exact opposite: Healing takes place within a state of hyperarousal. Whether in a rural African American church, a Guarani tribal ceremony, or a Zulu dance, the goal of the healing rituals is to get people even more excited—emotionally, physically, and spiritually aroused to an altered state of consciousness. This has been one of Keeney's most stunning discoveries from the time he started participating in global healing traditions.

Half the Story

Our culture has been swept away by a keen interest in the contemplative, meditative traditions of the East, combined with an almost passionate worship of what Herbert Benson (1990) called the "relaxation response." Our lives are so overstressed that most people are constantly looking for ways to find greater peace and serenity. We believe that by slowing things down as much as possible, remaining still, going into a relaxed state, we make the best context for healing to take place (there are other meditation traditions, such as the Buddhist "dead man yoga," and the Hindu *asparsa* yoga, which seek to exhaust the body and the mind to allow the spirit to soar).

"But that is only half the story," Keeney maintained. "The other half is what is being practiced by shamans around the world, most notably in Africa. When people come to the shaman, and say they have a chronic problem with stomach cramps or conflict in a relationship, they are *not* told to calm down. Instead, they are told this calls for a dance."

The community is brought together. Fires are lit. The drums are brought out and begin beating in a multi-polyphonic rhythm that makes sitting still almost impossible. The drumbeats become so intoxicating that the sounds seem to enter your body and soul; they make you move whether you want to or not. People begin to sway and move and shake in a convulsive-like fashion. Involuntary movements ripple through one's abdomen and chest and thighs. This is a very different sort of healing than the tranquillity that we hope to inspire in our own work.

"When you watch a full ceremony," Keeney said, "you find that people dance through the night. They dance themselves into exhaustion, until they fall into heaps on the ground. Then they rise and dance some more. They become so aroused that they actually reach a point where their nerves and muscles cannot perform any longer. They just collapse."

Ironically, it is through this intense stimulation that people reach a state of deep, reflective stillness that meditators would take years trying to achieve. They fall into this condition naturally, not by willing themselves to relax but by allowing themselves to become totally and completely excited.

"What we can learn from shamans around the world," Keeney summarized, "is that healing can be seen as a cycling between deep stillness and heightened plateaus of arousal, then back again to stillness, all through the night."

Keeney cited the work of Milton Erickson (1980) as one example of a therapist who put this principle to work. He liked to conduct 3-hour sessions at times, preferring to wait until his patients naturally went into a trance state when they were ready rather than artificially inducing it. "If you watch the natural cycles of arousal that people go through, you can work within those patterns. So this is the other half of the story that we have been missing in our culture."

Movement

The essence of shamanic practice in almost every culture Keeney has studied involves movement. All shamans lead their community in nonpurposeful, nonchoreographed body movements. This even can be found in the history of psychology, if we go all the way back to the days of William James, when there was much interest in automatism. This included the kinds of hypnotic trance states that produced automatic writing, in which the person had no recollection of the activity. It is also similar to the euphoric states of speaking in tongues that are characteristic of evangelical churches. Yet now these practices have been neglected by psychology, if not forgotten.

While studying the work of a famous Japanese sensei, Ikuko Osumi, in Japan, Keeney (1999b) discovered a familiar pattern that he had witnessed in both Africa and South America—the use of movement to produce healing energy. In the ancient Japanese tradition of *seiki jutsu,* the healer mobilizes and circulates the life force as part of a ceremony that emphasizes rapid, subtle shaking movements, almost imperceptible to an observer.

Ikuko Osumi, Sensei, revered healer of Japan and
master of the ancient healing art of *seiki jutsu.*

According to this healing practice, people become sick when
their life energy becomes low. It is necessary under such circumstances to fill the tank, so to speak. This procedure takes place by
preparing the body in a ceremony that takes place at a certain
time of day, at a designated spot, under other specific circumstances. The life force energy is inserted through the top of the
head. A series of exercises, practiced 20 minutes each day, is prescribed in order to maintain this energy. This is done through natural movements.

"This can be as simple," Keeney explained, "as the kind of rocking you might do in a chair. You reach a point where it feels like
you are no longer causing the chair to rock but it is rocking you. It

becomes an automatic movement, like a trance state, that pro duces a deep condition not so much of relaxation as arousal. Concentration is heightened, as are all the senses."

As Keeney described this practice, he rose out of his chair and demonstrated what he was talking about. His arms floated up in the air. His body began to vibrate, gently at first, then more and more visibly. He made moaning sounds. He started slapping his thighs like a sumo wrestler. He slapped his chest, his arms, then leaned forward and started blowing through his mouth. The vibrations now moved up his neck, making whooshing sounds out of his mouth. He looked and acted just like a Samurai warrior about to go into battle. And this analogy is not far off the mark. The practice was actually done by the Samurai for thousands of years.

Even today, disciples of this ancient tradition, including some CEOs of major Japanese corporations (executives and scientists of Sony), put themselves into life-energy vibrating trances before they negotiate an important deal. Keeney mentioned this as a shamanic practice that can be readily integrated into modern life, using subtle vibrational energy shifts to access greater inner resources.

One example of this occurred with a young woman athlete whose career had been interrupted by an injury. Keeney received a call from this woman's mother, a researcher at the Mayo Clinic in Rochester, Minnesota. She said that her daughter was a competitive college gymnast who had received knee surgery several years ago. Although the best doctors at the Mayo Clinic had worked with her, they were startled to find that after she recovered from surgery, she was unable to perform a forward somersault, the simplest of maneuvers.

The young woman was sent to various departments throughout the clinic, from surgery to physical rehabilitation to psychiatry. Among other things, the professionals made her a personalized audiocassette that guided her through some visualization practices before her gymnastic routine. Yet nothing worked, and the woman still found herself unable to execute a forward roll.

The Mayo Clinic gave up and suggested that perhaps she should try some alternative approach, such as hypnosis. The girl's parents subsequently went on a search to find an alternative treatment for their daughter and were given the name of the Milton H. Erickson Foundation in Phoenix, Arizona, a center world-renowned for hypnosis and innovative work in psychotherapy. After the director of the foundation listened to their story, he recommended that they have a meeting with Keeney.

When the young gymnast, now a college student in Wisconsin, came to Keeney's office, he told her about the Japanese method of arousing the life force. He demonstrated how to bring the force into her injured knee and suggested how she could start moving her body in a way that would draw the life force into her whole being. After 1 week of doing this, she reported that she could feel a tingling sensation in the joint. Then, to her great surprise, as well as to the shock of her coach, she spontaneously did a double somersault during a practice session.

"One week of this practice with the life force was able to bring forth what years of the best medical treatment available in the world was unable to accomplish."

As we are both rather conventional practitioners, Keeney could see our look of skepticism. He was losing us and knew that we were being polite and attentive, even though this stuff, which sounded "New Age," would never fly in our work. It was then that he clarified that this was an "Old Age" tradition, part of practices that have been used all over the world for thousands of years.

Rocking and Wiggling

Please, we begged, how can you relate all this to the kind of work that most of us do? There was no way we could imagine ourselves going into a Samurai or sumo wrestler stance as we faced our clients and students. But maybe this reflects our own inhibitions surrounding our bodies. Our culture does not permit such movements, except under the most rigidly prescribed contexts, such as a nightclub or an Orthodox Jewish synagogue.

"People should wiggle more," Keeney announced simply. "Probably the worst thing that any healer could do is to sit still in an office chair during a session. If you think about it, this flies in the face of everything we know about how people change in other cultures through the ages. They don't do it through talk and sitting calmly but through arousal and naturalistic trance states."

What immediately comes to mind is the image of children and their natural movements; they can hardly sit still for a moment. Kids are always fidgeting, rocking, squirming, giggling, vibrating with energy. It isn't until they get to school that teachers (and parents) are always admonishing them to sit still and stop that foolishness. Even by the time they are young adults, humans still find it virtually intolerable to remain still for more than a few minutes at a time. Yet that is what we demand of them when they sit in school, in assemblies, and in movies and plays. Even during religious worship in most traditions (except among Muslims, Orthodox Jews, and African Americans), congregants are expected to remain immobile and polite in the House of God—unless otherwise directed by the pastor-priest-rabbi-minister that it is time to rise or be seated.

Given the prohibitions against movement in our culture (and in the helping professions), we wondered how therapists could arouse clients and draw upon this as a resource?

"One option," Keeney offered, "is to move more often when you're alone. You can arouse yourself prior to seeing clients simply by turning on music that makes you want to move and shake and you can dance in the room. You can work yourself up."

Keeney remembered when he used to teach therapy to doctoral students in a family therapy program. There was all this time and attention directed toward what to say and do during a session but almost nothing mentioned about how to get ready for the encounter.

Compare this to the way a baseball hitter prepares himself to go to the plate. Everything he does uses rituals that increase arousal. He wiggles his butt, shakes his hips, circles his neck, moves his shoulders, touches his head. Then he glances at the batting coach, who looks just like a shaman with all the rigmarole that he goes through in his signals, touching his elbow, his belt, his nose, his forehead, on and on—between the two of them, they are doing an elaborate dance.

As another example, Keeney cited actors before they go on stage. They have their own rituals, as do musicians and any other performers. Teaching and counseling are no different. And he urges us to develop our own arousal-building patterns before we go "on stage." Again, these are not designed to loosen us up, but to activate our spirits and all our senses. Keeney believes that like shamans, we can do our best work when we are vibrating. He means this not only metaphorically but literally.

The Sound of Music

Then there are the things we could do when the energy in sessions lags. So many times we sit in sessions bored, lethargic, functioning on autopilot. We look at the clock and count the minutes until the end. We lapse into fantasy and leave the room until the appointed time for our return. We tap our foot in impatience, frustrated and sometimes even fuming that our time is being squandered. And while all this is going on, we have so many options other than sitting still.

"I think our clients have fantasies of us being eccentric people anyway," Keeney said. "I think this gives us license to do more creative things than ever imagined. There is nothing wrong with having a few percussion instruments in the office and, from time to time, shaking a rattle or banging a triangle or even pounding a drum. Whenever I have an opportunity to work with people, I want to have as many things available to me as possible."

"Like what?" we asked.

"I used to have a sound effects synthesizer from Radio Shack," Keeney said with a grin. "One of those electronic devices you can get for about $150 that simulates many sounds. It has the kind of sound effects they used to have on radio shows from the old days, things like the sound of a bullet, a cannon being fired, a windstorm, a broken glass. Just imagine the possibilities."

Indeed we can! Partners who have been talking about their conflicts begin to squabble and fight in the session. The therapist pushes a button, and you hear the sounds of cats squealing. Another time someone says something insightful, and you hit the applause button.

Keeney recalled when he worked with children in classrooms, and he brought his little sound machine with him. He invited the kids to script stories and then use the sound effects to bring them alive.

There was a time in his own life when Keeney was going through a difficult divorce with his wife. She was abusing alcohol and having fitful rages that affected their son, Scott, who was only about 6 at the time. Scott began having nightmares that kept him up at night. It was probably no coincidence that Scott's bedroom wall abutted that of his mother during her alcohol binges. His worst nightmare consisted of visions that a mean, hungry bear was hiding in the closet.

Keeney was concerned about what he could do to help his son. They had been driving in the car, talking about the situation and also discussing the kind of work that Brad was doing lately on Indian reservations. Scott was intensely curious about his father's work, and perhaps partly as a distraction from his fear of the scary bears, he kept asking his dad more questions.

Just at a point where they crossed the Mississippi River, a shadow passed over the car.

"Dad," Scott called out, "what's that?" He was pointing to the wingspan of a large, fast form that flew over the car, just buzzing the windshield.

"That's an eagle," Keeney explained to his son. "It is a most powerful, magnificent raptor in the sky. Isn't it something?"

"Yeah!" Scott agreed. Then he thought for a moment and said to his father, "Dad, what's an Indian?"

"Well, Scott, a true Indian is someone who loves the animals, loves people, loves trees, and loves the river. An Indian is someone who would think that eagle flying over us was a very important thing, a good sign."

Scott nodded his head. "I love those things, too, Dad. And I think that eagle is important. Does that make me an Indian, too?"

"Yes, Scott, in a way it does."

Keeney was seized by the moment, the very idea that an eagle would give them a sign. He started thinking in the Indian way, as his Ojibwa friends might think about things. And this gave him some inspiration.

Funny Medicine

"Where are we going, Dad?" Scott asked.

"Home, son, we're going home. I've got an idea about how we can take care of that bear you are afraid of."

They drove straight to Keeney's apartment and they authored a story together called "Funny Medicine for Children Who Are Scared of Bears." While Scott recited their story aloud, Brad played accompaniment on the piano.

This is what they created:

> *This funny medicine is for children who are scared of bears.*
> *Get the largest piece of paper you can find, maybe even one as*
>   *big as your bed.*
> *Draw a picture of the largest bear that you can draw.*
> *Makes its face really scary. Make sure you can see its teeth.*
> *When you have drawn this bear, take a red crayon and draw*
>   *its heart.*

Keeney and his son, Scott, creating the stories and songs "Funny Medicines for Children," as a way of helping them overcome fears.

Draw a picture of yourself inside the bear's heart. This will make the bear your bear. The bear will have you in its heart to protect you.

Take a piece of cloth that is your favorite color and cover the bear's chest as if it was a shirt. This way nobody can see the bear's heart.

Put the bear under your bed. When you go to sleep, know that your bear is protecting you. If any mean bear tries to mess with you, it will have to get past your bear.

Think of your bear whenever you are scared of anything. No ghost, no goblin, no monster or spooky thing can get past your bear.

Make sure you keep your bear's heart a secret. Tell no one how he protects you.

Brad and Scott published this intervention (Keeney & Keeney, 1993), along with some others, in the *Japanese Journal of Family Psychology.* This was the beginning of the sort of interventions that would become Keeney's trademark. At workshops, in presentations, and classes, with families and clients, he would use stories set to music to help people conquer their fears by creating representations of them that were much less frightening. Even today, when Keeney is invited to do a lecture or a presentation, he is more likely to order a grand piano or a set of drums for the stage, rather than an overhead projector.

"You don't have to be a musician," Keeney pointed out. "You can always play appropriate music at various intervals, depending on the level of arousal you want to create."

Keeney conceptualizes arousal on a different level than we are ordinarily used to seeing it. We may associate arousal as being out of control, whereas he looks at it as a natural and normal state that can be intrinsically healing. Rather than arousal being feared ("You are overexcited. Settle down."), fears can be embraced and used therapeutically.

Certainly, there are times when arousal can be detrimental. When couples are fighting, for example, when their heart rates get past a certain level, as they might during a fight or a spat of anger, there is not much opportunity for learning. People become more concerned with survival. But there are other times when arousal can open pathways, and other times when it shuts them down; the key is to recognize the difference and make appropriate shifts.

So far, we have been talking about the kind of arousal that might take place in conversation or in the context of a traditional therapy session. Keeney has in mind a deeper level of hyperarousal that can only be attained in movement.

"How could you imagine us doing that?" we asked him.

"There are so many ways," Keeney said. "You could send a couple for dance lessons, but with specific tasks that accompany the activity. You can't send people to dance with the Bushmen, but you can send them to polka or disco or samba or to a gospel church. The key is in creating a therapeutic task related to movement that contextualizes the problem in a different way."

The Worry Rug

One idea for integrating movement into his work occurred to Keeney when he was consulted by an elementary school teacher who worried excessively. Madeline was anxious about her job, her children, her parents, her health. Even after a year of therapy, the worries still persisted, and this is what led her to be referred to Keeney.

"I wonder if you can stop worrying about your worrying?" he said to Madeline, after she presented some brief background on her situation.

"Huh?"

"Never mind," he said with a smile. "Let's try something else that might put your mind at ease. I want you to go to a toy store. I assume there is one in the neighborhood?"

"Yeah," Madeline answered, a bit confused. "Sure. There's one I take my kids to sometimes."

"Good. I want you to go to that store and purchase a children's bank."

"You mean like a piggy bank kind of thing?"

"Exactly. But it doesn't have to be a pig. It can be any special form that strikes your fancy. Let yourself be led to one particular bank."

"Okay," she agreed. "Then what?"

"I want you to bring the bank home and put it in a prominent place where you can see it almost everywhere you go at home."

"What do you mean?"

"Well, like you could put it on top of the television set in the family room. How does that sound?"

Madeline nodded but was still confused about what was going on. This guy was *nothing* like her other therapist. He wasn't asking her lots of questions, nor was he even doing that thing that therapists do where they repeat what you say; he was just listening intently and then he gave her this weird assignment.

"Good," Keeney said, as if that was settled. "Now, what I want you to do is every time you catch yourself worrying for more than a minute—a full 60 seconds—I want you to put a quarter in that bank sitting on top of the TV."

"You want me to put money in the bank?"

"That's right. Every time you worry for more than a minute, you walk over to the bank, no matter where you are in the house, and you insert exactly one quarter. It's got to be a quarter. No nickels and dimes. Got that?"

"I . . . I guess so."

"You don't sound so sure," Keeney observed. "In order for this to work, you have to agree to be honest about this and really follow through. Are you prepared to do that?"

She hesitated for a moment, genuinely giving the matter some serious thought. "Yeah, I can do that," she finally said, this time with a certain authority. She looked amused by the whole thing, but by now she was so desperate, she'd try anything.

Indeed, Madeline did follow the instructions, and in no time the bank was full of her "worries." They talked about where she could donate the money, and once she identified an appropriate charity, Keeney explained that now she could stop worrying because she put the worries to work. Even if she couldn't help herself, she could at least allow her worries to help others.

A short time later, Madeline reported in a session that while she had been worrying earlier in the day, she found herself having a vivid daydream.

"What sort of daydream?" Keeney asked, always alert to the power of dreams and images.

"Well, I could see myself with a rug."

"A rug?"

"Uh huh. It was a small rug, like an Oriental rug of some kind. It was rolled up and rested in a corner of a room where nobody would bother it."

"Go on," Keeney encouraged. He could see a look on Madeline's face that almost looked like rapture.

"Well, I pictured myself taking the rug and rolling it out on the floor. Then I took off my shoes and my socks, and I stood in the middle of the rug." She stopped to look at Keeney, gauging his reaction. Keeney smiled and nodded encouragingly.

"So, as I was standing on the rug, I imagined that my mind just let go of all the worries. It was like gravity pulled them all through the bottoms of my feet. Then I'd kind of wiggle my toes, like they were being moved by the worries. I stomped my feet to shake the worries loose and they spilled out onto the rug." Madeline looked up again.

"Then what happened?"

"Well, then I took the rug outside and shook it out. I shook out all the worries real hard. When I was sure they were all gone, and the rug was clean and fresh again, then I rolled it up and put it back in the corner where it could be used again next time."

"I see," Keeney said with a huge grin. And see, he did indeed! It was a rather simple matter to instruct Madeline to follow through on exactly the plan she described in her daydream—to purchase a special "worry rug" that was similar to the one she had imagined. The arousal and the movement that took place as she banished her worries were just as effective in reality as they had been in

her fantasy. And from this interaction was born the template of an
idea that Keeney would soon use again and again in a variety of
forms and contexts.

Shaking with Force

Once upon a time, most of what helpers and healers did in their
work was to encourage troubled people to dance and sing and
move. Our helping professions have now evolved into therapeutic
endeavors that require prolonged stillness. People are asked to
remain in their seats for an hour or more at a time. They are
asked to tell their stories in the most quiet, relaxed way possible.
We add to this tranquilized scene by using hypnotic voices that re-
assure clients that there is nothing to worry about, that if only
they remain as calm as possible, everything will turn out just fine.

We are not suggesting that relaxation strategies do not have
their place in our overstressed, overscheduled world. We are,
however, offering an alternative way of looking at healing that
has a long tradition in the most ancient wisdom of cultures
around the world. It is not only by calming down that people find
peace, but also through the ecstasy that can be evoked by dance
and music (or even shaking out a rug).

Throughout the world, Keeney has discovered so many different ways that cultures evoke ecstatic movement. In Nova Scotia,
the blind Micmac medicine man Dave Gehue naturally shakes
when he touches others with his healing touch. His teacher, the
late Cree elder Albert Lightning, was also a "shaker" and would
find his body seized with ecstatic movements. Gehue believed that
the strongest medicine people always shake with the life force. In
his own words, "No shake, no shaman."

A shaking body is one of the truest signs of someone entering
the ecstatic state of shamanism. In fact, the very word *"shaman"*
refers to the excited, shaking body of the shaman. As mentioned
before, this is sometimes forgotten in the contemporary understanding and expressions of shamanism, where the primary emphasis is on using a technique of guided imagery to direct an
inner fantasy journey to another imagined realm. For the
shamans Keeney has met around the world, having such a flight
is only one of the experiences that are possible. What is most important to their practice, however, is having the energy of life
enter their bodies, where it vibrates, ripples, and shakes them

with its currents. A true shaman shakes and carries a song that connects him or her with the divine.

The Gods Are Crazy

On one of his trips to Africa, Keeney was seated on the airplane next to a South African physician. The man began talking about his career and said that he had been the doctor assigned to the movie *The Gods Must Be Crazy,* a comedy about the Bushmen whose lives were changed by a Coca Cola bottle that fell from a plane in the sky. At one point during the shooting of the film, the main Bushman character was brought to the consulting physician in a condition no one understood. He had gone into a deep trance and was completely unresponsive to conversation; his body quivered uncontrollably and had gone into a deep shaking.

The doctor conducted a preliminary examination but could find no reason to explain the shaking that was taking place. What the medical staff did not know was that the Bushman, according to his belief system, had entered a healing state and was restoring his heath and vitality. The next day the Bushman stopped shaking and was found to be completely ready for work.

Keeney pointed out that it isn't necessary to shake as intensely as that Bushman, but it may be worthwhile for almost anyone to spend some time exploring the multitude of benefits that can occur from unleashing the life force through body movements. "Remember the gymnast I mentioned earlier?" Keeney asked.

How could we forget?

"She found that the natural arousal of a shaking body is inseparable from the flow of her creative process. After working with me for several sessions, she showed me how she was progressing with her body movement practice. As she did so, she had a daydream, remembering a special box that her grandmother had once given her. I told her to be on the lookout for a dream in which she might encounter that box. The very next night she dreamed of the box and heard a voice tell her to open it. She did and found that it held a tiny snake, all coiled up. This didn't frighten her, but it made her curious. I told her that cultures throughout the world depict the coiled snake as a symbol of the universal life force, what the yoga tradition calls *kundalini.*

Keeney asked the gymnast to keep track of her dreams for the following week and to choose one word for each dream that would best represent the meaning it held. For the dream she had just had, she chose the word *snake.* When she returned for her next session, she was delighted to report that she had experienced three more powerful dreams. The first dream involved a frightening criminal entering her house. She hid in the closet and covered herself with a pile of clothes. When the intruder opened the closet door and lifted off the clothes, he looked at her and said, "There is no one here." He then left, and she was not harmed in any way. The word for that dream was *fear,* and they discussed how the last 3 years of her life had been filled with the fear that she would never be able to perform a gymnastic routine again. For 3 years, she had sought help in numerous forms, but she had not competed in a single competition. In this dream, however, she faced fear, and it did not come in. She was not available for fear to enter.

The second night she dreamed of being near the edge of a canyon. There she turned into a cloud and was able to fly over the canyon and over a forest that was right next to it. Her word for that dream was *cloud,* and it captured her feeling of being weightless and able to fly without effort.

In the third dream she had that week, she saw herself in a gymnastic competition, performing her routine with absolute perfection. She chose the words *desired reality* to capture the essence of that dream and noted that she experienced complete ecstasy in it.

The gymnast then took the words that she had chosen for her dreams and constructed a sentence with them that would capture what she had learned from her practice of shaking. The sentence she came up with was: "When you see the coiled *snake,* know that some will see *fear,* while you will see the secret to life, the life force that turns you into a weightless *cloud* and effortlessly moves you to your *desired reality.*"

The gymnast decided to focus on this sentence whenever she was about to perform her gymnastic routine. The very next evening she competed for the first time in 3 years. She placed in two of her events and led her team to first place.

Ecstatic Experience of the Shaman

When a shaman feels the inner heat, shakes with ecstatic energy, and hears or sings the sacred sounds, he or she may trigger a wide range of enhanced states of consciousness. One of these may be a magical journey up a rope to the sky, through a tunnel into

an underworld, or into an immediate transference of consciousness to another place and time in the mythopoetic landscape. At
other times, you simply feel weightless and timeless, as if strad-
dling eternity itself, being internally still with the purposeless
movements your body performs. All of the spiritual experiences
reported by mystics, yogis, and initiates of the world's religions
may take place for the shaman.

In this regard, the shaman is a conduit of raw spiritual experience, never predictable or fully controlled. Buddhist deep listening, Sufi whirling, Christian conversion, Bushmen shape-shifting,
or Zen awareness are all available as the conduit of spiritual
transmission. In this regard, the shaman is the bringer of religious experience, the rekindler of tradition, and the beacon of
hope for all things anointed with spirit.

In one sense, shamanism is about being open to the *Tao,* the
natural effortless dance between movement and stillness that is
life itself. Applied to psychotherapy and strategies of personal
transformation, each school of therapy can be experientially true
if the practitioner allows the process to flow naturally through
him or her. What this means, ultimately, is that the vessel is more
important that the content of what flows inside its arteries and
veins. Learning to be this empty vessel is the heart of shamanistic
training. Keeney cites the words of the Lakota medicine man
Fools Crow, who described himself as a "hollow bone." This notion of emptiness is found in all the religions of the world, and it
applies to being a whole therapist, helper, or healer. To be full of
wisdom is to be empty. To be moved by the spirit is to be still. In
these paradoxes lies a great truth for how to be more fully alive
(Keeney, 1996).

Becoming a shaman, a therapist, or a fully developed human
being is essentially the same process. We must seek to be aware
of all possibilities but yet allow the unique characteristics of the
situation at hand to move us to be perfect for that moment. This is
what Keeney calls a no-therapy for no-mind, or a no-shamanism
for no-transformation, or a no-behavior for no-purpose. This Zen-
like, paradoxical way of defining life turns everything we have
been taught upside down. With the shamanic view, we see that we
must learn to make ourselves available for the spirit of life that
waits for us to take a ride on its breath. Ultimately, we are all aim-
ing to be surfers of life, hoping that we can learn to catch a wave
and ride it through its resolution, and then wait eagerly and pa-

tiently for the next wave. Ecstatic experiences constitute these waves of life. Being ready to ride them is the only lesson worth knowing.

Finding Enlightenment

There are so many ways that we might shake and move within our own worlds, especially considering the relatively sedentary lives we lead. But that would mean putting this book down, standing up, loosening yourself up, and experiencing the power of what your body can do when it is freed from its usual constraints. Or, alternatively, you could follow Keeney's advice on how to initiate some introductory shamanic movement into your life:

> *Purchase a brand new wooden pencil. In a private place talk to the pencil, asking it to help you become enlightened through shamanic movement. Sharpen the pencil and keep it in a safe place. Only use this pencil to write the word* enlightenment. *Every day write this word at least once with the pencil, but never more than 12 times at a single sitting. Do this until it is impossible to hold the pencil any more.*
>
> *When it is no longer possible to write with the pencil, place it in a small box and seal it. On the top of the box write these words, "The Silent Pencil." Every night before going to sleep, get out the box and shake it like a rattle. Say the word* enlightenment *12 times while you are rattling the silent pencil. Do this until you have a dream about being enlightened, lightened, or lit.*

Chapter Twelve

Therapeutic Tasks and Ordeals

Earlier, we had introduced the metaphor of burning logs to describe the essential elements of a person's presenting communications. If you recall, we mentioned that a client could be asked to imagine that she had spent a hundred hours in therapy and was asked to select three salient words that summarized the essence of what these sessions were about and what she had learned. These are three burning logs that have particular meaning to the person and that symbolize the closest connections she feels to her story.

Because the shaman does not think much of talk without action, the next step is to imagine ways that these "logs" can be converted into prescriptions for action; this is typically called homework. Among shamans, much of their healing boils down to particular ordeals that they ask their clients to go through. This is not the same thing at all as asking a client to go home and talk to his spouse, to write in a journal for 30 minutes, or to exercise for a half hour each day—these are far too direct and literal.

In his book *Ordeal Therapy*, Jay Haley (1984) talked about his strategy of creating therapeutic tasks that were so onerous and distasteful that clients might cure themselves as an excuse so that they didn't have to come back for more. This is a start but does not capture the full picture of what a true shaman has in mind. Western helpers and healers, not to mention their clients, are quite literal-minded. When we prescribe tasks, these are supposed to make sense or at least be remotely connected to the desired treatment goals. If a person is having trouble with self-acceptance, then someone like Albert Ellis (2001) would prescribe shame-attacking exercises, in which the person might be asked to stand on a street corner and sing songs with a bag over his head. A strategic therapist like Cloe Madanes (1981) might prescribe the presenting symptoms as a homework assignment: "You want to lose weight? Okay, I want you to eat more this week." Following the tradition of Milton Erickson, this type of paradoxical assignment might sound crazy, but at least it was related to the problem.

The shaman would take an even less linear and rational route. "The shaman's goal," Keeney said, "is to work with the burning logs—to juggle them, shuffle them, play with them, in such a way that they create a particular ritual or task that interrupts the habituated patterns that are currently operating. This is what creates the possibility of new ways of being."

The burning logs are the important metaphors that a client believes have meaning for his or her life. It doesn't matter whether the shaman or the client understands these metaphors; what is important is that they are utilized in a session. They are the burning logs that provide the heat for change.

"This sounds like the old Chinese proverb," Jon added. "It advises that if you don't change your direction, then you will end up where you are headed. Anything a helper can do to change the direction of a person's misfortune may be helpful. And play or, as you say, 'playing with the burning logs,' is a good way to creatively get out of the client's stuck box."

As an example, a family complained to its therapist that "there is total silence about what anyone feels about being together." For this family, the key metaphors that kept surfacing in the session were "silence," "feels," and "together." Whereas a therapist or a teacher in our culture might do one thing with this material, a shaman might juggle these "hot coals" into a prescription for action:

Using a cassette tape recorder, each family member must do the following: Set the tape to record and then in SILENCE imagine saying everything you FEEL about being in your family. Do

*not say anything aloud. Say these things only in your mind.
Each person should record for no longer than 10 minutes.
After all members have recorded their feelings, gather the
family TOGETHER and play the silent tape. Set the volume at a
comfortable level, as though there was something to hear. Remain silent and listen to what you can't hear.*

This shuffling of the family members' "burning logs" stirs their
imagination, acts out their own predicament in an imaginative
way, and stimulates them to see, feel, hear, and act in new ways.
The task addresses what is most meaningful to them but does not
engage in any discussion of understanding, unless, of course, the
family members present a view of their new understanding. The
shaman, however, won't try to understand their new understanding but will listen for the key metaphors, the burning logs that can
be played with one more time, ad infinitum.

The Shaking Tent

In many indigenous traditions, the healing begins with a dream.
Someone in the community has a dream of some importance, and
this is brought to the shaman. Unlike a psychoanalyst, the highly
evolved shaman does not attempt to interpret this dream, make
sense of it, or even invite the person to find some meaning in the
images. Instead, the shaman gives the person some task or ordeal
to complete that is related to the dream.

This is not just an idea to Keeney but a reality, in terms of the
way he lives his own life. He first visited the Bushmen because he
had a dream that directed him to do so. He is still such a florid and
vivid dreamer that many of his life decisions are based on the messages that come to him in his sleeping visions. After all, a shaman
would give no more weight to what happens in his or her waking
life as to what happens when dreaming. Among some indigenous
peoples, it is believed that the only time one is truly awake is when
one is dreaming. And who are we to say any different?

The shaman's goal is often to bring the dream into the other
world, the natural world. For example, among the Ojibwa Indians, if you were to have a dream about an otter, or its metaphori-
cal representation, you might be asked to go hunt for an otter and
use its skin in some ritualized way. In fact, Keeney actually had a
dream quite like this, in which in the vision his grandfather told

him to go get the skin of an otter and make a bag to carry his things. This is what led him, originally, to consult with a medicine man, Ron Geyshick, among the Ojibwa Indians of Canada.

Keeney first flew to International Falls, Minnesota, and from there took a seaplane to the island in Lac La Croix that houses the reservation. The evening that Keeney arrived, it was very cold. The people had gathered together to meet him and hold a ceremony. They brought deer stew and moose meat to celebrate the coming together of the people and the practice of their oldest healing ritual, called the shaking tent. This is regarded as the most powerful and revered ceremony among the Ojibwa people.

A tepee-like structure is built out of poles that are lashed together and stuck in the ground, then covered with blankets but leaving the top open. This is where Ron, the medicine man, would sit.

Covered completely in this tent, the medicine man would sing songs and chant as the spirit moved him. It was believed that as the spirits shook the tent, so was it possible to receive messages of guidance. There are actually old photographs from the 1800s, now stored in the Smithsonian, that depict this ancient ritual.

Whenever someone in the village was sick or was visited by a sacred dream, he or she would visit the medicine man inside the tent. People stood in line and waited their turns. Each petitioner approached the tent and then asked for help. The medicine man then consulted with the spirit world and offered his verdict.

In this case, Ron, the medicine man, was in his 50s, although he looked like he had lived a much harder life. He wore a flannel shirt, jeans, and a hat with a tractor emblem on it, looking a bit like a lumberjack or a farmer. He was a man who had never smiled; at least, nobody ever remembered seeing him smile.

That particular night, freezing and nervous while waiting his turn, Keeney approached Ron, encased in his tent. He waited for his turn to speak to Ron, but all remained silent in the tent. Keeney looked back over his shoulder at his friends, who gestured that he should continue.

"Okay, then," Keeney said, feeling a little strange talking to a teepee. "I had this dream about my grandfather. He has always been very special to me, maybe even the most important person in my life growing up. He was a preacher, well, more like a medicine man like you. He was important in his community as a healer. And he is the person who has most guided my life."

There was no movement in the tent whatsoever. Keeney wondered if Ron was even still inside. With further encouragement from those behind him, Brad continued the story of his dream about the otter. "So," he finished, "my grandfather said I should go get an otter bag. I don't know what that means."

Brad heard voices inside the tent, as if there were several different people present. This was impossible, of course, because the dwelling was just large enough to cover Ron's body. Some anthropologists believe that the medicine man is just using ventriloquism to project and change his voice; true believers think these are the voices of the spirits.

While Keeney waited patiently, he noticed that a little bell on top of the tent was ringing loudly. This was a signal that the spirit was shaking the tent. The tent swayed violently back and forth. Keeney remained until the shaking stopped.

After everyone had their say and related their stories, Ron emerged from the tent and everyone gathered together inside a nearby shanty house. Just as they settled down, there was a lot of commotion and the men rushed outside with their rifles. For a moment, Keeney thought they might be under attack, raided by another hostile tribe or maybe by the Bureau of Indian Affairs. But they were on an island so remote and isolated, there was no way that anyone could sneak up on them.

Keeney went outside to join the men, who had formed a circle and were staring at the ground. As he approached them, one of the men pointed to a pile of dust that they had been staring at. "See that?" he asked.

"Yeah," Keeney answered. "A pile of dust. What's the big deal?"

"That, my friend, was an owl."

"An owl?" What the hell were they talking about?

The old man nodded. "That was once an owl and this is his powder, all that is left of him. There is a bad medicine man over yonder, and he has tried to harm us by sending this owl. It is a spirit owl that has been created to hurt us. But one of our men shot the owl and it turned to dust. That is how we know what it means."

As he finished the explanation, the old man shrugged, as if this sort of thing was not uncommon. In fact, all of the people were feeling rather celebratory because they had managed to defeat this evil medicine man once again. So then they all went back inside the shack.

Ron had positioned himself in a rocking chair and commenced to rock. Each of the people who had consulted the shaking tent then sat down, one by one, in an old rickety folding chair in front of him. It was not necessary to tell him your name or to repeat the story you had told; Ron somehow knew this already.

As soon as Brad took a seat, Ron looked at him and nodded. "Yup, it's time for you to have a pipe. But you need a special pipe and I know just the man who can make this for you. When someone needs a sacred feather, he can find one. And he can get you an otter bag to hold your pipe. His name is Nate."

As we heard his name, we were immediately startled. We recognized that this was the same person whom Keeney had described in his case "The Medicine Man Who Never Had a Vision," which we included in our book about unusual cases. This very story had cemented our relationships and landed us together in Namibia to dance with the Bushmen.

Keeney was just as surprised by his short audience with Ron, who indicated with a dismissive gesture that he was ready for the next in line. This person was told that he needed to drink a tea made from a combination of four different barks that were found in particular parts of the forest. The tea was to be consumed three times per day. And so on, throughout the evening.

When Ron was through and all the people in the community had received their instructions, they then held a feast, which is what always happens after such a ceremony. People laughed and giggled and teased one another. As Brad sat and talked with them throughout the night, he wondered how his dream would be brought into the world.

Constructing Rituals

Among many Native American groups, the task that is prescribed almost always represents a way to bring the dream into the everyday physical world. If someone dreamed of a horse with red stripes, the medicine man might order the person to find a horse and paint it accordingly, then ride it into the wind until the sweat from the horse washes the stripes away. Or the medicine man might ask the person to paint the stripes on a piece of bark and to always carry that totem with him. However it is formed, the point is always to take something from the deepest part of one's unconscious and to bring it out into the world.

"Why is this?" we asked him.

"As a shaman, I say to people that it is important to enact respect for the deepest parts of our minds and hearts. We need to

Keeney with Walking Thunder, Dine (Navajo)
medicine woman, and her mother.

show and tell the source of our dreams that we take it seriously. We give it the same attention we would anything in the physical world. It's like saying, 'You, my deepest unconscious mind, have spoken and now I am showing you that I listened. Now I will act on your behalf.'"

This, of course, is a very different way of thinking about homework. There are no logical prescriptions because the tasks that are assigned almost never make sense, at least in the ways we think about understanding.

"Dreams provide us with anchors," Keeney elaborated, "or buoys, if you wish, that mark areas of particular significance in the deep unconscious."

In the classic shamanic paradigm, a sacred dream holds a key metaphor that may be derived from conversation, and this is subsequently connected to some prescribed action in the world. So the key questions for the shaman to ask are

1. What are the key metaphors?
2. How can they be converted to some form of action that makes them come alive in the everyday world?

In developing the prescriptive action, it is completely unnecessary (and probably undesirable) that the homework or the ordeal make sense or logically flow from the discussion. Unlike in traditional therapy or teaching, where homework is intended to provide a structured practice of specific target skills, the work of the shaman utilizes significant themes in more dramatic (and mysterious) ways, those that are not limited to our conscious or surface understandings. If anything, such tasks are intended to disrupt usual routines, rather than add to them.

In his book *Improvisational Therapy,* Keeney plotted the method for constructing therapeutic tasks. Although this sounds like there may be an easily accessible catalogue of therapeutic prescriptions, Keeney has actually derived his own language from his early training as a cybernetic epistemologist. He speaks of such things as "rim markers" and "frame reversals" and "chunking" to plot the sequencing of interventions.

As we've mentioned before, Keeney functions more like a screenwriter, a film producer, or a jazz pianist than what we would ever imagine as a mental health professional. His prescriptions are thus not in any way conceived as logical or linear extensions of a presenting problem ("You are angry at your partner so tell her what you think and feel"). In the traditions of Milton Erickson, Jay Haley, and Carl Whitaker, not to mention pianists like Thelonious Monk or Cyrus Chestnut, Keeney improvises in creative ways that even he doesn't understand.

"What's your favorite medium for constructing therapeutic tasks?" we asked Keeney, hoping to pin him down to more specifics.

"That would be Rice Krispies."

"Huh?"

"I love using Rice Krispies, the cereal, as part of my ordeals."

We wondered what on earth he was talking about.

"I sometimes ask people to put a few heaping spoonfuls of Rice Krispies in their shoes. As you walk around in the shoes, you end up grinding the cereal down to a powder, all the while it makes this wonderful sound. So in a sense, with every step the person takes, he or she is transforming a familiar thing into something else. This, after all, is what we are trying to do when we help people."

To back up a little and summarize the process, Keeney likened his therapeutic stance to that of a careful listener with a butterfly net. He tunes himself as carefully as he can to the client and attempts to capture a metaphor from the client's primary unconscious process. He sometimes refers to this as the client's "meaningful noise."

"How do you teach this sort of thing?" we wonder.

"If you go into a bookstore," Keeney said, "you will feel that somewhere is a subject area, or a single volume, that you believe has valuable knowledge, but it is beyond the grasp of your understanding."

"Like your book *Aesthetics of Change,* for example," we kidded him.

"Sure," Keeney said good-naturedly. "It could be about the I Ching or postmodern theory, or a James Joyce novel, or cybernetics, or William Blake's poetry, or superstring theory in physics. Sometimes you buy these books almost like a sacred talisman. By definition, it is almost impossible to have a coherent grasp of their contents. Yet there are still lots of people who believe these books hold wisdom and important insight."

So it is with shamanic ordeals, Keeney contended. We don't have to understand what we are doing to still trust that they may be meaningful and, in turn, useful. Once he has located the primary processes or central metaphors or meaningful noise (and this is not difficult to do, if you ask the client), Keeney plays with these "burning logs" in such a way that they are converted into a theater of the absurd.

One Size Doesn't Fit All

There is a common practice employed by therapists and teachers of all persuasions that is based on the idea that certain things are good for people, all people, regardless of their needs and inter-

ests. Homework is thus often constructed in such a way that some
universal assignment is given to everyone, no matter what each
person's presenting complaints, identified issues, personalities,
past experiences, or stated goals are.

A teacher would ask everyone in the same class to complete the
same task, whether that is to write a paper about a particular
topic, conduct an identical field study, or prepare an oral presentation. The whole idea is that what is good for one is good for all,
and based on past experience, the teacher has determined that
everyone can and should profit from the same homework. There
is little (if any) consideration given to whether a student has already done such an assignment before in another class, or
whether the student's specific learning goals are even remotely
related to the structure. In some cases, there is even precious little room for each student to adapt the task to fit his or her particular resources, time constraints, or learning styles, much less
actual interests. "I'm the expert," the teacher says, "and I know
what is good for you—what is good for everyone, as a matter of
fact—so put on these shoes and walk around in them. No matter if
they are too tight or big, whether you like the style or not, or
whether you keep tripping as you wear them, you'll get used to
them after awhile. And if you don't, well, too damn bad!"

Even though therapy is supposed to be a highly individualized
learning structure, many practitioners also prescribe virtually
identical tasks and homework assignments to almost all their
clients. One therapist might ask everyone to complete "thought
journals" to monitor cognitive activity throughout the day. Another
thinks that beginning an exercise program is good to manage
stress and so routinely requires this commitment as an adjunct to
sessions. Many practitioners have their own favorite tasks that
they believe are good for what ails folks—reading an assigned
book, seeing a recommended movie, joining a support group,
tending a garden, practicing meditation, doing mental exercises,
completing worksheets, or some other standard practice.

The reasoning behind these generic tasks is quite sound and
uniformly accepted—we can't help people just by talking to them
for an hour a week; they've got to do something, to act, to apply
what they are learning, or to break loose from old habits that are
getting in the way. There are limitations, however, to stocking our
therapeutic warehouse with one kind of shoe to fit everyone. And
we are not talking about increasing the inventory to include just a

few different sizes and colors and styles. We are saying that a shaman has no warehouse at all or, at least, not one that contains a ready supply of articles made for walking.

If we are to take what shamans can teach us about the use of therapeutic rituals and tasks, then we must expand the range and the scope of what is possible. Rather than solely relying on logical, linear thinking about what is good for people ("You want to lose weight? Start working out."), we can also customize and individualize activities in ways that resonate more with a client's own experience and our own intuition. This is no different from the therapist who creates metaphors out of the client's own language and narrative, versus the practitioner who has a collection of ready-made metaphors already stored on the shelf, selecting a best fit according to the particular situation. Obviously, custom-made products are more meaningful and durable.

The very challenge of writing a book is that we are trying to speak to thousands of different people. Each of you is looking for something different. You bought the book for different reasons. You are at different stages in your lives. You are working in varied jobs, hold different values, and are following different paths. You speak a hundred or more different languages. You represent dozens of ethnicities and national origins. And your perceptual systems are individualized such that it can be argued that you are each reading different books.

If we gathered together a few dozen of you in the same room, we could ask you, from memory, what the last paragraph said to you (No peeking!).

"You said we are all different," one of you calls out.

"No, you really were saying that we are all the same in our differences," another says.

"You're both wrong," a voice says. "You were taking a position to get me to think about my relationship with my mother and how she always tries to control me."

"Huh?" the guy next to her says, "What the hell are you talking about? There was no mother mentioned in that paragraph. They were just trying to wrap up the chapter by summarizing a key point that therapeutic rituals work best when they are customized to individuals using the practitioner's intuition and the client's own resources."

"So you say," she argues back. "When I read that paragraph, I started thinking about my mother and what she . . ."

And on and on it would go.

One point we wish to make as we bring this particular discussion to a close (even if it is not the point that poked you) is that the whole prospect of trying to connect with, and influence, as diverse audience as might be reading these very words is that there is nothing we can say that would be useful or memorable to everyone. We didn't write a book with one interpretation, meaning, or intention but a book filled with many possible opportunities for understanding and misunderstanding. From this perspective, you are holding thousands of different books in your hands at this very moment, and one of them is customized to fit you.

Keeney Tells One More Story to Confuse You Further

There was a little kitten who told a little girl not to read the story you are now reading.

She read the story anyway.

The kitten turned into the girl. And the girl turned into the kitten.

The girl, who was now a kitten, begged the kitten, who was now a little girl, to read the story she was not supposed to read.

The kitten and the girl lived many lives, going back and forth between becoming one another.

One day they forgot who they had originally been.

They never remembered.

Then they forgot that they had forgotten.

At that moment they turned into the words that became the story you are not supposed to read.

Chapter Thirteen

Paradox
and Duality

"We live in a world in which the holders of ancient wisdom have been too easily trivialized," Keeney said, as we resumed our conversation. As the sun was starting to penetrate the surprisingly delicate leaves of this huge tree, we moved within the shade of our dining tent. Pesky flies renewed their attacks to suck the few beads of moisture from our bodies before they evaporated. From the tunnel viewpoint of the open tent, we could see termite mounds more than 10 feet high. They looked like sentinels in the form of oversized wizards' hats.

"You feel rather strongly about this," Jeffrey reflected mildly. We could see Brad's passion brewing.

"Everything in our culture is simplified, as if all understanding may be reduced to opposing forces—light and dark, good and evil, ugly and beautiful, sickness and health. Things are often expressed as polar opposites, including the role of healer: We are supposed to minimize pain and maximize gain."

In so doing, Keeney felt that we undercut the true complexity of life. This is so unlike many indigenous cultures, where things like good and evil are not seen as opposing forces but rather as part of the same thing. We thus fail to recognize the paradox in our ways of thinking because we think that if something hurts, you just get rid of it; if it is good, then get as much of it as you can.

Yet too much oxygen is toxic. If you eat too much, drink too much water, or exercise too much, it is also not good for you. If you give too many gifts to your children, this can become toxic as well. If you obtain too much knowledge, it can become toxic. It is in the interaction between opposing polarities that balance is found.

The implications of this observation are profound and not at all expected. "This means," Keeney said, "that it is good at times to become sick. It is good to have a marital fight. Gregory Bateson used to say that having a good marriage is like standing up in a canoe. If you try to stand straight without moving, so that everything remains perfectly calm, then you will surely topple over into the lake. The only way you can stand up in a canoe is to rock, to keep moving back and forth; once you remain still, you fall over. It is like this with a marriage as well: you need to have good arguments and crises to keep things in balance."

Keeney mentioned the consequences of avoiding sickness, which makes you a bigger target for the next disease that can take you out with one shot. Yet a history of previous sicknesses helps to immunize you against future ones. The immune system needs to be exercised to remain in top fitness. So it is with our personal lives, according to the shaman. We must go through pilgrimages of suffering, from which one can recover with even greater resources and imagination. You can't get the Holy Grail without slaying a few dragons (and getting burned) along the way.

Death and Resurrection

The key experience to becoming a shaman is enacting a death and resurrection experience. Almost every shamanic tradition sends the initiate into an ordeal, whether fasting, being bitten by poisonous ants, or submitting oneself to extreme physical or mental conditions. In each of these trials, the shaman must go through a death-like experience and walk through the fire, so to speak. We are not talking about the fire walking of a New Age workshop, where no pain is actually felt; we are speaking about being burned deeply and thoroughly by the fire—being thrown into the kiln to be remolded and reshaped.

Many shamans around the world, regardless of whether they live in the jungles, the deserts, the forests, the high mountains, or the plains, talk about their calling in terms of the suffering they have undergone. Throughout his various explorations, Keeney himself has been required to go through week-long fasts, praying for days without rest or nourishment. He has survived standing in a fire to burn his feet. In each of the cultures he has visited and lived, he has been invited to enter their spiritual worlds through a form of death and rebirth that was prescribed. For a shaman, you must lose your old life in order to find a new one as a healer. And there is no shortcut to this path.

Keeney will not find this the least surprising, but as these very words were being written, Jeffrey was visited by a student who waited shyly outside the door of his office. The student could see that Jeffrey was busy typing away on his computer, so she stood patiently, waiting to be recognized and invited inside.

Jeffrey could see her shadow looming over the entrance but still felt reluctant to stop the flow of words; he was on a roll. With a sigh to himself, he turned and greeted the student warmly. "Hey, there!" he said cheerfully, recognizing her from an undergraduate class he was teaching on leadership skills. "Come on in!"

Nadia arranged herself in the seat and seemed to gather herself together. She was older than the other students in this undergraduate class, perhaps in her late 20s. As is not uncommon of people in this part of the world, she exhibited features of several different cultures—part Latina, part Asian.

"So, what can I do for you?" Jeffrey said, seeing the student's discomfort.

In the ensuing half hour, Nadia told a brief story about the disappointment and discouragement she felt in being denied admission into the graduate program. She did not express the usual complaints or pleading that are often heard in such situations; rather, she was matter-of-factly wondering what she could do to strengthen her application for the next admissions process.

"Well," Jeffrey responded, "what was the problem in your application the first time? Why weren't you admitted?" He was not actually involved in the selection process, but he had noted that Nadia seemed like a very capable student in class and had done quite well on her assignments.

Nadia nodded. "I've had a hard life," she said. "Ever since junior high school, I've had a drug problem. Meth and speed. Cocaine. Some hard drinking. I don't even remember my high school years much and college was just a fog. So my grade point average doesn't meet the minimum required."

"I see," Jeffrey said, realizing exactly why she had been denied. She probably hadn't even made it to the interview stage because her academic record was not good enough.

"But that was many years ago," Nadia continued. "I went into rehab and got my life back together. I've been clean for over 7 years. But it's been hard for me."

Indeed, it had. There was a history of abuse in her family. Poverty as well. And she had struggled most of her life with her own cultural identity, being caught between parents who came from different ethnicities and backgrounds. Then she absolutely hit bottom, losing everything important in her life—her job, her friends, her boyfriend, her parents' trust and support, and, most of all, her own self-respect.

"I thought about killing myself," Nadia said casually. "I figured what's the use anyway since I was already dead? Nobody would care what happened to me, and I certainly didn't care about myself. Being dead was the same as being alive to me. I just didn't have the energy to die; it was too much trouble."

At this point, Jeffrey stopped the story for a moment and looked at Brad. They were meeting together sometime after this had occurred. "Isn't that amazing that this happened just as I was writing about the death and rebirth?"

"It is amazing, indeed," he agreed. "But there's one part missing."

"What do you mean?" Jeffrey asked.

"Just that a shaman would take this to the next step. The woman would have to give up. Perhaps she'd go to her grandmother and ask the old woman to talk about dreams. It might go something like this . . .

My grandmother, she is a bruja, a curandera. When I told her I didn't want to live anymore, she asked me about my dreams. I told her about my recurring nightmare, the way a man with eight arms came chasing me with a knife in each hand. He would cut me up and throw me away. My grandmother seemed to know what was going on. She held a cleansing ceremony for me that lasted through the night. She kept praying and praying over me. In her house, listening to the comforting sounds of her voice as she prayed through the

*night, I had a special dream. I saw my grandmother put to-
gether all the chopped up pieces of my body, bringing them together as a whole. When I woke up, my grandmother said I
looked different. And that is the way I felt. She told me that
God was making me a healer.*

Jeffrey nodded, hearing the familiar story of what so many
shamans describe about their own existential deaths and re-
births. Here was a young woman sitting before him who had gone
through the fire, who had her soul singed and her spirit suffo-
cated, but somehow, she had survived.

Jeffrey was just about to give Nadia the standard spiel in such a
circumstance, that she needed to raise her grade point average,
that she needed to demonstrate better her ability to succeed aca-
demically, when he glanced over at his computer screen. He could
see the vertical black line of the cursor blinking in the middle of a
sentence above, which was talking about how shamans must be
reborn through the trials they face in life. And now, sitting before
him, was a young woman who desperately wanted to be a helper
and a healer herself. That was her calling. That was the path she
was determined to follow, no matter how many rejections she experienced or obstacles she had to overcome.

It is not unusual among members of the helping profession that
we chose this work because of our own wounds and traumas that
we suffered. It is also relatively common that counselors, especially those who work in the area of substance abuse, are re-
cruited from among those who have experienced similar problems
and have recovered from them. This is not a requirement of the
job, most certainly, but there is no substitute for life experience,
rather than textbook learning.

In the few moments that Jeffrey glanced over at the computer
screen and then back toward this student who was seeking the
healing path, he recalled the words that he had just written. And
yet here was a new initiate who was facing him, someone who
had *lived* inside the kiln, who faced trials by fire and repeatedly
had her feet (and soul) burned. He didn't know whether or not
Nadia would gain admission to this particular program, but he
told her that this really didn't really matter much in the bigger
scheme of things. If this particular group did not choose her, that
would be their loss as much as hers; she would find somewhere to
pursue her studies. Of that, Jeffrey had no doubt.

Nadia smiled gratefully and extended her hand. "Thanks so much," she said. "I know what I need to do now. I always knew it, I guess, but now I've got some options. And some hope." Then she smiled in a way to signal that she really meant that, really felt that.

As Nadia walked out of the office, Jeffrey was left staring at the computer screen again. Just as he had been thinking and writing about the shaman's process of death and resurrection, a prospective apprentice appeared who had *lived* that exact journey. It is one of the paradoxes of learning to be a helper and a healer in our culture that we don't recruit and mentor the same kinds of prospects that healers would in other parts of the world. We might consider life experiences a little, but mostly, we are looking for the ability to take tests and write papers, the signs of academic success, and tasks that have little to do with the actual job at hand. Of course, our intentions are good and noble, but this is only one reason why shamans around the world consider our practices to be as strange and "primitive" as we might consider theirs.

Shamans all over the world talk about their own death and resurrection. It is not enough that they merely suffered or experienced trauma; they actually had to die from the ordeal—at least, existentially and spiritually speaking. "The Holy Rollers talk about this a lot," Keeney said, "but for a lot of them, it is just talk. Among shaman apprentices, they speak a lot about their waking dreams of being chopped up and eaten by monsters. Life gives you a bad deal. You surrender and allow yourself to die. Then you reach out for the sacred, and with a bit of luck and perseverance, there is a transformation. Without this death experience, it's all talk without serious intent."

Evil and Good Intentions

Paradox is so much a part of other cultures that ideas we ordinarily consider polarities are seen elsewhere as part and parcel of the same thing. Take good and evil, for instance. In Bali, the people believe that some people are destined to be good and others to be bad. They don't wish to change this, because everyone has a role that is important. If someone is called to the dark side, it is necessary that this person walk that road and not try to be something he or she is not. To do otherwise is to upset the balance of things. Besides, that person would just be replaced by someone else.

Through our cultural lens we tend to look at things morally, rather than ecologically. We would be appalled at former traditions in the South Pacific, where the people managed to avoid costly wars by conducting ritualistic battles every so often, in which a few individuals were sacrificed for the greater good.

This point reminded Keeney of the work of Victor Frankl (1962), the existential theorist and Holocaust survivor. Suffering not only provides a challenge for finding meaning but is *necessary* for creating greater meaning. This is the same insight that lies at the core of many world religions, even though helpers and healers in our culture become obsessed with finding the primary reason for suffering and then seek to obliterate it.

"Is it faulty genes?" Keeney asked. "Or faulty learning? Perhaps abusive parents? It is always something to blame. We are always looking for the alleged reason why things don't go according to plan, and in so doing, we chop the world into dualisms."

As a counterpoint to this perspective, Keeney mentioned places like Bali, Africa, and the Navajo reservation, where their ancient traditions respect the importance of both good and evil, pleasure and pain. Beauty is only possible when there is ugliness. Kali is the Hindu god of evil, and without evil, there would be no good, there would be no change, there would be no motivation to be different. Life is ordered around the tension of two or more forces; if one is cut off, then they both die.

How can there be a sunny day without a dark night? Without pain, we would never be able to delight in the occasions of pleasure. With every victory medical science has achieved over bacterial and viral infections, Mother Nature simply comes back with a new one. With each victory over Nature, we raise the stakes. The diseases get more dangerous and the odds of extermination rise at an exponential rate. We need to learn how to get in bed with sickness, danger, suffering, and evil, if we are ever to have a peaceful night's sleep.

Footsteps on the Roof

Several years ago, in 1999, on a balmy tropical day, Keeney and his photographer, Kern, arrived at the international airport in Denpasar, Bali. They had come to interview and photograph the traditional healers of Bali (called *balians*), with the assistance of a colleague, Mr. I Wayan Budi Asa Mekel (also known simply as

"Budi"). Budi was arguably the top guide in Bali, having served in that capacity for numerous prestigious institutions. More important, he was the primary source (and voice) of information for *Sekala and Niskala,* the two-volume book series on Balinese culture.

They landed at the airport to find that their luggage had not followed them. When they checked with the airlines, there were no records (or even clues) as to where their bags might have gone. They now had no clothes, which was a little annoying, but they were also missing all of their recording and photographic equipment, as well as their research materials.

Whatever apprehensions they felt after being the last disgruntled passengers to leave the terminal, Budi's smile changed everything. He reassured them that he could help them to resupply and would do everything in his power to locate their missing luggage. "Everything's gonna work out," he reassured them in such a way that they had absolutely no doubt.

After arriving at the village where they would spend the night, Keeney retired for an early night's sleep. He was jet-lagged, exhausted, and still frustrated that all his things had been lost. So when he was awakened out of a deep sleep in the middle of the night (which was during the day, according to his own biological clock), he was more disoriented and groggy than usual. He shuffled into the bathroom to relieve himself, then crawled back into bed.

KERBOOOOM! It was the loudest explosion that he had ever heard. It seemed like the whole room was collapsing from the force. His first thought was that the village must be under some kind of guerrilla attack. He shook his head and then realized that it must have been an earthquake. Paralyzed with fear, he froze in position, waiting for the world to split open and swallow him.

There was an eerie silence, then a loud stomping sound coming from the roof. "Damn, this is even worse that an earthquake!" Keeney said to himself in a whisper. Terrorists were attacking, now walking on the roof, preparing to take him hostage or even kill him. This was not the first time something like this had happened. A few years back, while teaching at the University of South Africa, he had been staying at the home of one of his colleagues when they had been attacked by intruders. When bullets started flying, only diving underneath his bed to hide had saved his life. A minute later, one of the intruders had started to look underneath the bed, when Keeney's friend opened defensive fire, chasing them away.

With survival instincts honed from the repeated rehearsals he had practiced, Keeney again dived to the floor for safety. Just before crawling under cover of the bed, he noticed that the stomping of the footsteps seemed to move farther away. Then, curiously, they seemed to return again in his direction. But the odd thing is that the steps didn't sound urgent and menacing as much as they just felt heavy and solid. In fact, whatever was up there didn't sound human at all, more like some kind of creature. Keeney's overactive imagination at this point conjured up a picture of some Hulk-like or Godzilla-like being stomping around. He again froze in terror when he imagined that he was actually living in some type of Stephen King horror story.

But alas, rather than the sounds diminishing, they seemed to be getting louder. With each crash of a footstep (if, indeed, the creature even had feet!), the building shook and material from the thatched ceiling rained downward. Keeney could hear rocks and sand sliding off the end of the roof as well. He decided to wait for the beast to pause before making some kind of dash to safety.

A minute later, Keeney made a run for the bathroom and started screaming out the window. "Hey. HEY! Kern! ARE YOU THERE!" he called out to his friend. Before he could finish the cry, the noise got louder, seeming to track his own movements and head toward his new location. "HELP ME ! IS THERE ANYONE OUT THERE?"

Keeney actually felt that he had strained his voice, he had been yelling so loudly. But there was no response. This was strange because he knew other people were staying close by. Why wasn't anyone answering? Where *was* everyone? And what the hell was that thing doing on the roof?

Time to take inventory. Keeney was pretty sure he wasn't dreaming, nor was this a waking dream or a hallucination. He did a reality check to be sure, just the way a pilot might check the controls before takeoff. He had plenty of time to do this because, now that he was camped out in the bathroom, the sounds were continuing on and on, hardly just a momentary "strange sound in the night."

Praying is always a good option in such a predicament, so Keeney decided to try that for awhile. He had plenty of time to pray to the Christian God of his grandfather. In times of panic, he only prayed directly to his most personal connection to the Divine, the deity figure of his childhood. But nothing would stop the sounds. If anything, they seemed to become worse, rattling the doors as if it was trying to come inside.

Keeney isn't sure why he made this connection, but for some reason he started thinking about his missing luggage. If only he'd had his sound and photographic equipment with him, he could record what was going on. After all, who would believe him?

Keeney recalled reading somewhere that the Balinese like to make magical drawings about phenomena that seem mysterious or dangerous and then use them for protection and guidance. If ever there was a time for such help, it was certainly now. "I know what I'll do," he said to himself, now talking out loud as a child would to himself in the dark. "I'll ask Budi to get some drawings for me so I don't have to put up with this nightmare again tomorrow night."

As soon as he said these words, the footsteps immediately stopped. This was a considerable relief, of course, but it also made Keeney feel increased vigilance and caution. Did this being, this thing, hear him? Was he somehow supposed to do something? Then out loud: "Am I supposed to make a book of the drawings?"

There was an immediate noise again, but this time not heavy footsteps. Instead what he heard sounded very much like a flock of birds flying nearby, even through the room, although he could see nothing of the kind.

"This is absurd," Keeney said to himself. "I don't believe in these things. I've never believed . . ."

Before he could finish the sentence, the stomping began again, shaking the building so hard that Keeney feared the whole roof would collapse.

"Hey! Okay already!" he yelled out toward the ceiling. "I'll do what you want—whatever *that* is [he said under his breath]. Tomorrow, I'll get right on that book you want. No problem." What he didn't say, but thought to himself, was that there was no way he was ever staying in this place again. He was out of there at first light.

At least now there was silence and relative peace (although the rafters of the roof were still creaking from the strain they had suffered). Nevertheless, Keeney remained holed up in the bathroom, still too afraid to open the door for fear that the creature would return.

It may have been a few hours later—Keeney isn't sure because he fell asleep—that he heard footsteps again, but these were clearly the human kind approaching his door. Suddenly, he just broke out crying. He was terrified, exhausted, and totally confused. As he threw open the door and saw Budi waiting with his angelic smile, Brad ran up to him and hugged him, crying hysterically. Budi just soothed him, as if he was accustomed to this sort of thing all the time.

Once he calmed down, Keeney called his travel agent right away, "Look," he said, "you need to book a room for me. Right away. Make it the Ritz Carlton. And get me out of this place." Keeney figured that no self-respecting spirit would ever reside at the Ritz Carlton.

"What happened to you?" Budi said with real concern, noticing how distraught Keeney was (even after the crying had stopped).

Brad told him the whole story, complete with as many details as possible. He had stopped caring at this point whether or not anyone thought he was crazy. He knew that all this had happened.

Budi nodded without expression, showing neither surprise nor the indulgent expression that Keeney expected. "The big god of the island has made you a visit."

"You've heard of something like this before?" Keeney said with excitement. "You mean this doesn't sound totally crazy to you?"

"Oh, no," Budi shook his head up and down, which in Balinese means the same thing as when we shake it side to side. "The people here know about this. You must get dressed and I will make arrangements for you to speak with someone."

"Can you just tell me what happened?" Keeney pleaded, not wanting to wait for an explanation. He'd had some very weird experiences in his life but nothing like this, which had literally shaken his world so completely.

"As I have told you," Budi said in a calm, soothing voice. "The big god has come to you. His name is Jero Gede Macaling. He is the god for all shamans. He lives on a small island called Nusa Penida. I have made an appointment for us to see the top *balian* in Bali. She advises the heads of our government and is highly respected by other *balians*. She is waiting to see you."

Mangku Alit was indeed an impressive woman, who was known for her unique ritual of going into a trance. She would burn pieces of coconut shell in a bowl, then hold the flames and smoke close to her face, and disappear into a trance, where she claimed to become the voice for various spiritual sources.

After initial greetings, Mangku wasted no time getting ready for the ceremony. Offerings had been brought by Budi, and the shaman's apprentices had made the appropriate preparations. As the smoke rose, carrying her into a trance, Mangku began to speak in the voice of Jero Gede Macaling:

"Yes, it is so," the husky voice said. Although it was speaking out of Mangku's mouth, she appeared only as a wispy form in the smoke of the coconut shells. "The god wants you to do this thing that you have been asked. You have been given his permission not only to write a book about our *balians* but to tell about the magical drawings. This has rarely been discussed, the left side of magic. Furthermore, you must visit other *balians,* go to the island that houses the shrine of Jero Gede Macaling, and then you must return to the room where all of this took place. Special offerings, prayers, and ceremonies must be made."

By this point, almost nothing that happened in Bali would surprise Keeney. So, upon completing the collection of drawings, he soon thereafter received a phone call from the aiport, informing him that his luggage had been found. It had simply shown up, with no explanation as to its loss.

Before leaving Bali, Keeney did visit the island of Nusa Penida, accompanied by several priests. He was taken to Pura Dalem Peed, the shrine of Jero Gede Macaling, where he sat with the religious healers. During the ceremony, Keeney felt someone kick him on the side of the head. When he turned to see who it was, he was surprised that no one was near him. The priests were very happy to hear this because the god initiates someone into the *balian*'s way of knowing by stepping on the person's head with his foot.

As he got up from the shrine floor, Keeney turned to see Mangku Alit standing at the entrance. "I didn't know that you were planning on visiting the island on this day," he said to her.

She smiled and nodded, acknowledging that it was a very auspicious day. To complete the final task set before him, in spite of his continued apprehensions, Keeney returned to the room on the main island, as he had been directed. Again he was awakened in the middle of the night, but this time not by heavy footsteps but by the soothing sound of the rain. Thinking nothing about it, he returned to sleep. The next morning, Brad found that it had actually been raining *in* the room because everything inside was thoroughly soaked. His papers were soaked on the desk. His clothes were wet, even though they had been inside an armoire with a tight door. Curiously, everything else in the room—the floor, the furniture—was completely dry!

Keeney gazing at the masked figure of Jero Gede Macaling,
the god of Balinese shamans.

"As I prepared to leave Bali," Keeney recalled, "Budi told me
that he and his workers had examined the roof of the room and
found that it was filled with sand and rocks. These materials were
not used when they put the roof together." He remembered the
sound of the stomping and how the sand and rocks had slid down
the roof. However, his memory carried no association of fear but
held a glimpse of a truth and a mystery he would never fully understand. He was taught that we must learn to live with good and
evil, terror and peace, suffering and joy.

Get Down and Dirty

We asked Keeney to relate this idea of paradoxes and dualities to
the practice of therapy.

"It makes it easier to have compassion for others, even those
you might judge critically. No matter what someone has done,
whether they have harmed their children or engaged in atrocities,
they are still no different from anyone else. We are all the same.
They were just stupid enough to act on the impulses that all of us
have within us."

"Isn't this just Rogerian unconditional acceptance?"

"In one sense, perhaps," Keeney said. "But Rogers's position can be seen as very arrogant."

"How so?"

"Thinking that you have to muster up some inner regard for others in order to love them. The paradox is that this actually maintains a bigger difference between you and those you help."

Seeing our confusion, Keeney expanded the thought. "It is as if you are the great blessed ones who see with compassionate eyes and love those who are beneath you."

"And how is what you propose all that different?"

"Shamans believe—they *know*—that they are just as messed up as anyone else. We are rascals just like anyone else. It is no accident that a great number of shamans have been drunks, womanizers, convicts, diseased, and subject to terrible misfortunes. In fact, the best qualification for becoming a shaman is that you have already survived the first lesson of ordeals."

Keeney cited the life of Lame Deer of the Lakota Indians in South Dakota as one example. His biography was written by Richard Erdoes (Lame Deer & Erdoes, 1973), an Austrian Jewish refugee from Hitler's Nazi regime. Keeney happens to know quite a bit about this story because he is writing an oral history of Erdoes, whose background is just as colorful as that of his Native American collaborators. In his biography of Lame Deer, Erdoes ended up writing the definitive Native American story, which chronicled the life of one of the most powerful medicine men.

"Yet Lame Deer was a drunk and a rascal," Keeney said. "I'm not saying you have to be a drunk or wounded in order to be a shaman. I'm not saying you have to rob a bank or commit murder. But if you sin, sin boldly; it brings you down to your own humanity. A good shaman knows that he or she is just as worthless as anyone else."

One crucial difference is that shamans learn their craft from their own trials and tribulations. In our culture, prospective helpers and healers go to school, where they sit in comfortable, climate-controlled classrooms and have polite conversations, listen passively, and read assigned readings, in order to join the guild. But true shamans are required to learn life lessons from pain and agony that come only through life experience.

Referring back to Carl Rogers's notions of unconditional acceptance of others, Keeney mentioned that the shaman is not saying to others, I do not judge you because I am a big person, but because I am as messed up as you are. Who am I to judge you when I am no better than you?

"That is the irony of the debate between Carl Rogers and B. F. Skinner many years ago. Rogers was saying that people are basically good and Skinner said that they, like all animals, are neutral, neither innately good nor bad. Skinner was actually closer to the mark, at least as far as shamans are concerned."

"So Skinner was the real humanist, huh?"

"Paradoxically, that is right. He is the one who said we are no better than pigeons. But it repulsed social scientists to have people trivialized, thrown into the same category as rats. Yet this actually produces a great spiritual insight to realize that we are no more divine than a sparrow. That is part of the most ancient wisdom of the world's oldest religions.

"Shamans are really the practitioners of the world's religions, as much, if not more so, than the Billy Grahams and the Dalai Lamas who are the voices of mainstream orthodoxies."

Keeney finds it interesting that intellectuals, scholars, theologians, anthropologists, and rabbis love reading the sacred texts of ancient religions and love hearing the old wisdom stories. They like to debate the finer points of the texts and argue about what things really mean. But when it comes down to the grassroots practice of religion, where we declare we are no more than a gnat, that is where most of them draw the line.

"If you want to go full force into shamanic tradition," Keeney said, "you can't just read a book about it. You've got to get down and dirty to experience things and lower yourself firsthand."

Authentic Compassion

So, how do helpers and healers use these ideas in their work? How do we not only live with the paradoxes of life but utilize them?

"First we must practice *authentic* compassion, not the sort that is faked by judgers and do-gooders. We must see ourselves in everyone whom we help and realize that we are all the same. This is true humility."

Keeney recasts humility as something other than modesty about one's achievements. He confronts the kind of arrogance and narcissism that pervades the field, where we pretend we are the same as our clients but know deep down inside that we are far better than they are.

"The greatest sins have little to do with the Ten Commandments. The latter are the sorts of lapses that come from stupidity or crimes of passion and impulsivity. Theft, murder, adultery, cheating, can all be pardoned if we truly understand forgiveness. But the greatest of sins is pride."

According to Keeney, pride is the result of narcissistic circular indulgence. A sense of false pride is what leads to arrogant good intentions. But the shaman does not hold such illusions: She knows that what may seem good can end up being evil in disguise. More of something can sometimes mean less.

And this is what leads the shaman (and some therapists) to prescribe paradoxical tasks, knowing that we can sometimes make things far worse by proceeding in a literal, linear way. When someone comes in and complains that he can't sleep, can't study, can't concentrate, can't get out of bed, we need to view these symptoms as teachers and guides. We must respect them. If we follow their direction, we can become a helping, resourceful presence.

Paradox as Treatment

"Whenever a family comes in," Keeney said, "and says there is a bad child who needs to be fixed, immediately you know there is an overly rigid good child as well. Clinical wisdom, from the shamanic point of view, might suggest to the parents that they should encourage the good child to loosen up as much as they get on the bad child. This helps address harmony and balance in the context."

Historically, Keeney pointed out that paradox was used in healing long before therapy ever rediscovered it. Shamans have been using paradox for thousands of years. All great rabbis, country preachers, and horse-and-buggy doctors knew about what worked and what did not. They might not have understood systems theory or ecology, but they learned how one could say what, on the surface, appeared to be the "wrong" thing, yet get the "right" result.

We do this intuitively when we say to a resistant client: "Yeah, there's no reason why you should trust me. *I* wouldn't trust me if I were you." And this, paradoxically, becomes the basis for trust.

The most obvious example of this from our field is the work of Milton Erickson. Keeney has been interviewing Erickson's daughter, therapist Betty Alice Erickson, for a book that portrays the master healer as our field's greatest wisdom teacher. Keeney considers it significant that Erickson began his journey the way most shamans do: by facing ordeals and obstacles that must be overcome. After surviving a bout of polio and being told by the doctor that he would never live through the night, Erickson told himself that he would stay up all night long without closing his eyes. He would stare at a dresser mirror positioned so that he could see out the window until the sun rose. Then, when he survived the night, he later resolved that although he could not walk, he would aim to paddle a canoe down the Mississippi River as part of his ordeal to become a presence in the world.

"This is the stuff of shamanic folklore," Keeney summarized. "To everyone who knows Erickson's work, his key principle was utilizing whatever the client brought to him. He made himself an ally of the symptoms, rather than seeing them as the enemy to be defeated." Gregory Bateson correctly defined Erickson's place in the history of psychotherapy, Keeney likes to quote, as "the Mozart of all the helping traditions."

Respect for Pathology and Sickness

One of the most interesting paradoxical ideas of the shaman is that symptoms and problems are not viewed as bad. A shaman would never use the language of diagnosis in the same ways we might talk about symptoms and pathology. The shaman would recognize and respect the suffering as a teacher and urge the client to do the same. It is seen as a gift that can become an ally, a guide, and a cotherapist, rather than an enemy. And, as Milton Erickson noted, the symptoms provide the direction for the course of intervention.

The Zulu shamans, or *sangomas,* have a favored method called "changing the mask." A young man was being pressured to leave the village and find a wife, but he refused. His family was disappointed, and many in the community were upset by this stubbornness. After speaking with the young man for some time, Credo Mutwa, the shaman we introduced earlier, learned that the boy was extremely attached to his mother; he worshiped her and was unwilling to leave her.

"If you could marry," Credo asked the man, "what sort of woman would you take as your wife?"

"Someone just like my mother," he said without hesitation.

Credo told the mother that she was to find someone in the community or a nearby village who looked as much like her as possible. The mother did this, located such a potential bride, and the son was satisfied. He married her and everything worked out.

A therapist in our culture might have labeled the young man as having an unresolved oedipal complex, an attachment disorder, or co-dependency. The Zulu shaman, however, used what the young man presented without labeling or diagnosing it as evidence of pathology. Such a thing is not feared or even named.

We had to take an intermission at this juncture because Brad and Jon got into an argument about whether diagnostically naming the problem is, in fact, a useful thing to do. Brad insisted that a shaman would never do such a thing, whereas Jon argued that it helped to get a handle on what was being presented.

"Maybe it helps *you*," countered Keeney. "But I'm not sure it helps the client."

"Some people feel more comfortable having a name for what is bothering them," Jon persisted.

"But to label and name it is to concretize it. Instead of adding more mystery to the situation, which is what a shaman would do, you extract the mystery the way a psychologist would do."

"But that's what I am!"

"Exactly!" Keeney replied.

"Okay, boys," Jeffrey intervened. "Where were we? You were saying that it's not good to make the problem more concrete."

"Yes," Keeney agreed, picking up the thread, "people come to us after they have already drowned themselves in self-reflection over an assumed life problem. They have talked to their friends about it. They have talked to their family about it. They have talked to themselves until they are sick of it. They lie in bed at night dreaming about it, and first thing in the morning, they start thinking more about their damn problem. It's a never ending soap opera rerun. Then they go to a professional who wants to talk about it even *more!*"

Keeney maintained that it is because we are so uncomfortable with ambiguity, complexity, uncertainty, and mystery that we insist on giving the problem a name. And this name, this diagnosis, fossilizes the situation, which makes it even more difficult for the client to escape from it.

"So, what would the shaman do instead?" Jon asked. "If he wouldn't name the problem, what would he do?"

Keeney shrugged. "He'd say this is life. It hurts."

Jon scoffed. "Shamans don't have to deal with insurance companies. They don't have to deal with managed care."

"Ah, but that is a different story," Keeney said. "Now you are talking about business and getting paid. I thought we were talking about helping people."

Looking to defuse the conflict, Jeffrey asked, "But, Brad, if a shaman was going to have a diagnostic scheme, what would it look like?"

"Wouldn't have one," Brad insisted.

"We know that. But let's say a Bushman shaman, one of the fellows down that path . . ." Jeffrey pointed toward the parting in the bush that led to the village.

Keeney said that such a *Bushman DSM and Treatment Manual* might look something like this:

1. Remove dirty arrows and those shot by malevolent spirits.
2. Clean those arrows that can be cleaned.
3. Insert more arrows.

"That's it?"

"Yup," Keeney said. "As I said, they're not very big on trying to resolve paradoxes or name things that, to them, should remain mysterious."

Of course, shamans disagree among themselves just as often as a group of therapists or teachers might do so. And within the different indigenous cultures, there is a great variety of methods used to assess problems. Some Shamans might gaze into crystals in a trance state, examine tea leaves, read palms, or examine the patterns of burning embers. The Bushmen like to use their senses of smell and taste. The Dine use hand trembling.

"And aren't they looking to give a name to the problem that is presented?" Jon pressed again. "Isn't there a difference to them between 'arrows' that need cleaning versus those that must be replaced?"

"Not really."

"What, then?"

Keeney smiled. "There is no answer. Let me tell you a fairy tale that explains the whole of psychiatry."

"Once upon a time a confused person came to a psychiatrist's office to seek help for her situation. Everyone was complaining about this person and she was miserable, finding herself very anxious and unpredictable. As the psychiatrist listened to her story, he felt very anxious himself. He became so worried and concerned about what she might say or do that he immediately gave her a tranquilizer. And the psychiatrist immediately felt less anxious and more relaxed."

We laughed in appreciation. "So, Brad, what you're saying is that the psychiatrist could have given himself the tranquilizer and achieved the same outcome."

"You got it. That's the way a cybernetician sees the situation. Things are circularly connected. The meaning of the client's behavior is found in the therapist's behavior, and vice versa.

"The difference between the Western therapist and the Bushman shaman is that the Bushman knows, respects, and honors this circularity. The Bushman doctor dances to feel better and, as a circular consequence, some healing of others may occur. He gives a nail in order to prepare himself for receiving one. The Bushman embraces these natural paradoxes of life and is not tempted to take a conceptual hammer and try to flatten the world of experience into any flat-planed view, explanation, and behavioral strategy for acting on others. That is the difference that makes a difference, my friends. Say yes to the circles of life and don't get lost in the illusory lines."

Chapter Fourteen

Love over Power

Most Westerners associate shamanism with the tales of Don Juan, as told by the anthropologist Carlos Castaneda. In his fictionalized account of Yaqui sorcery, Castaneda (1973) portrayed the shaman as someone who attains greater power through the drug-induced dream states that allowed for closer communication with the spirits. The general idea was that an apprentice sorcerer would, under the guidance of a mentor, journey into the spirit world in order to combat evil by accumulating power and overcoming bad intentions. This is not unlike the sort of classic, mythological tales depicted by Joseph Campbell (1990), in his historical review of heroic adventures throughout the ages. Myths of all cultures, from Hercules and Samson to Star Wars, portray the hero as someone who goes on a quest to obtain greater power or "the force."

Learning to Be a Shaman in Three Easy Lessons

As we discussed earlier, much of the interest in shamanic practices has flowed in two directions: either the use of hallucinogenic substances to induce altered states of consciousnesses or the use of other means (like drum circles or sweat lodges) to find greater power within each individual.

Keeney shook his head at this unimaginative state of affairs and the general reputation that shamanism has earned in our culture. "Some of these characters," Keeney said, "build businesses like Amway. They develop commercial drumming tapes. They run weekend workshops in 'How to Be a Shaman.' They have everyone in the audience do a little visual imagery so they can find their 'power animal,' like an elk or a rhino, and this is supposed to make all the difference. It's the same kind of pop psychology theater that sells everywhere."

Again Brad shook his head in disbelief. The very idea that someone could extract the essence of being a shaman in a weekend seminar seemed ridiculous. But this all feeds the very idea that personal power can be increased incrementally by following certain practices. And this power will give one greater control and influence over others to do one's bidding.

"It's no different with therapy," Keeney added.

"You're saying that therapy is just a quick-fix gimmick like these weekend shaman workshops?"

"In one sense, yes," Keeney answered. "But instead of looking for power, people are looking for knowledge. It's all the same thing. Everyone wants some sort of leverage to get them more of what they want. Even helpers and healers in our culture are always looking for ways to use their power to manipulate people to change. Yet in my own journeys, I have not found this to be the case. The elders I have been fortunate to meet, the medicine men and women, the witchdoctors and the healers, have not been about increasing power but about bringing forth and cultivating love."

We warned Keeney that he was now treading on sacred ground. Love is a four-letter word in our field. We *never* talk about love in the context of helping, whether as teachers, therapists, or physicians. Love conjures up ideas of romance, of the ethereal, of irrational feelings that can neither be measured nor even understood. It is the stuff of songs and stories but is never associated with what we do in our work.

Keeney likes to use the image of "Cupid's arrows" as a metaphor for the way mutually expressed feelings of love can pierce our hearts and open the door to deep experiences of intimate relationship. *Eros,* the passionate longing for skin-to-skin contact and sensual interaction, is one sort of love that Keeney likens to "red hot" arrows. *Familial love* and *agape,* the truest forms of brotherly and sisterly love, move us to think about how we can be present to others without concern for our own solitary satisfaction or gain. This love, brought about by Cupid's "blue-hot" arrows, is evident in parents who feel willing to make any sacrifice for their children. It also underlies meaningful social stewardship in the family and the community. Finally, *mystical* love, or *nomos,* the most powerful experience anyone can imagine, is the blissful realization and contact with Supreme Love, the mystic's union with the Divine. According to Keeney, this is the work of Cupid's "white-hot" arrows.

"I believe that the red, blue, and white arrows are actually different manifestations of one arrow," Keeney explained further. "They are derived from the single arrow of love. It is the amount of passionate heat that changes the color of the arrow. Moving from the red-hot arrow of love where each person wants to dissolve into the other, blue-hot love is more intimate and intense, where you forget and even sacrifice yourself and solely attend to serving the beloved. The hottest flame of passion turns the arrow white and pierces the deepest core of your heart, bringing mystical revelation, divine illumination, and classic spiritual awakening. Here the difference between you, the other, and the sacred originating source of love, all dissolve and become an eternal moment of undifferentiated ecstatic bliss."

Keeney cited many mystics and shamans who have found many paths that lead to the burning flames of the divine heart. One common description in this literature describes experiences in which the healer's insides felt like they were on fire.

"What about you?" we asked him. "When did you first feel the blue-white hot arrows strike you in the soul?"

Keeney smiled and nodded. He took a moment to consider how he wanted to frame the story, knowing full well how uncomfortable secular readers might feel about anything that smacks of religious fervor.

"I was 19," Keeney began, "when I had the most remarkable experience of my entire life. A year and a half before, I had won the international science fair and received scholarship offers to numerous universities. I arrived at the university as a complete nerd, with a slide rule dangling on my belt. That was a time when social protest and activism had spread across the country and, like so many others of our generation, my social consciousness was awakened and disturbed by the inequalities I found around

Keeney with his science project, which won
First Prize at the International Science Fair,
Fort Worth, Texas, 1969.

me. I turned to music, my other passion, and began composing songs as a means of expressing the feelings that were churning inside me during that turbulent time.

"One evening, as I walked by the university library, I felt a deep sense of peace and calm come over my entire body. As I continued moving, my body felt lighter and lighter until I could feel no weight at all. I could have sworn that I was gliding across the sidewalk. My legs continued to move, but I had no sense of moving them. They walked me right into the campus chapel, where I sat down on the front pew."

Keeney mentioned that one of the things that made this altered state so remarkable for him at the time was that he had been so sheltered, he had never tried drugs of any kind, nor had he even tasted alcohol. About the closest thing he had known to a transcendent experience was when he played or listened to music. Yet once he entered the chapel, he felt a fire in his belly, as if a divine force was touching him. "This ball of fire slowly and surely crept up my back, and as it did, I began to feel multiple heartbeats within my chest. It continued climbing upward through my throat and finally all the way to the top of my head. As this fire worked itself up, my body became hotter by the moment. Sweat dripped from every pore and I began shaking. I felt like I had been struck by some kind of lightning bolt. I jerked and began to shake all over, ripples of energy pulsing through my abdomen, legs, feet, arms, and hands.

"Most important, my heart opened in some kind of mysterious way. I felt love in a way I never knew was possible. There was no one I could imagine, even the worst of enemies, who did not deserve to be the object of this love. I was having a genuine mystical experience, the sort of thing written about by the early Christian, Sufi, Jewish, Buddhist, and Hindu mystics. It did not stop with the heat and body shaking and deeply felt emotion. I began to weep. Water flowed from my eyes, along with the sweat from my pores, and that ball of fire came right out of the top of my head. It came out as steam or a white cloud and situated itself about 5 feet directly in front of me.

"The light was a white oval-shaped light about the size of a person. Its edges were not finely formed, but soft and irregular like those of a cloud in the sky. Inside this light I saw one saint after another, beginning with Jesus. As I looked at this vision, I felt more heat and love and rippling currents across my skin. There was direct communication, a divine communion that took place as I looked into the eyes of the holy ones standing in front of me. I felt the transmission of love, a love that carried wisdom, peace, joy, and unspecified knowing. It was not a knowing of words with narrative structure, but a connection to something vast and beyond intellectual comprehension.

"I hypothesized that I was being rewired and hooked up to the primal source of love. I knew that the greatest wisdom, most important knowledge, purest creativity, most important power, and deepest mystery were entirely rooted to this divine love. The whole of my body experienced, right there and then, the greatest truth a human being can ever realize. I witnessed, firsthand, what my grandparents and parents had taught me since I was old enough to hear their words: 'God is love.' 'In the beginning was love.' 'All that is important is love.' 'Of all the gifts, love is the greatest gift.'

"This experience did not last just a few minutes. I sat in that chapel throughout the night. It was difficult to move myself out of the rapture I felt, though I finally managed to stand up and walk back to my dormitory room, but doing so with my head bowed over. Whenever I looked up, I felt the light returning and I was afraid that I would succumb and never come out of it again. This was because the luminosity I beheld was so beautiful, sweet, vast, and glorious that it would be difficult, if not impossible, to look away from it again."

It was years later that Keeney heard about people who had near-death experiences, describing a light at the end of a mystical tunnel. They reported how difficult it was to walk away from the light and return to their daily lives.

I know just what they were talking about," Keeney said, "but in my case, I had a near-life experience. I came face-to-face with the power that gives life its heart and soul. I was never the same after that evening in the chapel."

The Orchid Grower

From that age of 19, Keeney felt motivated, if not possessed, to seek out others who had experienced similar transcendent experiences of love. He pursued this mission quietly and secretly, not wanting anyone else to know about what happened. Perhaps others would think he was crazy or some kind of religious freak. It was better to proceed as cautiously as possible. And this, in part, is what led him to move away from conventional psychology toward the wider traditions of ancient healing practices.

Keeney fondly recalled the work of Ikuko Osumi, one of the most renowned healers in Japan and a master of *seiki jutsu* whom we mentioned earlier. Even with her remarkable healing abilities, it is not power that is most associated with her practice.

"I have never in my life," Keeney recalled with a smile, "met anyone who is so dedicated to the care of her patients. Everyone whom I have taken to see her says the same thing. She screens everything out of her awareness except being completely present and mindful toward those she is helping. Most of the patients who come to see her have already been abandoned by experts in the most noted hospitals around the world. She puts them in a bed right next to her in her own home. She attends to them. She watches them and observes every aspect of their being. She feeds them. She makes them a special tea or prepares a special dish, noting how they respond with total concentration. She checks their pulses in the ancient Oriental way. She gives them massages and tells them how important it is for them to rest. Her life is totally devoted to caring for her patients."

Keeney shook his head, still amazed that anyone could be so selfless and so committed to helping others. It is one thing for a therapist to spend an hour a week with a patient and give this person our reasonably undivided attention (when we aren't lost in our own plans and fantasies), but Ikuko actually invites the patients to live with her! She is famous throughout her land for growing orchids, those that cannot easily survive. She sees her patients as rare orchids as well, each one requiring constant individual attention.

Osumi, Sensei, teaches the side of love that is deeply caring without any need for sentimental display. She doesn't ask her patients whether they love her, in order for her to be a loving presence. Like Florence Nightengale, she offers herself without any conditions, other than the patients' willingness to accept what she has to offer. This is the love of an archetypal nursing mother. What needs to be done is done quietly and completely, with no hesitation or burdensome qualifications.

Little Seagull Man

While spending time in the lower Amazon basin of Paraguay, Keeney (2000) also spent time with the Guarani shamans. They call themselves "inhabitants of the forest" and still practice the ancient ways of their people.

In one particular village where Keeney spent some time, the chief shaman was named Ava Tape Miri, which means "little seagull man." Miri is a stocky man, with distinctly Indian features and wispy gray facial hair. He wears a bandanna around his head and beads around his neck. He had been an outlaw for many years and part of a gang before he took on the spiritual leadership role of his tribe. He had a dream one night, in which his father appeared to him and introduced him to the spirit world. From that time onward, he became a man of love.

Usually, when people think about shamans and medicine people of the Amazon, they imagine shamans as warriors doing battle against the forces of evil with spiritual spears. Yet in Keeney's investigations with the Guarani and many other cultures, this is not at all what appeared to be the dominant role of healers.

The Guarani are among the most impoverished people on Earth, absolute outcasts. They own virtually nothing. Yet when Brad came to Little Seagull Man, the shaman said to him, "All that I own are my songs. I will give them to you."

To shamans, the most important thing is their song, the music that was given to them in dreams and visions. Little Seagull Man took several days preparing to give his sacred song to Brad. This song was a bridge to the spirit world. It was the most important aspect of his life. When he was ready, he announced to the village that everyone should come to the ceremonial hut, which had a thatched roof and a spirit canoe. The women stood along the back wall and used long, hollow bamboo poles to pound out a rhythm into the dirt.

Dum, da dum, da dum, da dum, da dum.

Then the singing began, a low chant in which the shaman offered a song to the spirits. The men held hands as they moved their feet up and down, all in a line, the women behind them. The shaman led them in front with his rattles. The drum poles continued to pound a beat, dum da dum, da dum, da dum.

The shaman turned to face the men. They moved forward as a group, dancing their way out of the hut to circle the spirit canoe, Keeney in the middle of them. They danced like this all night, although occasionally one of the shamans would feel a surge of energy and jump into the air with a shriek, "Ayeeeei!"

After they danced through the night, morning arrived. Little Seagull Man addressed Keeney in front of the people. "I am now ready to give you my song."

What struck Brad most about this moment was how intimate it felt. Here was this man who had spent the last several days doing little else except prepare to sing a song for this visiting White shaman whom he had known for several years. Here was a man who had been a killer and a bandit and was now the most gentle and loving of souls.

Little Seagull Man sang the song to Keeney. He sang it with such passion and feeling that tears fell down his cheeks. Then he collapsed. He was so exhausted after finally sharing his gift that he passed out and remained on his straw mat for the rest of the day in order to recover.

Keeney is still in awe of how giving such people have been to him. "They open their hearts without any fear. They will give anything they have. It is the same with the Bushmen." As he said this, he looked meaningfully in the direction of the three women shamans who were resting by our camp. Early in the morning, the three of them walked more than 5 miles just to find a special root that they wanted to give to Keeney, the Big Doctor. The only thing they wanted in return was to be touched by him, to shake with him.

It's All about Love

Among all the expressions of love that Keeney has ever experienced, the most memorable occurred in Black churches. "It is in these genuine churches where people welcome you with open arms, no matter who you might be. This is a place to love one another. I learned more in these rural churches than I ever learned from the books written by noted theologians at Harvard Divinity School. I am talking about people who have an unbelievable capacity to be stewards to one another and love one another. Their understanding of Christianity is very different from the kind of Christian message you might hear from multimillion-dollar evangelists in a huge organization."

For some time, Keeney was a member of the New Salem Missionary Baptist Church, a congregation consisting almost entirely of parishioners from rural Louisiana who had been involved in the Civil Rights Movement. "This was a congregation so poor that the building had no plumbing. Some of the people had no means of transportation and had to walk the long way to church. Others had no medical care. And it seemed like every month they were burying one of their young people who had been killed in gang violence. But they went to the church for healing. And for love. This is the most powerful shamanic prescription known to man and woman."

Keeney sees the mission of therapy as not so different from what goes on in these churches or among the Guarani. Our mission is to love others, to forgive others, and to work as wisely as we can to bring love to one another. "People need to be understood with compassion. They need to feel that no matter how difficult their lives might be, there is a community, a healing presence, that can love them and rejoice in their lives."

Therapy, of course, is a secular field and—at least, in our culture—is not always associated with the realm of the spiritual. But as we've said before, shamans make no such artificial distinctions. Therapist, minister, teacher, healer—they are all the same thing.

"How you love the other is the making of who you are," Keeney said. "To know love, you must love. To receive forgiveness, you must forgive. To be at peace, you must extend the hand that offers peace."

This does sound remarkably like the sermon of a minister.

"That may be so," Keeney agreed. "And, as long as we're doin' church right now, I want to make sure that you know that I do not give the concept 'power' any importance in my work."

Like his mentor Gregory Bateson, he sees "power" as a very troubling metaphor. This is a strange thing for Keeney to say. Anyone with that sort of charisma and magnetism, who attracts a herd of admirers at any gathering, surely must enjoy the power that comes with influencing others. Yet he feels that any perception of "influence" gets in the way of helping others. These days, he prays before and after any public performance, asking to be an empty vessel, available for helping others. He works hard to experience himself as "small," yet that may paradoxically lead to his being more influential with others.

For most helpers and healers, power and love are not mutually exclusive. Keeney, however, notes how we talk a lot about benevolent power, or influencing power, in our field. Jay Haley (1989) has said that all human interactions are about power and even wrote a book on the power tactics of Jesus Christ. Salvador Minuchin (Minuchin & Fishman, 1974), Cloe Madanes (1981), and many other family theorists also postulate that much of what therapists should do is take power positions to realign the power hierarchies of those they are helping. Several of Jeffrey's (Kottler, 1991, 2000, 2001, 2004) own books are loaded with sections that are devoted to how to develop more power, so as to become a more influential model for those we help. After all, we can't help people if we can't command their interest, attention, and respect. Keeney struggles to see things differently.

He continues, saying, "Isn't it interesting that it seems perfectly acceptable for therapists to talk about ways to attain more power, but almost nothing is ever mentioned about how we can practice more love, except in the context of religious practice? That is one of the reasons the work of Gregory Bateson had such a huge impact on me."

We asked Keeney what he meant by that, and he said that when he first began to spend time with Bateson, he had asked Bateson why he had decided to walk away from the field of psychotherapy and devote his later years to studying other subjects. Bateson told him it was because therapists were too addicted to the metaphor of power. Cybernetics offered Bateson an alternative worldview that looked at things in terms of whole patterns, rather than in terms of the sort of power relationships between presumed isolated entities (such as therapist and client) that were (and are) still so prevalent.

"What do you see as an alternative to this?" Keeney once asked his mentor.

"I don't see people in terms of power," Bateson replied. "I see them in terms of mind."

Keeney was skeptical and challenged the older man to make this discussion far more personal. "If other people seek power," Keeney pressed, "what, then, is it that you seek in your life, if not such power?"

"I seek shame."

At the time, Keeney had no idea what Bateson meant by this but chose not to press it further. It was only many years later that he finally understood the significance of this answer. By shame, Bateson was emphasizing his realization of being a small part in a much larger system and ecosystem. He didn't cultivate the pride of a heroic cowboy who acted like he was a lone soldier against the world. Rather, he accepted the limitations of his role in the larger system of human relationships and biological complexities of a fragile planet with limited resources. In that way, Bateson's thinking was like that of a shaman in many ways; he held no illusions about the superiority of human beings over other creatures or of himself above others. He had conducted fieldwork with several indigenous cultural groups and had the opportunity to witness other ways of construing a world. So when he developed a theory to explain how people interact with one another in particular ways, he preferred the more systemic language of cybernetics over the language of psychology, which was largely based on metaphors of Newtonian physics (inner drives, personality mechanisms, self-esteem, and psychic energy).

Many of Bateson's contemporaries did not take him very seriously. They called him naive or eccentric, with little practical appreciation of the real world. His disciples excommunicated him from their inner circle because he was considered a crank who refused to acknowledge the idea that "power" was the most important notion in understanding human relations.

From the books and manuscripts that were piled up around his house or the dense, intellectual structure of his ideas, one would think that Bateson really worshiped Platonic knowledge, rather than power. But Keeney is convinced that most people never understood that Bateson's real life's work was about systemic wisdom, relational "I-Thou" love, rather than the "I-It" notions of influence and power. He looked for the relational patterns that connect, whether they be between patient and symptom, family members, or people and redwood forests. He cultivated the larger systemic view, one that did not mock nature with arrogant assumptions about controlling and exploiting the resources of oth- ers and of the planet. This deeper view of relationship, rather than the surface view of linear science and control, touched the poetics of sacred vision and left him standing with a sense of awe and wonder toward the natural world.

Keeney's other significant academic mentor, Heinz von Foerster, was one of the most respected cyberneticians in scientific history. He, too, devoted his life to helping others see the world cybernetically or, as he preferred to say it, "recursively." By this, Heinz meant that the observer was always in the observed and the therapist was always inside the view (and understanding) of the client's situation. Keeney adds, "I can summarize both Bateson's and von Foerster's epistemology or way of knowing in one sentence: 'Everything must dance together before anything can be known.'"

Before von Foerster passed away, Keeney visited him at his home in Pescadero, California. Lying in bed with a respirator, the old scientist motioned Keeney to sit by his side. He placed both of his hands on Keeney's head and said in a whisper, "You have been

a good son. I give you my blessing. Please continue this work."
And similar to both his mentors, Keeney has traveled the world
and discovered relationship and love in many fascinating places—
whether in the song of a Guarani shaman, in a pulsating group
hug of Bushmen women, or in the ecstatic worship of the Black
Church.

Chapter Fifteen

Shamanic Principles Applied to Everyday Life

Thus far in this book, we have looked at the ways that shamans operate in different cultures and how these ideas might be applied to the work of helpers and healers. Yet we know that one of the distinct privileges of being a helper is that the things that we do to assist others are equally effective with ourselves. In fact, the more helpers and healers are able to apply in their own lives that which they teach their students and clients, the more credibility they have, and the more skill with which they are able to apply these principles to helping others. Likewise, in looking at the practice of shamanism, all of the things that we have been talking about not only can be applied to your own life but *should* be done so.

On Not Understanding

We have fallen hopelessly in love with technology. We have come to worship our televisions, telecommunication devices, computers, and other electronic conveniences. Yet with all these marvels of engineering, our lives have evolved in ways that are diametrically opposed to those of the indigenous cultures we have discussed. In no way do we wish to romanticize these ancient peoples who live with poverty and chronic disease, who have a life expectancy about half of our own. On the other hand (and you knew this was coming), these ancient wisdom traditions have much to teach us about the ways we could be living our own lives.

Keeney became quite animated at this point in our discussion. He paced back and forth, gesturing with his arms; we had never seen him so serious. "As a result of the ways we live," he began, "the ways we learn, the ways we try to love, the ways we try to understand and make meaning in our lives, we only end up in a dark abyss of bewilderment, despair, and confusion."

"Wait a minute! Are you actually suggesting that the search for meaning and trying to understand things only make things worse?" After all, as teachers and supervisors and therapists, this is what we do for a living: help people to understand where they have been, where they are now, and where they might like to go next.

Keeney held up his hand, asking for patience. It was not that he had any particular problem with meaning-making activities, it was just that such efforts can be advanced by alternatives that are not so directly and implicitly mediated.

When he saw our looks of confusion, he explained, "Our culture is committed to making understanding and control a priority. Yet the more we try to control ourselves and others, the more out of control both become."

"This is the paradox so central to your work in cybernetics."

"Exactly. It is the lesson of all ecological systems. The role of understanding in our culture has been a striking example of our effort to gain an illusion of mastery over the world and our internal experience."

It is certainly true that we attempt to manage anxiety, uncertainty, and fear by entertaining the idea that we can truly understand what is happening to us and within us. As along as we can say, "I understand," then we lessen our worries, even about things we really can't control in any way. Once we say we understand something, then we don't have to think about it anymore.

Consider our favored theories of helping and healing. If we are really honest with ourselves (and with others), we would have to admit that there is no way that we could ever understand how people learn and grow; the process is just too complex and multi-dimensional. So we pretend that our current theories explain a process that we can never understand. We can't live with the reality that we are doing a job that is incomprehensible—that when we do help anyone, we are never really sure how it happened. We convince ourselves (and others) that we do understand and thereby give ourselves the comfort we need to proceed with what we do. Otherwise, we would remain mute.

Work and Play

The ethos of shamanic cultures is quite different from what most of us are used to. Rather than worshiping understanding, they value the exact opposite: surprise and mystery. They remind themselves every day that surprises come their way and how out of control they are to singularly influence the course that life takes. "Rather than seeking to reduce mystery through the illu- sion of understanding," Keeney said, "they feed it. They behold mystery with wide-eyed wonderment. They look at all the ways to feel enchanted by everyday life, from finding food to looking at the stars. They fill their lives with a sense of magical play."

We were about to object, more than a little defensively. Jeffrey's day as an administrator often involves a sequence of serial meetings, none of which seem particularly useful but which are nevertheless filled with folks who take what they are doing very seriously. From the first dawn e-mail check-in, and all throughout the day, his time is partitioned in measured intervals of 1-hour blocks of time. Play is what takes place on the walks between meetings (although Fridays are *always* saved for surfing).

And then Jon. What do we say about Jon? This is a guy who works *five* full-time jobs. He is a faculty member. He is a therapist with a thriving private practice. He is a consultant. He is an author. He is a film producer. Jon is so busy and scattered that he sometimes juggles two or three jobs at the same time. While producing a therapy video, he sits in the production control room, overseeing the unfolding drama, as he reads student papers and chats on his cell phone to a client in crisis. His life is so busy with work commitments, he has no time to actually read a book; instead, he listens to books on tape as he transports himself from one work venue to another.

As we think about the ways we manage our own lives, we look across the way and see several Bushmen sitting in the shade, chatting with one another. Even though it is 10 in the morning, their work day is over: They've helped around the village to organize a few things and now they can rest and relax. We "listen" in on their conversation through a translator and learn that most of what they talk about is us, these strange White people sitting in portable chairs, working so hard to make sense of what they are doing. They think this is pretty amusing, because they have so little interest themselves in making sense of their own lives. But they are polite and cordial hosts; they will humor us as best they can. But still, they wonder why Jeffrey runs around so frantically with his camera and tripod, taking pictures of everything. They wonder why Jon can't sit still and keeps standing up to do something else, or why he plays with a handheld video game or a tape recorder, rather than listening to his friends speak. But the Bushmen shrug: They don't care to understand or alter these strange practices; they accept them as the way things are.

Meanwhile, Brad keeps joining with the Bushmen throughout the day and night, hugging, shaking, making sounds, and falling to the ground. We go over to the Bushmen elders and ask, "Bo [Brad's Bushman name] is a very big doctor in our country because of the love in his heart. What do you think of him here?"

"He is a big doctor and we love to give and receive nails with him," Cgunta, the oldest Bushman doctor, responds.

"He is a powerful person," the women doctors join in. "We have never seen anyone more powerful. He is a good dancer and his talent comes from the Big God."

Jon asks, "How is it different dancing with a White doctor?"

"We don't see any difference. We are sharing the same thing that comes from God. Bo is a Bushman. He has the same flesh that we have."

"When he's away, we dream of dancing with him. We send him nails and take care of him. Our strongest doctors protect him."

"Are there other White doctors that come?" Jon asked.

One of the other men shook his head. "There are none."

"So, then," Jon pressed, "why did it take so many years for a White person to become a Bushman doctor?"

Cgunta shrugged. "It is the Big God who made the decision. Bo is what he is supposed to be."

✕ You Are Where You Are Supposed to Be

So, we wonder, how is it possible to learn to sit still, to stop working so frantically, to apply these lessons from shamanic cultures to our own lives?

"For one thing," Keeney said, "it is not necessary to go to the Navajo Reservation, or Japan, or Bali, or the Amazon, or Tibet, or to come here to the Kalahari. In fact, doing so may make things worse."

We asked what he meant by that and were told that it is be- *see page 242* cause of the ways we do things in our culture. When people go on some sort of pilgrimage or vision quest, it is with a spirit devoted to understanding. Just look at the ways we were operating in the middle of Namibia: we were outfitted with all our devices—digital, single-lens reflex, video, and rangefinder cameras; tape recorders (three!); reference materials; laptop computers—all designed as instruments of understanding. We could be playing with the Bushmen, but we seek to study them.

We treat travel adventures the way we would search a bookstore for the next self-help manual. We seek to become transformed through our understanding of a new phenomenon. We think that by understanding ourselves or some aspect of the world that has previously been unfathomable, that this will somehow change our lives for the better. Yet often afterward, we end up feeling just as empty and hungry for something more.

"One of the key lessons I have learned from shamans and spiritual teachers," Keeney said, now speaking to you, the reader, directly, "is that everyone is exactly where he or she is supposed to be. As you read these words, you are doing so because you are looking for something else other than what you have and what you know. *But right now you are where you are supposed to be.*

"It is a shamanic challenge for you to consider that the gods, the forces and spirits of Nature, and your own ancestors, have brilliantly arranged every experience in your life to be what it has been—no matter how difficult or challenging or confusing that may have been for you. They are all part of what makes you unique."

This is indeed a challenge for those of us who try to understand things for a living. And after all, is that not what we believe helpers and healers are all about? We are supposed to understand the process of learning and growth. We are supposed to understand why people have problems and what is getting in their way. We are supposed to understand the process by which we work because we will be asked to explain it later. And furthermore, we are supposed to help others understand themselves better, not to mention understand the rest of the world and why everyone behaves the way they do.

Keeney issued the challenge that we should stop looking back to understand, particularly when this leads to excuses for why we can't have what we really want and need. "What the world needs more of," Keeney concluded, "is not more understanding but more mystery."

Seeking Mystery and Surprises

What if we were to surrender the obsession with understanding? What, then, would we do instead?

The alternative to understanding is honoring mystery. "Personally," Keeney confessed, "I want more mystery and surprises in my life. I want to feel enchanted. I want to bring back the sense of childlike wonder as often as I can."

This is an important principle not only for the way Keeney conducts his life but for the way he does therapy. We've mentioned earlier his case of the medicine man who never had a vision. This Native American healer had tried everything he could think of to overcome his shame. He fasted. He went on vision quests. He tried his best to understand what was going on and approached the solution with grim determination.

When he consulted Keeney, this White shaman, about his problem, they did not spend more than a minute or two actually talking about the problem. Brad didn't care why the medicine man was not having visions. He was not interested in exploring the origins of the problem or the cognitions or feelings that accompanied it. If anything, he wanted to help the medicine man to think less about the situation and to stop trying to understand what it might mean. Instead, Keeney wanted to induce greater mystery into the situation. That is what led him to suggest that they retire into a darkened room so that they might chant and pray. And that is why he created a series of rituals and ordeals for the man to complete that would move him away from grim understanding and toward creative action.

The dilemma of helpers and healers is that they often lock themselves into helping practices that become routines. We stop seeing people as individuals, and we start applying our favorite methods with a degree of indifference or, at least, something less than complete passion and commitment. How many times have you heard yourself tell the same stories or share the same anecdotes that you have told a hundred times before? As good as a metaphor or a teaching story might be, there is a fundamental difference between making up a customized intervention for the first time and repeating something that has become a well-worn (but still potent) habit.

Even if clients can't tell the difference between the first and the hundredth performance, it is still important to model in our own lives that which we want our clients to do. People become captured by their routines. We eat the same things for breakfast every morning. We dress ourselves by putting the same sock on and the same shoe on, in the same sequence. We leave the house at the same time. We commute using the exact same route. We sit at the dinner table with our lover or partner and have the same kinds of conversations that we have so many times previously. When we get together with colleagues over coffee or tea, we talk about the same kinds of things. And when we help people, we tend to draw upon the same resources and strategies that we have mindlessly employed in similar circumstances. At times, it feels like our whole lives are on autopilot.

Of course, habits are helpful and convenient. They help us to save time and energy by freeing up energy and decisions that might otherwise be directed toward more significant areas. It is because we don't have to think about what to have for breakfast that we can think about other things instead.

We can still add more mystery, play, tinkering, and risk taking to our lives—*if* we are willing to surrender some of the drive toward understanding.

Mindful Prayer

Here's where it gets more than a little tricky. All shamans, at least those who have what Keeney considers the "right stuff," are organized by prayer. Whether mystery is represented by God, Krishna, Jesus, Buddha, Mohammed, the Sacred Bear, or Brown Rice, all shamans relate to something divine and mysterious. This prayer might not take place in a formal house of worship but could involve meditation in Nature, mystical experience, a vision quest, or having deep conversation with a loved one.

By and large, helping and healing outside of a religious context are secular enterprises. We have separation of church and state

not only in our constitution but also in the foundations of our helping professions. So where this becomes challenging is that Keeney
insists that without some kind of prayer, there can be no shaman.
Some alleged gurus have tried to sell a kind of secular shamanism,
in which you shake a few rattles or play a drum, but the core of all
shamanic healing is a recognition that there is something that is
bigger than all of us, something beyond understanding.

In all the time we have been together, we have not once seen
Brad pray in any recognizable way. We asked him about that.

"Keep in mind that praying out here is all about dancing, shaking, singing, and touching. You actually haven't seen anything but
praying, but not the kind of praying you're familiar with. We
should go to a Black Church. I'd love to show you some praying
there."

"Say Amen, somebody!" "Yes, Jesus. Yes!" Brad shouts, as if he
were suddenly transported to a church in the backwoods of
Louisiana.

"And finally, you might be interested in knowing that when I
wake up in the morning, and particularly when I go to bed, I voice
out loud, or speak inside my head, and ask for direction and guidance and to be taught in dream."

We nod our heads in recognition. We have already learned to expect that any new morning Brad might announce his intention to
undertake some major new course of action in his life. We find this
both amusing and interesting, but also aggravating at times. It was
a dream that led him to the Kalahari in the first place. It was a
dream that guided him to accept our writing this book with him.
But it was also dreams that led him to cancel or reschedule certain
plans and to do something else that had taken greater priority. Now
that we think about it, it seems interesting that telling someone you
have changed your mind because of a dream sounds pretty flaky,
yet telling someone the same thing "upon reflection" or "in conversation with someone" is perfectly acceptable and rational.

"So, how does this dream stuff, this mindful prayer, work for
you?" we asked.

Keeney nodded, thinking about how to frame his response. "My
experience is similar to what I have heard among the Bushmen. It
is a letting go of control. The trembling and shaking begin only
after you are prepared to surrender control."

Jeffrey nodded his head (though not in understanding), remembering his own experience at the dance.

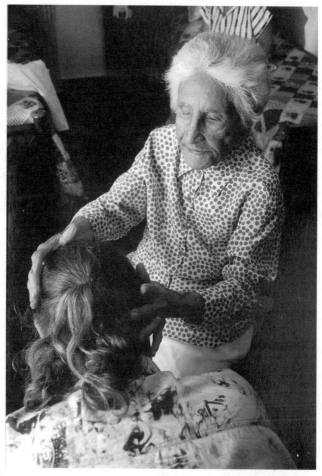

Otavia Pimentel, a Brazilian healer in her 90s blesses
Keeney. She told him, "Sometimes I dream so much
that I fall out of bed."

"It feels to me as if I live a life in vibration, play, love, and
prayer. Any time I see someone in therapy or in any sort of helping relationship, I never begin without a simple, silent prayer. And
my prayers are moved by all the ways different people have
touched me from around the world."

"So," Jeffrey pressed, still uneasy about this subject, "how
would a secular therapist like me, an avowed cynic about conventional religious practices, create such a prayer? It could not in-

clude a reference to God or to any of the usual referents in prayers that I so mistrust. But I still consider myself profoundly spiritual."

Keeney shrugged. "I don't know. I wish I could help you with that. Maybe . . ."

"Maybe surfing is my prayer," Jeffrey blurted out, before Brad could complete the apology.

Both Jon and Brad laughed, not because they found this so amusing but because it actually fit so well.

"I didn't know I knew the answer before I asked the question."

"The particular prayer doesn't matter, no more so than the choice of a religious practice. But I have my doubts whether, if you were born in a Buddhist home, another world religion would carry you as deeply as the one you grew up with as a child. I think that being a pilgrim through other world religions is useful when it returns you to your own home. I also believe that there is really no such thing as an atheist." As he said this, he looked meaningfully at Jeffrey. "Perhaps one's god is reason or whatever else you regard as most important."

To Keeney, whatever deeply touches and accesses a person's soul is his or her religion. For the Bushmen, their prayer is dancing, not beseeching the Lord in a church. For the Dine (Navajo), it is walking, all the while noticing the beauty in front of them and behind them. And for most therapists and other healers, we have our own ritualized professional "prayers" that we call upon to give us strength and serenity. For some, this might involve reviewing one's clinical notes, going into a brief meditative trance, or organizing one's thoughts. Whatever we do, we try to free our creativity and focus our concentration. We try to keep ourselves nimble and totally aware so that we might best respond to whatever comes up in the session. This is just another kind of prayer. "But," Keeney challenged, "how deep does your way of praying take you? Does it make you rock and shake?"

Experimentation and Risk Taking

This talk about religion and prayer prompted Keeney to answer a question we didn't think to ask.

"People sometimes ask me if I believe in reincarnation. I say it is irrelevant to me. It is not even very interesting to me whether a person thinks he was King Henry, or Socrates, or a merchant of Venice. But I do believe that reincarnation provides a useful metaphor for the life we have in this lifetime. Namely, we are basically living the same life over and over again. We recycle our own biography. We find ourselves constituted by habits and routines so it is as if we wake up every day and live the same life over. The goal of those who believe in reincarnation is be free of bondage: They are hoping to be turned into something else that will be more enlightened and free than they currently feel. But to me, it is all about the wish for more creativity and choices, the desire for more surprise and mystery."

It is true that our lives, and the stories we follow, all proceed along a linear chronology. We are always linking things in terms of whether they occur in the beginning, the middle, or the end. As therapists, we organize our work into these same stages of intake, working stage, termination, and so forth. Yet to the cybernetician or the shaman, patterns always repeat themselves in endless loops, each with small changes along the way.

Therapists notice how their clients (as well as they themselves) often end up in a relationship with a person similar to the one they left before. They might even become involved with someone who is like the person who married their parent. Just like their clients, therapists find themselves caught in recycled loops that they feel unable to break free from. That is why shamans (perhaps more than therapists) constantly think in terms of disrupting habitual cycles in order to introduce something new.

In the first chapter of the book, we talked about how Credo Mutwa, the Zulu shaman, cured his own melanoma by building a statue to honor this "goddess." In relating this story to Brad, Credo didn't venture any guesses about how this miracle occurred. Yet it would be familiar to many therapists that he employed a method of utilizing his symptoms, rather than seeing them as an enemy to be defeated.

Several times, we asked Keeney to relate his points to the everyday lives of helpers or healers. What are we to do with this? Build statues to honor our nemeses?

Brad was reluctant to give us any generalizations. "It always depends on the unique situation at hand," he said again and again. He enjoyed paraphrasing William Blake, "Evil takes place within the generalization. Good can only be delivered through the particular deed."

seem to be resisting this," we challenged him. "We are at
d of the book. We are at the end of our adventure together."
vve looked around to see our guides dismantling the tents and
breaking camp. We were about to have our farewell dinner under
the stars and watch the sky light up with the sunset. Already we
could see the blackened silhouettes of the huge termite mounds.

"You seem to be feeling some resistance to going any further,"
we pressed Brad again. "It is like you have run out of energy. The
heat and the dancing have taken everything out of you."

Keeney shrugged apologetically.

"Maybe it is also because you are a shaman that you don't like
rehashing and explaining things."

Creating Something New

Reluctant to surrender (and wanting to tie things together), we
asked Brad how we might reawaken his imagination and passion.

"To create something new?" he responded.

"Yes. How would you apply what you normally do, as a healer
and a shaman, to the reader this very moment?"

Keeney smiled, clearly warming to the task. "First, I would invite readers to think about each page they have read in this
book."

He paused for a moment, looking out toward the horizon in the
vanishing light. It was as if he pictured all the audience of readers
in the middle distance and was addressing each one of you in a
most personal way.

"I would ask each one of you to make a decision about which
page in this book was the most challenging and difficult for you.
Think about what chapter caused you to struggle the most. What
bothered you and got underneath your skin?"

Keeney waited for a moment, giving you, the reader, a chance to
reflect on this question and really think about the chapter, then the
page, that troubled or disturbed you the most. This was the page
in which you found yourself thinking that you could not possibly
accept those ideas or apply them to what you do or your own life.

"Have you identified this page?" Keeney asks you again. "Now,
what I want you to do is to tear this page out of the book."

You might think he is kidding, but surely by now you have come
to realize that few things he might do would be expected. Remem-

ber: Keeney is a shaman who respects the importance of surprise and mystery. So, how much do you trust this kind of wisdom? Will you do what he says and actually rip a page from this book?

"Examine the page that you have identified (and ripped out) that most disturbs you. Now select the single *sentence* on that page that you find most troubling, or the one that challenges you the most."

Keeney pauses to give you time to accomplish this task. He is a patient man, so take your time.

"Within this sentence, select the single *word* that is most offensive, or that contains the essence of the challenging thought or idea, which in turn symbolizes the whole page that struck you as most bothersome."

For this next task, you will need to retrieve a pair of scissors because—you guessed it—Brad wants you to excise this word from the page.

"Now, after you have cut out this word and held it in the palm of your hand, ask yourself where in the world you might store it. In other words, where do you want to keep this word that represents your greatest challenge in this book?"

Keeney is grinning hugely now, so contagiously that we can't help but smile back in appreciation.

"Do you put it inside your pillow?" he asks. "So you can sleep with it each night underneath your head and let it enter your dreams? Do you place it in the glove compartment of your car so it can accompany you wherever you go? Do you keep it in your dresser at the bottom of your underwear drawer? Do you put it in a safe deposit box? Do you plant it in your garden? Do you leave it on the table at a restaurant so someone else might pick it up?"

"Do you flush it down the toilet?" Jeffrey contributes to the options.

"Or mail it to Brad?" Jon adds.

"Or hand deliver it to the Bushmen?" Jeffrey says.

"Do you put it on the mirror in your bathroom," Brad adds, "so that every day you stare at it when you contemplate your own reflection?"

"Do you put it in a glass of scotch and drink it?" Jeffrey says.

"Do you use it as a salutation to end all your letters?" Brad continues his list. "Do you put it in an ice tray and freeze it inside an ice cube? Do you mix it with your toothpaste and brush your teeth? Do you fold it up and place it inside your belly button?

Balinese shaman Jero Mangku Srikandi
blessing Keeney's shamanic odyssey.

Then put a band-aid over your navel and write on it: 'My greatest challenge.'"

This, dear friends, is what it means to be a shaman.

Coming Full Circle: Back to Where We Started

"We're just about out of fuel."

"What do you mean, we're out of fuel?" Keeney shouted over the sound of the engine. They'd been lurching along for hours, driving through the heart of the central Kalahari Desert, the second largest expanse of endless sand in the world. They were probably still in Botswana, unless they had somehow crossed over into Namibia. It would certainly be easy to do, because what had earlier passed for a road now dwindled to a track in the sand.

"Keep going," Keeney ordered, trying to line up the map with some recognizable feature of the landscape. But it all looked the same—as far as they could see, endless brush and sand were speckled with a few spooky-looking camelthorn trees. If they didn't figure out their location soon, they'd end up sleeping in the truck until someone else came along.

Peter was a colleague and a fellow professor at the University of South Africa in Pretoria, where Keeney had been working as a visiting professor. One condition of his appointment had been that they arrange for someone to take Keeney into the Kalahari so that he could spend time with the Bushmen, the oldest known continuous culture on Earth. Peter had graciously volunteered for the job, and although he might have been an able academic, he had done a poor job of planning for this journey. They didn't have proper equipment or the necessary spare parts if something broke down, and now they were about to run out of gas in the most remote place in the world. There'd be no rescuers any time soon.

"Look! There!" Peter pointed in the direction of what appeared to be a road heading west toward some trees and possible shade.

"No, Peter, just keep following straight," Keeney insisted again. He looked over at Nelson, their third companion, sitting in the back seat. He was a university student who had come along as their interpreter. Hearing no advice from the only Native African present, Keeney insisted again, "We're getting close. I can feel it."

It was then that Keeney looked back and saw that he was no longer traveling alone. Their jeep was followed by a ragged caravan of other vehicles keeping pace behind them. He had not noticed this before, but now he recognized everyone in the other trucks. Following closest behind him were the Guarani shamans from the Amazon; then those from the Cree, Dine, and Ojibwa Nations; as well as others from Japan, Australia, Bali, Mexico, Brazil, and all the other places that he had visited during the past years.

Keeney shook his head, realizing that he had been having a waking dream, reliving his first visit to the Bushmen. He looked around, surprised to find himself still underneath the baobab tree watching the last of the light from our last night together. He looked first at Jon, then at Jeffrey, as if reorienting himself to the time and the place.

"It is the two of you who are the shamans," Brad said. "We have now returned full circle to the beginning. And you have evoked some mystery for me, just as you have awakened the wind."

We swear that at this exact moment, the wind started to pick up. "We should be aware of the wind," Brad said in a hypnotic voice, "and how it reminds us of the inventiveness that flows naturally when it is evoked by another who cares enough to call it out."

Epilogue

Bradford Keeney

When Jeffrey Kottler and Jon Carlson first proposed the idea of writing a book about my work, I immediately felt great joy because it meant that what I had witnessed and experienced in my odyssey into diverse global healing traditions could provide the same inspiration and encouragement for others that it had for me. I was thrilled that we would be able to introduce a broader audience to some of the amazing people I have met in my journeys. The longer I stayed out in the field, the more convinced I became that the teachings of other cultures must be heard. We have forgotten and, dare I say, disrespectfully ignored many of our elders. This is particularly true for psychotherapy, one of the youngest folk healing traditions on the planet.

At the same time, I felt somewhat uneasy about being called a "shaman" because I believe, in part, that you can't be a shaman if you say you are a shaman. This stems from the fact that being a shaman requires a disassociation from any sense of self-importance or expertise. The authentic shaman, in other words, aims to be an empty vessel, even absent of any identity of being a shaman. When the Bushmen, as well as other cultural leaders, say I am a kind of natural shaman, I take that to be a reference to how my spiritual awakening left me open to spiritual feelings and ecstatic forms of expression. This way of initiation is known to yogis throughout history whose *kundalini* awakenings left them ready to teach and work with others. And it is what my grandfather meant when he said I was reborn into a new life in spirit.

Personally, I don't care whether someone, including myself, thinks I am a board-certified, union card–carrying shaman. As a matter of fact, I spent most of my adult life trying to keep this part of my experience secret. But it was impossible to cover it up. People who didn't even believe in shamans kept calling me a shaman. Now, if you ask me whether I really believe that I am a shaman, I would say, in my heart of hearts, I am not a shaman. I don't think that shamanic journeys are that important (although I have experienced quite a few such journeys), and I don't like to take plants that make me hallucinate. What I like is dancing with the Bushmen, sitting in religious ceremonies, and swaying to the beat of gospel music in a Black Church. I agreed to let Jeffrey Kottler and Jon Carlson call me a shaman if they would allow me to explain why I don't care whether I am really a shaman or not. At the same time, I think it is quite interesting that all of the shamans I have ever met from other cultures agree with what I am telling you now.

Getting past my own embarrassment (and fear) at having to be the subject of a book, and with anxious trepidation, I cautiously accepted this project as an opportunity to help others know that the flickering lights of other wisdom traditions still provide illumination for how we might conceive of helping one another through the everyday struggles of life. I ask the reader's forgiveness in my having to prop myself up as a literary device for telling a great story that has relatively little to do with me. I always wished I could take every therapist, teacher, helper, and healer to the Kalahari, the Amazon, St. Vincent, Black churches throughout Louisiana, Bali, and on, and on, throughout the world. You would meet some of the most loving and sometimes eccentric characters imaginable. Out there are people who know how to care for others, without getting entangled in naïve sentimentalism. They know how to cleverly intervene so as to disrupt problematic habits and cycles of self-destruction, without being strangled by any illusions of Machiavellian power games. There are gentle and kind teachers whose ability to forgive and love and laugh qualifies them as saints. I wanted you to meet these people. They changed my life and my way of thinking about helping others. I believe they can do the same for you.

My desire to introduce you to these voices of cultural wisdom led me to join Jeffrey and Jon in creating this recollection of voyages into the ways of cultural healing. I was skeptical at first as to whether they would be able to have open ears and eyes, but their curious and kind manner, sprinkled with good wit and humor, often matched the wisdom I had found in so many faraway places. Although I was placed in a position to teach them, they, in fact, without pretension or advertised purpose, taught me as well. I learned that it was possible to come home and find warm and generous wisdom in my own backyard. Most important, their making of this book takes you on a journey to encounter the characters I always hoped others could meet.

This book appears at a time in my life when most of my primary mentors have passed away—Gregory Bateson, Heinz von Foerster, Franciso Varela, Carl Whitaker, Milton Erickson, Bushman doctors Mantag and Motaope, the St. Vincent Shaker Pointer Warren, and my grandfathers and grandmothers, Reverend W. L. and Virginia Keeney, and Auburn and Bess Gnann. Yet I feel, more than ever, that their spirit and ideas are alive today. Wisdom, like other cultured delights, gets better with each passing year.

There is an ancient custom, practiced by most indigenous cultures, that begins or ends a story by recognizing those who are an inseparable part of it. As a former family systems therapist, I, too, enthusiastically underscore the importance of my family context. Raised by a country preacher father and grandfather; a schoolteacher mother; a farmer, inventor, and construction worker grandfather; and hard-laboring grandmothers, I was taught to see how the suffering of everyday life could be embraced with an open, caring heart and become transformed into soulful grace. They, like the global shamans and healers I met throughout the world, emphasized that love is the greatest teacher.

My journey was never carried out on my own. My loving wife, Mev Jenson, and my kind and dream-filled son, Scott, were there with me. They, too, have been touched by the great mysteries of life, and their experiences have been a source of significant teaching to me. I have learned that there is no significant spiritual life independent of one's significant relationships. Soulful healing and growth take place in relationship. My odyssey has not taken place inside a cave but in intense interaction with those I love. And finally, I express an enthusiastic hug to Jeffrey Kottler and Jon Carlson, who helped bring me back home so that what I learned from others may, in turn, be passed on. Kottler's masterful writing and Carlson's witty and insightful participation in our discussions have helped bring these wisdom traditions to others. Using a language that is clearer and more accessible than my own, they have helped bridge old premises of cultural wisdom to hearts that desire to help others in their times of need and suffering. I have learned from Jeffrey and Jon and have felt healing in their presence. Most important, we have become brothers on a journey we now share together.

Books by Bradford Keeney

(1983). *Aesthetics of change.* New York: Guilford Press.

(1983). *Diagnosis and assessment of family therapy.* Rockville, MD: Aspen Systems.

(1985). *Mind in therapy: Constructing systemic family therapies* (with Jeffrey Ross). New York: Basic Books.

(1986). *The therapeutic work of Olga Silverstein* (with Olga Silverstein). New York: Guilford Press.

(1987). *Constructing therapeutic realities.* Dortmund, Germany: Verlag für Modernes Lernen.

(1990). *The systemic therapist* (Vol. I). St. Paul: Systemic Therapy Press.

(1990). *The systemic therapist* (Vol. II). St. Paul: Systemic Therapy Press.

(1992). *Improvisational therapy.* New York: Guilford Press.

(1993). *Resource focused therapy* (with Wendel Ray). London: Karnac Books.

(1995). *Shaking out the spirits.* Barrytown, NY: Station Hill Press.

(1995). *The lunatic guide to the* David Letterman Show. Barrytown, NY: Station Hill Press.

(1995). *Crazy wisdom tales.* New York: Barrytown Press.

(1996). *Everyday soul: Awakening the spirit in daily life.* New York: Riverhead.

(1998). *The energy break.* New York: Golden Books.

(1999). *Gary Holy Bull, Lakota Yuwipi man.* Philadelphia: Ringing Rocks Press.

(1999). *Ikuko Osumi, Japanese master of seiki jutsu.* Philadelphia: Ringing Rocks Press.

(1999). *Kalahari Bushmen healers.* Philadelphia: Ringing Rocks Press.

(2000). *Guarani shamans of the rainforest.* Philadelphia: Ringing Rocks Press.

(2001). *Vusamazulu Credo Mutwa: Zulu high sanusi.* Philadelphia: Ringing Rocks Press.

(2001). *Walking Thunder: Dine medicine woman.* Philadelphia: Ringing Rocks Press.

(2002). *Shakers of St. Vincent.* Philadelphia: Ringing Rocks Press.

(2003). *Ropes to God: Experiencing the Bushman spiritual universe.* Philadelphia: Ringing Rocks Press.

(2003). *Brazilian hands of faith.* Philadelphia: Ringing Rocks Press.

(2003). *Balians: Traditional healers of Bali.* Philadelphia: Ringing Rocks Press.

(2004). *The Gods are crazy: My story of becoming a Bushman shaman.* Inner Traditions Press.

References

Bateson, G. (1972). *Steps to an ecology of mind.* New York: Ballantine.

Bateson, G. (1979). *Mind and nature: A necessary unity.* New
York: E. P. Dutton.

Benson, H. (1990). *The relaxation response.* New York: Morrow.

Campbell, J. (1990). *Transformations of myth through time.* New
York: HarperCollins.

Casanowicz, I. M. (1926). *Shamanism of the natives of Siberia.*
Washington, DC: Annual Report of the Smithsonian Institution.

Casteneda, C. (1973). *The teachings of Don Juan: A Yaqui way of
knowledge.* New York: Simon and Schuster.

Eliade, M. (1968). *The sacred and the profane: The nature of religion.* New York: Harvest Books.

Ellis, A. (2001). *Overcoming destructive beliefs, feelings, and behaviors: New directions for rational emotive behavior therapy.*
Amherst, NY: Prometheus.

Erickson, M. (1980). *The collected papers of Milton H. Erickson,*
edited by Ernest L. Rossi. New York: Irvington.

Erickson, M. H., & Haley, J. (Eds.). (1967). *Advanced techniques of
hypnosis and therapy: Selected papers of Milton H. Erickson.*
Boston: Allyn & Bacon.

Frankl, V. (1962). *Man's search for meaning.* Boston: Beacon
Press.

Gwynne, S. C. (1997, October 20). Is my aura showing? *Time, 4.*

Haley, J. (1973). *Uncommon therapy: The Psychiatric techniques
of Milton H. Erickson, MD.* New York: W. W. Norton.

Haley, J. (1984). *Ordeal therapy.* San Francisco: Jossey-Bass.

Haley, J. (1989). *The power tactics of Jesus Christ and other essays* (2nd ed.). New York: W. W. Norton.

Harner, M. (1973). *Hallucinogens and shamanism.* New York: Ox-
ford University Press.

Harner, M. (1982). *The way of the shaman.* New York: Bantam.

Hoppal, M. (1987). Shamanism: An archaic and/or recent belief
system. In S. Nicholson (Ed.), *Shamanism: An expanded view of
reality* (pp. 76–100). Wheaton, IL: Quest.

Jones, E., & Bloch, D. (1993). *Family systems therapy: Developments in the Milan-systemic therapies.* New York: Wiley.

Jung, C. (1961). *Memories, dreams, reflections.* New York: Vintage Books.

Keeney, B. (1979). Ecosystemic epistemology. *Family Process, 21,* 117–129.

Keeney, B. (1983). *Aesthetics of change.* New York: Guilford Press.

Keeney, B. (1985). *Mind in therapy.* New York: Basic Books.

Keeney, B. (1990). *Improvisational therapy.* New York: Guilford Press.

Keeney, B. (1994). *The lunatic guide to the* David Letterman Show. Barrytown, NY: Station Hill Press.

Keeney, B. (1996). *Everyday soul: Awakening the spirit in daily life.* New York: Riverhead Books.

Keeney, B. (1999a). *Gary Holy Bull, Lakota Yuwipi man.* Philadelphia: Ringing Rocks Press.

Keeney, B. (1999b). *Ikuko Osumi, Japanese master of seiki jutsu.* Philadelphia: Ringing Rocks Press.

Keeney, B. (1999c). *Kalahari Bushmen healers.* Philadelphia: Ringing Rocks Press.

Keeney, B. (2000). *Guarani shamans of the rainforest.* Philadelphia: Ringing Rocks Press.

Keeney, B. (2001a). *Vusamazulu Credo Mutwa: Zulu high sanusi.* Philadelphia: Ringing Rocks Press.

Keeney, B. (2001b). *Walking Thunder: Dine medicine woman.* Philadelphia: Ringing Rocks Press.

Keeney, B. (2002). *Shakers of St. Vincent.* Philadelphia: Ringing Rocks Press.

Keeney, B. (2003a). *Ropes to God: Experiencing the Bushman spiritual universe.* Philadelphia: Ringing Rocks Press.

Keeney, B. (2003b). *Hands of faith: Healers of Brazil.* Philadelphia: Ringing Rocks Press.

Keeney, B. (2004). *Balians: Traditional healers of Bali.* Philadelphia: Ringing Rocks Press.

Keeney, B., & Keeney, S. (1993). Funny medicines for children. *Japanese Journal of Family Psychology, 7,* 125–132.

Kottler, J. A. (1991). *The compleat therapist.* San Francisco: Jossey-Bass.

Kottler, J. A. (2000). *Doing good: Passion and commitment for helping others.* Philadelphia: Brunner/Routledge.

Kottler, J. A. (2001). *Making changes last.* Philadelphia: Brunner/Routledge.

Kottler, J. A. (2004). *On being a therapist* (3rd ed.). San Francisco: Jossey-Bass.

Kottler, J. A., & Carlson, J. (2002). *Bad therapy: Master therapists share their worst failures.* New York: Brunner/Routledge.

Kottler, J. A., & Carlson, J. (2003). *The mummy at the dining room table: Eminent therapists reveal their most unusual cases.* San Francisco: Jossey-Bass.

Kottler, J. A., & Carlson, J. (2004). *My finest hour.* Boston: Allyn & Bacon.

Lame Deer, J., & Erdoes, R. (1973). *Lame Deer: Seeker of visions.* New York: Touchstone.

Larsen, S. (1976). *The shaman's doorway.* New York: Harper & Row.

Lipset, D. (1980). *Gregory Bateson: The legacy of a scientist.* Englewood Cliffs, NJ: Prentice Hall.

Madanes, C. (1981). *Strategic family therapy.* San Francisco: Jossey-Bass.

Maranhão, T. (1986). *Therapeutic discourse and Socratic dialogue.* Madison: University of Wisconsin Press.

Maslow, A. (1969). *The psychology of science.* Chicago: Henry Regnery.

Maslow, A. (1970). *Motivation and personality.* New York: Harper & Row.

May, R. (1976). Gregory Bateson and humanistic psychology. *Journal of Humanistic Psychology, 16,* 33–51.

Minuchin, S., & Fishman, C. (1974). *Families and family therapy.* Cambridge, MA: Harvard University Press.

Mutwa, V. C. (1964). *Indaba my children: African tribal history, legends, customs, and religious beliefs.* Johannesburg: Blue Crane Books.

Mutwa, V. C. (1971). *My people.* Middlesex, Great Britain: Penguin Books.

Mutwa, V. C. (1986). *Let not my country die.* Pretoria, South Africa: Sigma Press.

New Yorker. (1995, August 14). "Above and Beyond," *16.*

Tyler, S. (1987). *The unspeakable: Discourse, dialogue, and rhetoric in the postmodern world.* Madison: University of Wisconsin Press.

von Foerster, H. (1974). *Cybernetics of cybernetics.* Urbana: University of Illinois Press.

von Foerster, H. (1981). *Observing systems.* Seaside, CA: Intersystems Publications.

Walljasper, J. (2003). (July–August). The luckiest man alive? Bradford Keeney travles the globe searching for the secrets of soul. *Utne,* 46–54.

Watts, A. (1961). *Psychotherapy East and West.* New York: Ballantine.

Watzlawick, P., Beavin, J., & Jackson, D. (1967). *Pragmatics of human communication.* New York: W. W. Norton.

Watzlawick, P., Weakland, J., & Fisch, R. (1974). *Change: Principles of problem formation and problem resolution.* New York: W. W. Norton.

Whitaker, C. (1982). *From psyche to system: The evolving therapy of Carl Whitaker,* ed. J. R. Neill & D. P. Kniskern. New York: Guilford Press.

Whitaker, C., & Napier, A. (1978). *The family crucible.* New York: Harper & Row.